SO-BZN-735

# THE DEFINITIVE GUIDE TO ADDICTION INTERVENTIONS

Written for a broad audience of medical and behavioral healthcare professionals, *The Definitive Guide to Addiction Interventions: A Collective Strategy* introduces clinicians to best practices in addiction interventions and bridges the gap between the theory and practice of successful intervention. Synthesizing decades of fieldwork, Louise Stanger explores the framework for successful invitations to change, what they look like in action, and how to adjust approach by population, and Lee Weber serves as editor. The authors summarize and compare intervention models in use today, and explain the use of family mapping and individual portraiture as clinical tools. The text also teaches clinicians to troubleshoot common situations as they help move clients toward positive life decisions. Practical, ready-to-use clinical tools follow the text in downloadable worksheet form.

**Dr. Louise Stanger Ed.D, LCSW, CIP, CDWF** is a lecturer, clinician, trainer, and renowned interventionist. Her work has been featured in the *Huffington Post*, the *Journal of Alcohol Studies*, *Recovery View*, *Sober Way*, and various other magazines and scholarly publications. In addition, the *San Diego Business Journal* listed her as one of the top ten "Women Who Mean Business," and she was ranked as one of the top ten interventionists in the country.

**Lee Weber** is the founder and editor of Addiction Blog, with over a decade's experience in communications, online content creation, community development, and writing. Her mission is to connect families and individuals struggling with addiction to necessary and appropriate treatment options.

# THE DEFINITIVE GUIDE TO ADDICTION INTERVENTIONS

## A Collective Strategy

*Louise Stanger and Lee Weber*

Routledge
Taylor & Francis Group

NEW YORK AND LONDON

First published 2019
by Routledge
711 Third Avenue, New York, NY 10017

and by Routledge
2 Park Square, Milton Park, Abingdon, Oxon, OX14 4RN

*Routledge is an imprint of the Taylor & Francis Group, an informa business*

© 2019 Taylor & Francis

The right of Louise Stanger and Lee Weber to be identified as
authors of this work has been asserted by them in accordance with
sections 77 and 78 of the Copyright, Designs and Patents Act 1988.

All rights reserved. No part of this book may be reprinted or
reproduced or utilized in any form or by any electronic, mechanical,
or other means, now known or hereafter invented, including
photocopying and recording, or in any information storage or
retrieval system, without permission in writing from the publishers.

*Trademark notice*: Product or corporate names may be trademarks
or registered trademarks, and are used only for identification and
explanation without intent to infringe.

*Library of Congress Cataloging-in-Publication Data*
Names: Stanger, Louise, author. | Weber, Lee, author.
Title: The definitive guide to addiction interventions : a collective
    strategy / Dr. Louise Stanger, Lee Weber.
Description: New York, NY : Routledge, 2019. | Includes
    bibliographical references and index.
Identifiers: LCCN 2018023499 (print) | LCCN 2018024433
    (ebook) | ISBN 9780429461408 (E-book) | ISBN
    9781138616578 (hardback) | ISBN 9781138618039 (pbk.) |
    ISBN 9780429461408 (ebk)
Subjects: | MESH: Substance-Related Disorders—therapy | Crisis
    Intervention
Classification: LCC RC564 (ebook) | LCC RC564 (print) | NLM
    WM 270 | DDC 362.29—dc23
LC record available at https://lccn.loc.gov/2018023499


ISBN: 9781138616578 (hbk)
ISBN: 9781138618039 (pbk)
ISBN: 9780429461408 (ebk)


Typeset in Bembo
by Swales & Willis Ltd, Exeter, Devon, UK


Visit the eResources: www.routledge.com/9781138618039

This book is dedicated to the hundreds of thousands of families whose lives are ravaged by substance abuse, mental health, chronic pain, and other disorders. To all the sleepless people, the loved ones whose hearts are breaking, who don't know what their loved ones are doing, may there be professionals at every level of care who are able to reach out and help.

Also, to all the pioneers who have written in this field, I salute you for your work. May we see in the next decade research that helps us determine what strategies work best.

To my editor Lee Weber, who believed in me and taught me Macedonia is just a phone call away, thank you.

And to my family, my husband John for his unwavering belief in me, and to my daughters Felicia, Sydney, and Shelby, who taught me that a wild idea is always worth living.

This is a work of nonfiction. A textbook. Nonetheless, some of the names and personal characteristics of the individuals cited in case studies have been changed to disguise identity and protect confidentiality. Any resulting resemblance to persons living or dead is entirely coincidental and unintentional.

# CONTENTS

## PART 3
# Troubleshooting 187

# ILLUSTRATIONS

## Figures

## Tables

# ERESOURCE WORKSHEETS

To download accompanying worksheets, please go to: www.routledge.com/9781138618039

# PREFACE

Substance abuse requires intervention and treatment.

So, how do you get someone from refusal of treatment to a "yes" without setting them up in a surprise? Without shame or disrespect? Without an ambush?

This book aims to show you how.

In fact, we want to bridge the gap between the theory and practice of successful addiction intervention. We will present you with a definitive guide for how to successfully identify, refer, and track clients in early substance use disorder treatment. To do so, we'll show you how to combine the invitational family systems approach to interventions with clinical tools for implementation.

How did I get here?

Why does this process call to me when there are a plethora of models already existing?

I was first introduced to formal interventions by Dr. Frank Picard, who in 1989 penned the book *Family Intervention* in opposition to Vern Johnson's classic book of three years earlier, *Intervention: How to Help Someone Who Doesn't Want Help*. This was the time, at least in Southern California, when the Minnesota Model was held in high esteem and Hazelden was thought to be the industry leader in the field. Betty Ford was just starting, and in San Diego the Scripps McDonald Center was considered a pacesetter. Folks from Minnesota were heavily recruited.

As a lecturer at San Diego State University, I was given the task of developing the inaugural mandated three-unit graduate school course for social work and other related master's degree candidates that focused on substance abuse. In doing so, I relied on community partners to bring people in to guest lecture.

One evening, a good friend and colleague, Ed Lacey, brought to my classroom Dr. Frank Picard, who at the time was the director of a private treatment center named Springbrook, based in Oregon, and had penned a book entitled *Family Intervention*. As he spoke, my eyes widened, my mouth dropped open, my ears perked up, and I listened and absorbed. He must have read my mind; he knew my family! I was intrigued with what he had to say and how he perceived this to be important family work.

I recall listening to Frank with the reassurance that I had found my calling. I was great in times of crisis. I loved drama and intrigue. I had a deep desire to help people become all they could be.

I was hooked from that moment on.

I had the good fortune of direct tutelage from Dr. Picard on intervention cases. He, of course, did a variation on the surprise method of intervention, something you'll read about further into the book. So, my early years of practice utilized that methodology.

But something about the surprise method did not feel right to me.

Over the years, I transitioned from a solo practitioner to a team approach when performing interventions. Along the way, I have had the good fortune of taking several intervention courses, reading everything written on the subject, and having the benefit of training in other modalities. In addition to being a proud member of the National Association of Social Workers (NASW) and a licensed clinical social worker, I joined national intervention groups such as the Network of Independent Interventionists and the Association of Intervention Specialists. I also continued to engage in my own continuing education, being trained in a variety of different modalities, including motivational interviewing, solution-focused therapy, cognitive behavioral therapy (CBT), and most recently becoming a Certified Daring Way/Rising Strong Facilitator. I believe there is honor and synergy that comes from professional affiliation.

With experience, I adopted what I now call a Collective Intervention Strategy (CIS). These are my own processes that come directly from my experience working with thousands of families in over 30 years of social work practice. And the proof is in the pudding. I offer a guarantee to the families that work with me.

I guarantee that everyone participating in a collective intervention will learn more about substance abuse, addiction, process disorders, chronic pain, and mental health disorders. I guarantee that participants will better understand how these disorders affect people in general, as well as their specific family situation. I guarantee that families will uncover the hidden stories around the addiction and their loved one, creating a more accurate picture of reality. And I believe that everyone who experiences this approach to intervention will experience relief.

Often families come to me when their imagination, their hope, is gone. I ask them to:

*"Imagine"*
*Imagine not having to wonder where someone is.*
*Imagine what would it be like for you to not worry at night about your*
*loved one.*
*Imagine not having to call the police.*
*Imagine not having credit card bills from unknown places.*
*Imagine not worrying about who your spouse/daughter/son slept with or where*
*they are.*
*Imagine not being raged at.*
*Imagine not thinking, "It is all my fault."*
*Imagine not throwing away bottles, not stumbling over drug paraphernalia.*
*Imagine not wondering what these little white plastic bags of sugar are hidden*
*under the bed and in sock drawers.*
*Imagine not wondering what that smell is — whose bongs these are.*
*Imagine not getting a call from the hospital, from the dean of students saying*
*your student overdosed.*
*Imagine not having to wonder where all your money went.*
*Imagine the kids not cowering when mommy's drunk or when dad comes home*
*screaming.*
*Imagine brothers and sisters not having to drive with their sister who is loaded*
*and behind the wheel.*
*Imagine not being afraid to leave your 3-year-old with grandma, with grandpa.*
*Imagine not being lied to, not being cheated on, no more secrets.*
*Imagine.*
*Imagine not having to imagine!*

When we work toward a common goal of health, openings appear where there were none. It is my hope that this book will lead you toward a healthier, happier practice, and that you can continue to help others rise to their best possible selves.

Together, we can, for amazing things happen when we open ourselves up to change.

Warmly,
Dr. Louise

# PROLOGUE

## An Embarrassment of Riches

In writing this textbook, we have tried to be thorough in both words and deeds. Ultimately, something is always left out or could have been stated better. Our hope is you use this book as a guide that whets your curiosity and propels you into further training, research, and supervision.

May you discover the joy in moving others to change. We hope that you create your own legacy in a world filled with families who are wounded and who deserve the opportunity for health and wellness, to live full and satisfying lives, no matter their race, creed, religion, or sexual orientation. We hope that each of us can rise to our best possible selves.

In gratitude,
Dr. Louise and Lee

# PART 1

# Models of Intervention

# 1

# AN UNDERSTANDING OF ADDICTION

## The Brain Disorder of Addiction

In August 2011, the American Society of Addiction Medicine (ASAM) declared that addiction is:

> A primary, chronic disease of brain reward, motivation, memory and related circuitry. Dysfunction in these circuits leads to characteristic biological, psychological, social and spiritual manifestations. This is reflected in an individual pathologically pursuing reward and/or relief by substance use and other behaviors.[1]

It was about time. There has been longstanding controversy over whether people diagnosed with addiction have choice over their behaviors or not. Two decades of advancements in neuroscience convinced ASAM that addiction needed to be redefined by what's going on in the brain.

Research shows what we in the treatment industry saw manifest: the disease of addiction is centered in the brain. Many clinicians have observed that addiction is reflected in individuals pathologically pursing reward or relief by substance use or other behaviors. But now the science is catching up.

When ASAM officially noted the chemistry and biology behind addiction, a wave of relief could be felt among me and my colleagues. The moralizing, blaming, and stigma could now be addressed. Still, the ravages of addiction are gaining ground, not only in the United States. Addiction is a worldwide problem.[2]

Let's take a look at some of the assumptions that this book is founded on. Having a grasp on what is happening around us can help us find the appropriate motivation to be better clinicians. Let's take a look at some of the numbers. For additional background on the global pandemic of addiction, see our Chapter 1 eResource companion at: www.routledge.com/9781138618039. Further, you can access a checklist in Worksheet 1.1 (Quick Reference to Substance Use Disorders).

## The Definition of Addiction

I hold with the ASAM definition of how addiction manifests:

> Addiction is characterized by inability to consistently abstain, impairment in behavioral control, craving, diminished recognition of significant problems with one's behaviors and interpersonal relationships, and a dysfunctional emotional response. Like other chronic diseases, addiction often involves cycles of relapse and remission. Without treatment or engagement in recovery activities, addiction is progressive and can result in disability or premature death.[1]

In other words, addiction reinforces itself.

As clinicians, we must have a clear understanding of how addiction is centered in the brain. Psychoactive substances affect neurotransmission and interactions within reward circuitry of the brain, leading to addictive behaviors that replace healthy behaviors. At the same time, memories of previous experiences trigger craving and renewal of addictive behaviors. Meanwhile, brain circuitry that governs impulse control and judgment is also altered in this disease, resulting in the dysfunctional pursuit of those same rewards.

The cycle of drug use goes like this:

> *Use a drug. Feel good. Use again. Feel good. Repeat until numb.*

It is important to note here that the lexicon of addiction is evolving. A new and important distinction has been made in recent years for concise understanding. According to the National Institute on Drug Abuse (NIDA), the National Institutes of Health (NIH):

> Continues to use the term "addiction" to describe compulsive drug seeking despite negative consequences. However, "addiction" is not considered a specific diagnosis in the fifth edition of *The Diagnostic and Statistical Manual of Mental Disorders* (DSM-5)—a diagnostic manual used by clinicians that contains descriptions and symptoms of all mental disorders classified by the American Psychiatric Association (APA).
>
> In 2013, the APA updated the DSM, replacing the categories of substance abuse and substance dependence with a single category: substance use disorder. The symptoms associated with a substance use disorder fall into four major groupings: impaired control, social impairment, risky use, and pharmacological criteria (i.e. tolerance and withdrawal).[3]

Why is this distinction important? What are the diagnostic implications of no longer viewing substance abuse and substance dependence as two distinct, separate conditions?

The earlier DSM-IV division into two disorders was guided by the concept that "dependence syndrome" formed one dimension of substance problems, while social and interpersonal consequences of heavy use formed another. While related, DSM-IV placed dependence above abuse in a hierarchy; the separation made it impossible to diagnose abuse when dependence was present.[4]

So, what implications does this new definition have for clinicians? The change from categorizing substance abuse and dependence as separate issues into one new disorder does not affect clinicians dramatically. The DSM-5 aims to help clinicians more clearly diagnose and categorize addictions (substance use disorders). This mainly affects you if you are an individual clinician, particularly for reimbursements. In fact, I often view the DSM-5 as a billing tool used for insurance reimbursement; its categorization is applied for billing.

Therefore, clinicians may need to update intake questionnaires or billing systems accordingly. Additionally, you need to know the DSM-5 when in a clinical setting or while sitting down with a client or their family; DSM-5 criteria for addiction will guide the discussion and your case notes. Additionally, if you're teaching, you want to share this definition with students.

This is not to understate the clinical relevance and incredible usefulness of diagnostic tools. The DSM-5 is absolutely critical for recognition and identification of addiction. The new combined condition – substance use disorder – allows clinicians to set the diagnostic threshold for the disorder at two or more criteria *and* classify the severity indicators of the condition as mild, moderate, or severe.

What are these new criteria for diagnosis of addiction? The new DSM-5 describes substance use disorder as a problematic pattern of use of an intoxicating substance leading to clinically significant impairment or distress, as manifested by at least two of the following, occurring within a 12-month period:[5]

1. The substance is often taken in larger amounts or over a longer period than was intended.
2. There is a persistent desire or unsuccessful effort to cut down or control use of the substance.
3. A great deal of time is spent in activities necessary to obtain the substance, use the substance, or recover from its effects.
4. Craving, or a strong desire or urge to use the substance.
5. Recurrent use of the substance resulting in a failure to fulfill major role obligations at work, school, or home.
6. Continued use of the substance despite having persistent or recurrent social or interpersonal problems caused or exacerbated by the effects of its use.
7. Important social, occupational, or recreational activities are given up or reduced because of use of the substance.

8. Recurrent use of the substance in situations in which it is physically hazardous.
9. Use of the substance is continued despite knowledge of having a persistent or recurrent physical or psychological problem that is likely to have been caused or exacerbated by the substance.
10. Tolerance, as defined by either of the following:

    (a) A need for markedly increased amounts of the substance to achieve intoxication or desired effect.
    (b) A markedly diminished effect with continued use of the same amount of the substance.

11. Withdrawal, as manifested by either of the following:

    (a) The characteristic withdrawal syndrome for that substance (as specified in the DSM-5 for each substance).
    (b) The substance (or a closely related substance) is taken to relieve or avoid withdrawal symptoms.

*Note:* Current national surveys of drug use have not yet been modified to reflect the new DSM-5 criteria of substance use disorders, and therefore still report substance abuse and dependence separately.

## Trauma and Addiction

Trauma can be broadly understood as a stress that causes physical or emotional harm from which you cannot remove yourself. Clinically, trauma is an overwhelming experience that cannot be integrated, and elicits animal defensive mechanisms and dysregulated arousal. However, not everyone reacts to similar traumatic situations in the same way; trauma is subjective, meaning what matters most is the individual's internal beliefs and their innate sensitivity to stress. This is why people who witness the same event can have differing responses.

> *Trauma is both objective (something has happened) and subjective (this is how I feel about something).*

Trauma is indigenous to experiences of substance abuse, mental health, and chronic pain. In fact, trauma leads to a cascade of biological changes and stress responses that are highly associated with post-traumatic stress disorder (PTSD), other mental illnesses, and substance use disorders.[6] Some possible brain changes can include changes in limbic system functioning, hypothalamic–pituitary–adrenal axis activity changes with variable cortisol levels, and neurotransmitter-related dysregulation of arousal and endogenous opioid systems. In addition to biological changes triggered by trauma, people can also adapt harmful emotional and psychological patterns that lead to self-medication through the use of drugs and alcohol.

When does trauma arise? Trauma can stem from abuse or neglect, a frightening experience such as witnessing a murder, a car, boat, or airplane accident, during war, at school bullying and shootings, sudden life changes, not being told about something, or near-death experiences. Trauma also occurs in homes where a parent(s) used substances or when growing up in an environment where the expression of how one feels is not cultivated.

One of the most destructive forms of trauma is recurrent name-calling and humiliation, bullying, and embarrassment. The definition of trauma also includes responses to powerful one-time events, such as accidents, natural disasters, school shootings, public shootings, crimes, surgeries, deaths, and other violent events. It also includes responses to chronic or repetitive events, such as child abuse, neglect, combat, urban violence, concentration camps, battering relationships, and enduring deprivation.

The main point we'd like to make here is that the clinical tools outlined in this book will help you assess clients for possible trauma-related disorders. Given the prevalence of traumatic events in clients who present for substance abuse treatment, skills such as family mapping, retrospective biopsychosocial analysis, and portraiture are key to identifying and bringing trauma into the light. Appropriate diagnosis and treatment of trauma-informed substance use disorder are imperative to healing.

## The Complexity of Chronic Pain

To continue, we need to understand that the treatment of chronic pain is also connected to the problem of addiction in the United States. Pain is cited as the most common reason Americans access the healthcare system.[7] It is a leading cause of disability and it is a major contributor to healthcare costs. In fact, Americans with category 3 or 4 pain are likely to have worse health status, use more healthcare, and suffer from more disability than those with less severe pain.[8]

How prevalent is the problem of chronic pain?

Some 133 million people experience chronic pain in the United States[9] – 1.5 billion people globally.[10] Approximately 76.2 million, or one in every four Americans, have suffered from pain that lasts longer than 24 hours, and millions more suffer from acute pain.[11] In fact, 65% of all people will experience chronic pain once in their lifetime. Pain affects more Americans than diabetes, heart disease, and cancer combined.

> *To put growing numbers in perspective, one must first distinguish between acute and chronic pain.*

Acute pain is short-term, typically brought on by a physical ailment such as inflammation or injury, and clears up when the source is treated and heals.

Chronic pain, however, is long-lasting, generally over three months of persistent pain. Chronic pain is believed to be a disease that causes changes in the nerves and persists long after the initial source of the pain heals.

To add fuel to the fire, pain is big business for the healthcare industry – an estimated $560–635 billion is spent annually to manage pain, including healthcare expenses, lost income, and lost productivity at work and home.[12] Physical therapy, surgery, and nerve blocks are common forms of treatment, as well as alternative treatment approaches such as acupuncture, mindfulness, and massage therapy.

Still, many Americans – through no fault of their own – turn to prescription drugs to address their chronic pain. This has inadvertently given rise to the opioid epidemic – a catch-22 whereby the very cure for pain coupled with overprescribing sparks an addiction that can cause serious harm. Though most patients who are prescribed pain pills use them responsibly, research shows close to 5 million Americans are taking prescription pain medication in unsafe ways.[13]

Since chronic pain is a serious condition that can cause months and even years of pain, people who use painkillers long-term can develop problems such as hyperalgesia. Hyperalgesia is a condition wherein a person becomes overly sensitive to pain. Doctors and researchers have linked this phenomenon to opioids. Essentially, the prolonged use of pain medication to treat pain develops a change in the person's nervous system, so that their pain threshold goes down and sensitivity goes up.

To summarize, chronic pain can be an obstacle to addiction treatment. However, the clinician who is prepared with a correct understanding of the condition and who is armed with treatment options can most help people move to change. Knowing your audience and their needs is at the heart of successful addiction interventions.

## Beyond the Triple Threat of Dual Diagnosis

Until the 1980s, it used to be that clients coming in for treatment were typically corralled into two discrete camps: the mentally ill or the substance abuser. Each had parallel treatment and discrete funding streams. As that decade drew to a close, so appeared the term dual diagnosis, a clinical moniker that appropriately (finally!) acknowledged the reality that those who experienced substance abuse disorders were almost always in the throes of one or more concurrent mental health disorders that needed treatment.

## Tertiary Issues Concurrent with Addiction

As a seasoned interventionist, I've seen clients from both sides of the mental illness/substance abuse spectrum, as well as clients with an avalanche of additional problems that I describe as the *triple threat*, those who experience a tertiary issue either as a result of a prior condition (i.e. disorder or illness) or one that is exacerbated by additional factors (i.e. physical, legal, traumatic, etc.).

> *Traditional diagnoses sometimes miss the mark, to the detriment of the patients and their families.*

While three may be a crowd, we are at peril if we ignore the needs of this cacophonous threesome, foursome, fivesome, with its unique storylines, pains, and pathologies. These folks and their families present a diagnostic quandary with their kaleidoscope of competing and equally important issues. Figure 1.1 illustrates the possible complexity of tertiary conditions that co-occur in cases of substance use disorders.

## A Tidal Wave of Loss

Like a tidal wave that comes crushing to shore over the past year, the president, states, national news media, and families who have lost loved ones have cried out in crushing alarm about the tragedies of opioid addiction and overdose. With the increasing amount of untimely death, the tide has turned, and there is not a news media outlet that does not feature this dilemma.

> *I'm an educator at heart, and reading about these rising tides, as well as observing in my daily work with clients and families, I'm concerned for the long-term health and vitality of our nation.*

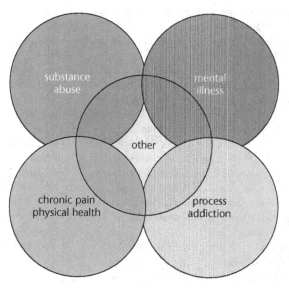

**FIGURE 1.1**  A diagram of tertiary issues concurrent with addiction

How can we begin to address such a harrowing substance abuse problem that is impacting millions of people? We must put our ideological differences aside and begin on the national, state, and local level to create policies and programs that support health and wellness. We must have a conceptual framework that spells out goals, objectives, and directives for folks at all levels. We must fund research that allows us to develop best treatment practices.

Insurance companies must work hand in hand with behavioral healthcare specialists to find the best treatment options that are equitable and fair to all Americans. Healthcare providers, doctors, nurses, and administrators must educate their patients and offer alternative pain management solutions.

We must develop educational programs that are consumer-friendly that speak to the risks involved for all these. In short, we must fund, educate, and inform. As a nation, we must be willing to treat these addictions with wholehearted vigor and determination.

## References

1. American Society of Addiction Medicine (2011) *Public Policy Statement: Definition of Addiction*. Rockville, MD: ASAM. Available at: https://asam.org/docs/default-source/public-policy-statements/1definition_of_addiction_long_4-11.pdf?sfvrsn=a8f64512_4 (accessed March 4, 2018).
2. UNODC (2012) *World Drug Report*. New York: United Nations Publications. Available at: www.unodc.org/unodc/en/data-and-analysis/WDR-2012.html (accessed March 4, 2018).
3. National Institute on Drug Abuse (2016) *Media Guide: The Science of Drug Abuse and Addiction*. Bethesda, MD: National Institutes of Health. Available at: www.drugabuse.gov/publications/media-guide (accessed March 4, 2018).
4. Hasin DS, O'Brien CP, Auriacombe M, et al. (2013) DSM-5 Criteria for Substance Use Disorders: Recommendations and Rationale. *The American Journal of Psychiatry*. 170(8): 834–851.
5. American Psychiatric Association (2013) *Diagnostic and Statistical Manual of Mental Disorders* (5th ed.). Arlington, TX: American Psychiatric Publishing. Available at: http://dx.doi.org/10.1176/appi.books.9780890425596 (accessed March 4, 2018).
6. Center for Substance Abuse Treatment (2014) *Treatment Improvement Protocol (TIP) Series, No. 57*. Rockville, MD: Substance Abuse and Mental Health Services Administration. Available at: www.ncbi.nlm.nih.gov/books/NBK207191/ (accessed March 4, 2018).
7. Stanger L (2018) *Are Your Clients in Pain?* San Diego, CA: SlideShare. Available at: www.slideshare.net/LouiseStanger/presentations (accessed March 4, 2018).
8. National Center for Complementary and Integrative Health (2012) *National Health Interview Survey*. Bethesda, MD: National Institutes of Health. Available at: https://nccih.nih.gov/research/statistics/NHIS/2012/pain/severity (accessed March 4, 2018).
9. Nahin RL (2015) Estimates of Pain Prevalence and Severity in Adults. *Journal of Pain*. 16(8): 769–780.

10. Global Industry Analysts, Inc. (2012) *Pain Management: A Global Strategic Business Report*. Available at: www.strategyr.com/Pain_Management_Market_Report.asp# sthash.pHEprTUP.dpbs (accessed March 4, 2018).

11. National Institute of Nursing Research (2010) *Fact Sheets: Pain Management*. Bethesda, MD: National Institutes of Health. Available at: https://report.nih.gov/ nihfactsheets/Pdfs/PainManagement(NINR).pdf (accessed March 4, 2018).

12. Institute of Medicine Committee on Advancing Pain Research, Care, and Education (2011) *Relieving Pain in America: A Blueprint for Transforming Prevention, Care, Education, and Research*. Washington, DC: National Academies Press. Available at: www.ncbi.nlm.nih.gov/books/NBK92521/ (accessed March 4, 2018).

13. MedlinePlus (2011) Safely Managing Chronic Pain. *NIH MedlinePlus Magazine*. 6(1): 4. Available at: https://medlineplus.gov/magazine/issues/spring11/articles/ spring11pg4.html (accessed March 4, 2018).

# 2

# CURRENT MODELS OF INTERVENTION

## A Recent History of Interventions

Interventions – as we know them – were first modeled in the mid to late 1980s. In truth, the intervention process was known by only a handful of people until a decade ago. The public was simply not informed. With the advent of the HBO television show *Interventions*, the dialogue between family and identified loved one/client/patient became public knowledge. Then we saw a proliferation of interventionists, trainings, and books hit the market.

> *Like all embryonic professions, the styles, ethics, and role of an interventionist have become subjects for debate.*

Simultaneously, the substance abuse field exploded with the development of thousands of new addiction treatment centers, an industry that is still experiencing explosive growth. SAMHSA's report titled *Projections of National Expenditures for Treatment of Mental and Substance Use Disorders, 2010–2020* estimates that addiction treatment spending from all public and private sources is expected to total $280.5 billion in 2020, which is an increase from $171.7 billion in 2009.[1] In fact, according to this same report, spending growth in the addiction treatment industry is estimated at 4.6% annually.

Over the past decade, it has appeared that a proliferation of interventionists (trained and untrained) have emerged, trying to help wounded families. The context is still akin to the Wild West; many interventionists have little credentialing, formal postgraduate education, or training. There are, of course, standout trainers in the field: Ed Storti, Jeff and Deborah Jay, Dr. Judith Landau, Brad Lamm, Candy Finnigan, Ken Seeley, and the recently deceased John

Southworth, to name a few. Others have starred in the HBO *Intervention* series: Heather Hayes and colleagues, who offer trainings across the country, including Dr. Jessica Rodriquez, Patti Pike, Jean Campbell, and Bill Maher, and across the pond in the UK Ian Young.

But what is their role in the context of growing addictions and business opportunity? For the purposes of this textbook, with the exception of the action model, I have tried to contain my discussion of interventionists and styles, and referenced those that have actually written and published books on the subject. I offer this:

> *Interventionists are charged with creating possibility and hope for folks ravaged by mental health and substance abuse disorders in a humane, systemic way designed to help all those involved.*

Working with wounded, trauma-ridden folks is a serious business. Interventionists are charged with helping loved ones and their families get the help they need in a compassionate, caring, ethical manner. Folks call upon interventionists when their hope is dashed. Admissions and business development professionals often refer to interventionists when they cannot close a sale, when the presenting problems are just too darn complicated.

Make no mistake: I do not believe a three- or five-day course in and of itself turns you automatically into an interventionist (even though some offer consultation afterwards). A course can, however, arm you with knowledge and information on how the process works, expose you to different approaches, and provide a springboard if you choose to do more work, and takes advantage of supervision as you develop your skills. A course helps inform those who have careers in admissions or business development, are part of the clinical team, or are generally interested in how this fits within treatment and aftercare.

## Theoretical Foundations for Interventions

There are many theories that help inform the practice of addiction interventions. These theories attempt to explain human behavior and help us in our understanding of what it takes to get a person to "yes" in the context of addiction treatment. A commonality in these theoretical frameworks is their view that individuals make decisions and apply learning to support their own best interests. Further, each theory helps us understand how we might motivate a person to change. Here, we have summarized a few of the most influential working theories used in the practice of addiction intervention:

- *Systems theory* describes human behavior in terms of complex systems. It is premised on the idea that an effective system is based on individual needs, rewards, expectations, and attributes of the people living in the system.

Per this theory, families, couples, and organization members are directly involved in resolving a problem, even if it is an individual issue.

- *Psychodynamic theory* was developed by Freud, and it explains personality in terms of conscious and unconscious forces. This social work theory describes the personality as consisting of the id (responsible for following basic instincts), the superego (attempts to follow rules and behave morally), and the ego (mediates between the id and the ego).
- *Psychodrama* is an action method often used as a psychotherapy during which clients use spontaneous dramatization, role play, and dramatic self-presentation to investigate and gain insight into their lives.
- *Psychosocial development theory* is an eight-stage theory of identity and psychosocial development articulated by Erik Erikson. Erikson believed everyone must pass through eight stages of development over the life cycle: hope, will, purpose, competence, fidelity, love, care, and wisdom. Each stage is divided into age ranges from infancy to older adults.
- *Rational choice theory* is based on the idea that all action is fundamentally rational in character, and people calculate the risks and benefits of any action before making decisions.
- *Social learning theory* is based on Albert Bandura's idea that learning occurs through observation and imitation. New behavior will continue if it is reinforced. Per this theory, rather than simply hearing a new concept and applying it, the learning process is made more efficient if the new behavior is modeled as well.
- *Sociometry* was developed by Joseph L. Moreno, MD, as the study of the formation of groups. It includes many exercises and activities designed to allow participants to see how they interact with one another, and offers groups the experience of practicing conflict, cooperation, and cohesion.
- *Transpersonal theory* proposes additional stages beyond the adult ego. In healthy individuals, these stages contribute to creativity, wisdom, and altruism. In people lacking healthy ego development, experiences can lead to psychosis.

## Social Work Practice Models

In addition, it can be helpful to look at practice models used in social work as potential tools during addiction interventions. Why the crossover? The National Association of Social Workers describes the principle mission of social workers thus: "Social workers aim to enhance human well-being and help meet the basic human needs of all people, with attention to the needs and empowerment of people who are vulnerable, oppressed, and living in poverty."[2] Therefore, our work in addictions and the mission of social work are keenly aligned. In fact, social workers have historically been providing essential services for people who experience substance abuse disorders for decades.

In my experience, successful addiction interventions are based on sound social work principles. These interventions start at the beginning of an individual or family's needs and work from the foundation of unconditional positive regard. Still, there are many different practice models that influence the way behavioral healthcare professionals choose to help people meet their goals.

While we do not have time to delve into all the details in this book, it can be helpful to outline the basic theories, concepts, and techniques of how social work practice models can be best used in interventions. Here are some of the major social work practice models currently used in various roles:

- *Cognitive behavioral therapy* focuses on the relationship between thoughts, feelings, and behaviors. Social workers assist clients in identifying patterns of irrational and self-destructive thoughts and behaviors that influence emotions and give homework assignments that can help change these unhealthy patterns.
- A *crisis intervention model* is used when someone is dealing with an acute crisis. The model includes seven stages: assess safety and lethality, rapport-building, problem identification, address feelings, generate alternatives, develop an action plan, and follow up. This social work practice model is commonly used with clients who are expressing suicidal ideation or have experienced direct trauma, and originated at the Simmons School of Social Work.
- *Narrative therapy* externalizes a person's problem by examining the story of the person's life. In the story, the client is not defined by the problem, and the problem exists as a separate entity. Instead of focusing on a client's depression, in this social work practice model a client would be encouraged to fight against the depression by looking at the skills and abilities that may have previously been taken for granted.
- *Problem-solving* assists people with the problem-solving process. Rather than tell clients what to do, social workers teach clients how to apply a problem-solving method so they can develop their own solutions.
- *Task-centered practice* is a short-term treatment where clients establish specific, measurable goals. Social workers and clients collaborate and create specific strategies and steps to begin reaching those goals.

In sum, each of these practice models can be used to help a person who is experiencing a substance abuse and/or mental health disorder into treatment. The methods are different; indeed, not all of these models consider the complexity of human behavior. Still, they all want someone to go from A to B. They combine elements of motivation and change, are oriented to quick solutions, and are designed to be done quickly in a short-term intervention.

## What Is an Intervention Model?

There are several intervention models currently in practice. These can best be categorized as either surprise, systemic, action, or invitational. Below, we'll look at the characteristics of each. In the next chapter, we'll examine how the Collective Intervention Strategy (CIS) encourages you to identify and make best use of these models. Before we take a deeper look, however, let's first understand the definition of a model.

Models are general explanations that are supported by evidence obtained through the scientific method. A theory, on the other hand, tries to explain human behavior – for example, by describing how humans interact or how humans react to certain stimuli.

The models we illuminate below are practice models. These describe how interventionists can help move someone to change. As such, they also describe how behavioral healthcare professionals, licensed social workers, marriage and family therapists, psychologists, addiction counselors, and certified intervention professionals may implement theories. In turn, these models attempt to provide practitioners with a blueprint of how to help others based on the underlying theories of motivation and change.

While interventions can and do take place inside such environments as home, work, school, hospitals, and jails, the protocols are different – often idiosyncratic – based on a person's training, background, and expertise.

> *In this book, I posit that there is not one true model of addiction intervention. Rather, a variety of different approaches are currently in use that purport success in moving persons through the stages of change from a precontemplative state into action (i.e. entering treatment).*

Hence, Prochaska and DiClemente's transtheoretical stages of change model may be most helpful in looking at clients as we move them to change. Likewise, interventionists owe a great debt of gratitude to seminal theoreticians such as Salvador Minuchin, an originator of structural family therapy, Monica McGoldrick, a family therapist who wrote on genograms, Virgina Satir, the founder of transformational family therapy, and Irving Yalom, the psychotherapist and existentialist who developed the theory and practice of group psychotherapy. Without the seminal work of these practitioners, the successes of today would not be possible.

## Common Strategies Used in Intervention

The strategies used in all intervention models to some degree involve an understanding of:

- family systems theory;
- human behavior and lifestyle development;
- motivational change theories;
- mental health disorders;
- characteristics of substance abuse disorders;

- characteristics of process disorders; and
- characteristics of chronic pain and other medical conditions.

Indeed, many models for addiction intervention employ some, all, or a combination of strategies. Still, the basic requirements are not exclusive. Indeed, the Collective Intervention Strategy (CIS) that we'll outline in the next chapters requires an understanding of how to complete a biopsychosocial assessment based on retrospective analysis, as well as 12-step facilitation, motivational interviewing, cognitive behavioral, and solution-focused therapy from both the therapeutic and business research communities.

While clinical strategies provide the backbone to successful interventions, your own personal style will necessarily alter outcomes, for good or bad. For this reason, it can help to assess your own clinical assumptions and style before you dive into the practice of interventions. See Worksheet 2.1 (Self-Assessment of Your Clinical Style), then use the findings to adjust and/or commit to training, supervision, or skill updates.

There are a handful of variables that add to the support of an effective treatment plan. Working with another person or having a team member present in an intervention to partner with you is one strategy that truly helps. This is often called a "second chair."

History has long proved the value of teamwork and partnership. In the treatment world, we all know that the best programs at their core are interdisciplinary and collaborative in their approach. In truth, no single professional can be all things to all clients. Even the most experienced physician would be remiss if they did not recommend the opinion or the support of a second physician. Teaming provides a more robust service and gives families, friends, and their loved ones a more comprehensive service. See Chapter 5 for more on the benefits of working in a team during addiction interventions.

## Efficacy of Intervention Models

Before we begin any discussion on the efficacy of drug or alcohol interventions, it will be helpful to make a specific distinction and agree on what exactly an intervention is. The 2015 publication *Field Trials of Health Interventions: A Toolbox* defines the medical practice of health interventions thus:

> We use the term "intervention" to apply to any activity undertaken with the objective of improving human health by preventing disease, by curing or reducing the severity or duration of an existing disease, or by restoring function lost through disease or injury.
>
> Interventions can be classified into two broad categories: (1) preventive interventions are those that prevent disease from occurring and thus reduce

the incidence (new cases) of disease, and (2) therapeutic interventions are those that treat, mitigate, or postpone the effects of disease, once it is under way, and thus reduce the case fatality rate or reduce the disability or morbidity associated with a disease. Some interventions may have both effects.[3]

To be clear, the type of drug or alcohol intervention we discuss in this book is the latter type of intervention; it is an invitation to treat the medical condition of substance use disorder(s). But how effective are these interventions, as shown in medical literature?

First, clinical, professionally guided interventions are a necessity. In 2016, the U.S. Department of Health and Human Services reported that of the 21.1 million persons classified as needing substance use treatment, only 3.8 million received it.[4] The same study broke it down even further: for those who needed but did not receive substance use treatment, *only 4.5% reported a perceived need for therapy*.[5] Another way to say this is that 95% of those who need substance use treatment do not realize that they have a drug or alcohol problem. Therefore, one of the greatest problems in initiating addiction treatment is that those who require treatment do not even recognize the need for therapeutic help. As we explore in later chapters, many people who need addiction treatment live in denial of a problem.

However, when an intervention is not supervised, it often does not occur. Studies have shown that the clear majority of networks do not implement a planned confrontation without professional help. For example, in one randomized clinical trial of 130 significant others offered manual-guided 12-hour intervention planning, 70% coached in a specific intervention model did not go through with it, but among those who did, most (75%) succeeded in getting the identified loved one (ILO) into treatment.[6] In another study, only 7 of 24 social networks confronted the ILO to seek treatment, even after counseling about the process.[7]

Second, the immediacy of response is critical to the effectiveness of an intervention. For example, crisis intervention literature demonstrates the benefit of an immediate response in people faced with crises.[8] Similarly, one research team funded by the National Institute on Drug Abuse found that same-day or immediate response to a family's call for help led to 83% treatment engagement.[9] A similar rationale has been employed with the community reinforcement training approach to engagement: the clinician attempts to see the client on the day of the first call.[10,11]

Further, interventions have been found to affect some populations more than others. For example, in the NIDA-funded study above,[9] Judith Landau et al. found that parents were more likely to get addicted individuals engaged than spouses, a finding supported earlier by colleagues, Meyers[12] and Szapnocznik.[13] The study also reported improved results with cases in which at least one parent was involved as a participant, matching that addicted individuals are closely involved with one or both of their parents.

The end conclusion?

*Parents can be a powerful resource for inducing ILOs to seek help.*

In my experience, when treatment resistance is addressed by family groups who face addiction as a medical brain disease, they can initiate change. Together, family units can destigmatize addiction and its treatment. Further, addicted brains are thought to manifest dysfunction of neural circuits underlying interception, self-awareness, and appropriate social, emotional, and cognitive responses. When families are correctly informed about the science that underlies the "hijacking" of the brain, it is easier to take emotional distance from the hurt and pain of the manifested behavior. Empathy becomes possible through this understanding.

## Limitations of Intervention Models

At present, only a handful of limited studies and literature reviews report on the efficacy of different intervention models. Further, none compare success rates by type of intervention. Specific therapeutic interventions for substance used disorders have been tested in a variety of clinical trials, including and not limited to motivational interviewing (MI). In fact, MI has a robust history in hospital, college, prison, and religious settings. Additionally, there are a plethora of evidence-based studies that examine the efficacy of specific types of therapies in clinical settings.

Still, the only research on intervention has been conducted within emergency room hospital settings using short-term motivational interviewing.[14,15] We'll cover motivational interviewing in depth in Chapter 5; it has been used to intervene with folks suspected of substance abuse in hospitals, and also in jails, to help people get treatment.

From my perspective, all intervention models are limited because of the lack of empirical study. Interventions mainly take place outside of a controlled environment, such as hospitals and jails. These highly structured settings define the context in which brief motivational studies done by Miller[16] and Rollnick[17] have been performed. Combined with the idiosyncratic nature of the providers, how might findings be applied to real-life situations? If one can become an interventionist without clinical training or professional licensure, how can we rely on reporting standards? The field is open to investigation and discourse, and is ripe for research.

One of the limitations of research into efficacy is that it's very difficult to track interventions. Interventions do not take place in institutions such as short-term hospital settings, prisons, or college campuses. Nor do control groups exist. Most interventions are facilitated by independent providers performing a service outside clinical settings; they take place in a home or in a boardroom.

So, we need to ask ourselves, "How do we move or think out of the box?" "How do we qualify success with data?" Further, research studies require backing money and collaboration. One research grant, for example, could be used toward gathering data collected via self-report; another could initiate an introductory, qualitative research project with a snowball questionnaire via phone calls. We could outreach to the membership of CIP, NII, AIS, social workers, and marriage and family counselors. We could ask:

- How many interventions did you do this year?
- What styles do you use?
- How many clients went to treatment?
- How many refuse treatments?

From my experience as a principal investigator for NIH, NIAAA, and U.S. Department of Education college-based interventions and family-based intervention studies, there has not been a major university or federal grant that tests any single intervention model. However, the National Council on Alcoholism and Drug Dependence claims that most interventions have an incredible success rate: 90% when led by a certified professional.[18]

Psychosocial interventions for the treatment of substance use problems cover a broad array of treatment interventions, each with their own varied theoretical backgrounds. While we do not have the time to examine these in detail, the following therapies are noteworthy in that each of them has been used to bring people struggling with substance abuse to a place of "yes":

- 12-step facilitation;
- cognitive behavioral therapy;
- motivational interviewing;
- psychodrama; and
- solution-focused therapy.

In conclusion, it is generally agreed that interventions aim to elicit changes in a person's substance misuse behaviors, cognitive, and emotional states, and that the interaction between therapist and patient helps facilitate this. Professional interventionists employ these evidence-based therapies in the practice of a drug or alcohol intervention. But what do these interventions look like? What are some of the clinical factors of each?

## The Surprise Model

The surprise model was first developed by Dr. Vernon Johnson, the grandfather of intervention, and is described in his landmark book *I'll Quit Tomorrow: A Practical Guide to Alcoholism Treatment*.[19] Dr. Johnson tested the model in hospitals and was an avid follower of the 12 Steps of Alcoholics Anonymous. Also known as the "Johnson model," this approach is perhaps the most well-known model of intervention, gaining popularity in recent years through reality television shows.

During a Johnson intervention, members of the ILO's social network participate directly in the process, often secretly or without the person's knowledge. In short, folks gather together and surprise the individual with the guidance of a facilitator to invite them to go to treatment. It is felt that if one is surprised, they will have less time to ruminate and their defenses will be lowered. The idea is that when startled, the identified client will be more likely to say "yes" to treatment.

Following the surprise model, interventionists meet with concerned loved ones a few times before a formal direct meeting to plan a surprise. The formalized process includes a progressive interaction between the clinician and the family or friends for at least two days before meeting with the ILO. During this time, interventionists help plan the intervention and educate the family about substance abuse and its prevention. Participants are coached about offering information in an emotionally neutral, factual manner while maintaining a supportive, non-accusatory tone.

The surprise model teaches family members how to present incontrovertible evidence to the loved one that a problem exists. The desired outcome is engagement – and retention – in addiction treatment. The main steps used in a surprise intervention include:

1.  The interventionist responds to the "first caller" or "concerned other" and determines key stakeholders. Usually, the person calling the interventionist (i.e. the person paying) helps guide the formation of the family group.
2.  Then the family/friends group holds a pre-intervention meeting. The pre-intervention meeting is held without the ILO's knowledge. During this meeting, key family members plan who will attend the intervention. They also decide on treatment options and begin recovery messaging via written letters.
3.  Then the family surprise and confront the ILO in a group setting. This is called the intervention. The intervention is a surprise meeting, held without invitation, meant to lower the ILO's defenses. During the intervention, family members read their personal letters out loud to urge an ILO into treatment. Letters encourage the loved one to enter treatment or face a series of consequences. The letters are designed in a specific way. They address how much the person cares for the individual, they share why the person's heart is hurting, they contain evidence of how relationships have been damaged, and they also set boundaries.
4.  If the ILO will not enter treatment, the family may choose to cut ties or impose other boundaries and consequences.

5. When treatment begins, the family resumes with their daily tasks.
6. If a relapse occurs, the family performs another intervention.

To produce the desired outcome, this type of intervention is highly scripted and organized. Concerned loved ones confront substance use and talk about the damage that drinking and drug use has caused them personally. The interventionist serves as facilitator for the process.

## Efficacy of the Surprise Model

Advocates of surprise interventions urge us to believe that confrontations present ILOs with the facts needed to get past denial of a substance use disorder. Through the intervention, the ILO is challenged to persist in the belief that nothing is wrong. Indeed, landmark studies seem to support the idea that social networks can be become highly influential in motivating an ILO to seek treatment. A 1989 study indicated that alcoholics who were confronted by their family group were significantly more likely to enter an alcohol detox or rehabilitation program and to remain continuously abstinent than were non-confronted alcoholics.[20]

However, evidence on the efficacy of the surprise model is weak at best. While this intervention approach is widely acclaimed as effective, it has been subject to relatively little evaluation. Most reports are uncontrolled assessments of family confrontation training that claim a higher rate of treatment. Still, little is known about the longer-term impact of these interventions on all participants and their relationships.

The 1999 randomized clinical trial of 130 concerned significant others mentioned earlier[6] may provide us with some insight. These family members were offered one of three counseling approaches: (a) Al-Anon facilitation therapy to encourage involvement in 12-step programs; (b) a Johnson intervention; or (c) CRAFT community reinforcement and family training. Outcomes of previously unmotivated problem drinkers in treatment engagement were: (a) 13%; (b) 30%; and (c) 64%, respectively. The study reasonably concluded that *teaching family members' skills to modify contingencies for drinking behaviors was more effective than a traditional confrontational intervention in yielding a higher rate of treatment engagement.*

Why such a discrepancy? Researchers posit that many families who are introduced to the surprise method decide not to go through with it. They simply find the style unacceptable. In truth, there are camps on both sides of the fence: some maintain that surprise is the best way forward, while others prefer an invitation style. After 30 years of experience, the style one adopts has a lot to do with what the individual interventionist has been trained in or comfortable with, and the situation as it unfolds.

## Limitations of the Surprise Model

At the time, Dr. Johnson encouraged something revolutionary: in the face of addiction, placing focus on the ILO and their resulting change in behavior became the priority. What was so new? His style of confrontation was intentional. A surprise intervention aims to lower defenses and to overcome denial. The main goal was for people to accept help and attend treatment. However, we have seen that there are inherent flaws in this model.

Often, surprise model interventions generate great upset and distrust. As noted in the 2017 Surgeon General's report *Facing Addiction in America,*[21] "Confrontational approaches in general, though once the norm even in many behavioral treatment settings, have not been found effective and may backfire by heightening resistance and diminishing self-esteem on the part of the targeted individual."[22]

ILOs report feeling disrespected, ambushed, and shamed. They report feeling cornered or pressured into treatment. It's no wonder that many of them drop out of treatment. In fact, dropout rates seem to increase as relapses occur. Many ILOs who were subject to the surprise model of intervention reported this type of rebellious thinking:

> At first, I stopped my drug and alcohol use because of the pressure from the Intervention, but then I found myself thinking, "I'm not going to be told what to do!" so I started using again.

Just imagine, you're the ILO struggling with a substance abuse or mental health disorder and this whole cadre of people descends upon you. Well, we know that substance abuse and mental health disorders are beset with shame and feeling awful. If clinicians set up an ambush or an adversarial relationship by surprising you at the very start, they've got to work through that first.

The fact is that the Johnson model yields questionable long-term results. One study of outpatient treatment retention in the late 1980s found that ILOs who came to treatment after a surprise intervention started off strong in treatment, but had high rates (55%) of dropping out after eight to ten weeks.[23] Another 1996 study of 210 cases found that individuals who went through the Johnson model of intervention were most likely to enter treatment. However, treatment retention was also found to deteriorate over the course of treatment.[24] Why might this be?

To begin, the main technique used during the Johnson method is bargaining. The list of consequences of noncompliance to treatment demands is a clear threat. Concerned loved ones are instructed to outline the action they will take if the ILO does not seek treatment. Little time or care is spent in case management or aftercare planning. Family therapy or coaching throughout the process is absent.

And the result of a surprise intervention? Often surprise interventions result in a defiant, rebellious response. But more than that, families risk much harm to individuals and the system. The highly confrontational aspects of the method can destroy the relationship with the ILO and/or chase them away forever. Or the surprise model confrontation can lead to ILOs "going over the edge" if strongly confronted, including mental breakdown or suicide attempts.

It's worthwhile noting the popularity of the surprise method here. Since its origin, the surprise model has been expanded upon by Dr. Frank Picard, author of *Family Intervention*,[25] who spoke of the necessity of including loved ones in the process, Debra and Jeff Jay, authors of *Love First*,[26] Ken Seeley, who was instrumental in starting the TV show *Intervention*, Candy Finnigan, who was also on the show and who wrote *When Enough Is Enough*,[27] John Southworth, and Ed Storti, author of *Heart to Heart*,[28] among other books. The way many iterations of this type of intervention are described, especially by Ed Storti and Jeff and Debra Jay, involve a great deal of compassion and motivation. In fact, these variations have worked well with thousands of clients.

Indeed, many colleagues have successfully softened the surprise method approach and crafted new styles that encompass a fine art of motivation and change theory. For example, Jeff and Debra Jay today restrict their trainings mainly to clinicians. In another example, Ed Storti has broadened the scope of the intervention team to include treatment providers that speak with the identified client about their facility. He has also been known to successfully step off a plane, have 10 minutes to prepare a family, and be successful. Is it his method or is it his own charisma that makes it happen? These individuals have made traditional interventions modern, adding their own special way of presenting, doing, and training.

### Advocates of the Surprise Model

- Vern Johnson: *I'll Quit Tomorrow.*
- Frank Pickard: *Family Intervention.*
- Candy Finnigan: *When Enough Is Enough.*
- Jeff and Debra Jay: *Love First.*
- Ed Storti: *Heart to Heart.*
- Ken Seeley: *Intervention 911.*
- John Southworth and associates: Mr. Southworth died in 2017 and was influential in the creation of trainings across the country, partnering at times with Ken Seeley.

### The Invitational Model

The invitational model of interventions is an iteration of the ARISE model – developed by Dr. Judith Landau, MD, and James Garret, CSW, authors of

*Invitational* Intervention,[29] and Brad Lamm's break free model, outlined in the book *How to Help the One You Love*.[30] These methods evolved mainly as an alternative to the surprise model. An invitational intervention relies on systems theory and assumes that families are competent, strong, and resilient in the face of major problems such as addiction.

At its most basic, invitational intervention is a combination of systems theory, family theory, and the Johnson model. They avoid confrontation and rely on willing participation by the ILO and the selected accountability team. According to founding practitioners, this style of intervention does not require threats or consequences; they state that less than 2% of families even talk about consequences. So, there are often no letters involved. No bargaining. No ambush. Instead, emphasis is on family education, developing strategy, and communication. The desired outcome is not only on treatment engagement of the ILO, but also includes long-term intergenerational family well-being and recovery.

In an Invitational Intervention using the ARISE model, the family has a chairperson who helps organize members and works directly with the interventionist. The interventionist or clinician guides the family strategy and facilitates two to five face-to-face sessions. They complete a family genogram, conduct interviews with family members, coach family members on crafting recovery messages, and direct conversations toward change. Some interventionists focus on a specific "change plan" customized to the ILO's needs for treatment. Finally, the group invites the ILO to change. If there is no movement by the last meeting, the group sets limits and consequences in a loving, supportive way.

The main steps used in an ARISE invitational intervention are:

1. Respond to the "first caller" or "concerned other" to establish a basis of hope, identify who to invite to the initial meeting, design a strategy to mobilize the support group, and teach techniques to successfully invite the ILO to the first meeting. At the same time, the interventionist can suggest a recovery message and get a commitment from all invited individuals to attend the initial meeting, regardless of whether the ILO attends.

2. If treatment does not start after the initial meeting, the interventionist facilitates between two and five face-to-face sessions, with or without the ILO present. The goal of these meetings is to develop motivational strategies to attain the goal of treatment engagement. The ILO is invited to each one of the group meetings. They are also told that since the discussion will revolve around them, they may want to attend to provide input and have their views considered. This alone often succeeds in getting the ILO to attend because most people do not like to be talked about without both hearing what is said and having a voice in the discussion.

3. If these meetings fail, this model reverts to a more traditional style such as the Johnson surprise model.

4.  If, after many opportunities to enter treatment, help is still refused, the family group sets limits, boundaries, and consequences for the ILO in a loving and supportive way. This final limit-setting approach is a natural consequence and does not come as a surprise. The family group commits to supporting each other in the implementation of the agreed upon consequences.

5.  Upon treatment completion, interventionists follow up with aftercare to address subtle and not so subtle change in the entire group. Meetings are held via regularly scheduled weekly family class sessions via telephone and the Internet.

## Efficacy of the Invitational Model

Luckily, the National Institute on Drug Abuse has sponsored empirical study on the application of the invitational model using the ARISE method – A Relational Intervention Sequence for Engagement – in varied age, gender, and race groups.[9] The study found that the invitational intervention successfully engaged ILOs into substance abuse treatment or self-help in 83% of the cases. This level of success was achieved without excluding any cases who asked for help, and with an average of only one session and one to two phone calls, totaling 88 minutes of clinician time (median = 75 minutes, range = 5–375).

One of the surprising findings was that invitational intervention using the ARISE method achieved engagement very rapidly. Fifty percent of engagers entered treatment within one week from the first call, and 84% within three weeks.

The main benefit of extending an invitation is you're not ambushing the ILO, but you're inviting them to change. Every day, people are invited to change, in every treatment center, in every clinical venue, by police when you get a DUI, but in terms of meeting a family where they are without force, I hold that it's more respectful to offer an invitation.

## Limitations of the Invitational Model

The main limitation of the invitational model is that the invitation itself can be a major stumbling block to treatment initiation: if the ILO does not show up, refuses to come, or the family has not extended an invitation, interventionists step into a surprise scenario. Strategies and tactics must be altered. In these cases, clinical skills are of extreme necessity.

Another limitation of the invitational model is that it may be more successful in some relationships than others. For example, parents may be more likely to engage children in addiction treatment than spouses. So, while parents may be influential in getting adolescents, teens, or young adults to accept help, invitations to change addressed to partners by their partner may not have as much impact.

### Advocates of the Invitational Model

- Speare and Raitner: *Systemic.*
- Garret and Landau: *ARISE: Linking Human Systems.*
- Brad Lamm: *Breakthrough Interventions.*

## The Systemic Model

Systems theory has been in use in social work since the 1970s. Founded on the principle that the whole of an organism is greater than the sum of its parts, this theory has been used to observe patterns and the way relationships are organized in living systems. Applied to families, clinicians evolved practices from treating individuals to treating entire families.

The main idea is that an individual personality and identity can change along with changes in family dynamics. And the goal? The goal is to discover and change the current systemic rules that sustain dysfunctional patterns or relationships. The major underlying principles of family systems interventions are that, first, each individual is doing the best that they can, and second, blame can evolve into an understanding of the overall context of the problem, leading to systemic change.

The systematic family systems model, or systemic model of addiction intervention, was introduced by Dr. Wayne Raiter, PhD, MA, LICSW, and Ed Speare about 15 years ago. The focus of a systemic family systems intervention is systemic health. Rather than focusing solely on the person who is diagnosed with a substance use disorder, the family systems model addresses the entire family together. The theory is that as the people in the family system get healthy, the ILO must change as well. The practice is one of group counseling.

This model of intervention includes three phases: systemic intervention, systemic treatment, and systemic reintegration. In the first phase, interventionists focus on shifting the family paradigm away from shame-based to positive and healing interactions. The second phase, systemic treatment, focuses on identifying appropriate help for each member of the group, as well as the system as a whole. This phase can last for months or years, as clinical treatment of the ILO moves from the acute phase to a treatment maintenance phase. Finally, the reintegration phase focuses on reintegrating the ILO into a new system that supports recovery.

It is important to note that this model is not time-based. Instead, the process assumes at least a one-year involvement from the interventionist, which gives the family system time to go through treatment, reintegrate, and work on relating and living skills.

In contrast to the surprise model, the systemic model has been designed to be nonconfrontational, nonjudgmental, and invitational. Rather than planning secretive meetings that lead to an ambush, an intervention specialist works with the family to invite the ILO to a series of meetings. Then the entire family participates in an interventionist-led workshop, which generally takes place over two days or, in a series of up to five meetings held on separate days.

Here's what the process usually looks like:

1. A concerned family member must contact an interventionist about the ILO.
2. Several family members meet or talk with the interventionist, and plans for the workshop are made.
3. The interventionist coaches a lead family member on how to invite the addicted individual to the workshop, although it will take place regardless of whether the individual decides to attend.
4. Family members attending the workshop are often asked to do some preparation, which may include attending Alcoholics Anonymous/Al-Anon meetings and completing some assigned reading.
5. The family attends the meeting. Each family member learns about their different treatment options. These may include addiction or codependency treatment, among others.
6. The interventionist usually maintains contact with the family for up to a year, following up either in person or via telephone.

During family meetings, the interventionist leads discussions on the nature of addiction. Note here that additional clinical skills are required for the best outcomes. For example, the model employs didactic therapy and interactive research skills. Individual and family therapy sessions, as well as family educational groups, can be built into the model. Furthermore, interventionists that examine generational patterns can identify extended family issues – going back four generations – to inform the intervention approach. Raiter considers this important to identify and develop healthy coping skills for the system.

Families learn about the clinical nature of addiction in the family systems approach. During the meetings, interventionists cover topics such as neurobiology, intergenerational issues, how addiction affects the family, and the process known as enabling. Interventionists discuss how communication styles should be modified to allow members to express themselves clearly. Finally, the group addresses the physical and mental impact of addiction on the ILO.

The strength of this approach is in developing new norms for the family such as healthy boundaries, constructive communication styles, and functional operating systems. As part of the process, everyone involved learns about addiction. Family members learn about and identify their own patterns of dysfunction. The interventionist helps each member of the family understand the role they play in the system of addiction, with the goal of having every family member commit to a plan of recovery.

Finally, when family members learn to set boundaries, engage in self-care, and stay safe around the ILO, the family is then able to invite the ILO to accept treatment. The hope is that a commitment by every family member will encourage the addicted individual to accept help. Still, the family may or may not discuss a member's specific behavior. Instead, they may focus on addiction as a concept, with the goal of learning all they can about how addiction can be eradicated from the entire family. Or family members can prioritize their own recovery.

What treatment options does the systemic model offer to family members? Families can opt to continue, complete, or end the intervention meetings. One natural follow-up is group therapy. In group therapy, members might commit to learning how to interact with the ILO without letting the addiction drive the relationship. Or families can enter individual counseling to learn how to address codependency.

## Efficacy of the Systemic Model

We currently do not have research that specifically targets the systemic model for outcomes in treatment initiation or retention. However, evidence from research on the application of family systems theory to social work and public health abounds. Italian psychiatrists, for example, in the 1970s reported better outcomes treating individuals diagnosed with schizophrenia when they worked with an entire family rather than the individual patient.[31] These pioneers successfully illustrated that symptomatic behavior of one individual can be part of a transactional pattern that is peculiar to the family system in which it occurs.

Later research has shown that:[32]

1. When developmental needs of individuals within a family are not being met, family members are likely to experience problems.
2. Within a family, any action by one member will affect all other members and the family as a whole. Each member's response will in turn prompt other responses that will affect all members, whose further reactions will then provoke yet more responses. Such a reverberating effect will in turn affect the first person in a continuous series of chains of influence.
3. The way to change the symptom is to change the rules of the family.

Further, the popularity of systems theory and the practice of family therapy has arisen from effectiveness in enabling rapid change for families experiencing problems. Indeed, the efficacy of family therapy in addiction treatment has shown that families who are subject to primary therapeutic grouping and intervention in the system of family relationships exhibit:

- increases in engagement of treatment for the ILO;
- increases in treatment retention for the ILO;
- reduction of the ILO's drug and alcohol use;
- improved family and social functioning; and
- discouraged relapse rates.[33]

Why is family therapy work effective for substance use treatment? There are currently a wide variety of family therapy models in use. Indeed, the practice is influenced by many diverse schools of thought. Still, multiple factors probably account for the effectiveness of family therapy in substance use disorder treatment. Of note are factors central to the practice of family therapy, including:

- acceptance from the therapist;
- determining accountability;
- increased awareness of the need for change;
- improved communication; and
- improved family structure and organization.

Each of these factors increases the family's motivation to change its patterns of interaction and opens up individuals to create personal change. Family therapy also views substance abuse in context, not as an isolated problem. Values include family solidarity, self-confession, support, self-esteem, awareness, and smooth re-entry into the community.

In the systemic model, everything changes. The idea is that an addicted family member gets help through treatment – later rejoining a healthy family system. But what if nothing changes? The strength in this model is that families can adapt. If one member of the system does not commit to change, the others must adapt. As the family learns to communicate in healthy, supportive ways, change can occur further down the road.

### Limitations of the Systemic Model

The systemic model of intervention may not be appropriate in cases of extreme addiction or drug dependence. When an ILO does significant damage to their lifestyle, health, mental health, and social functioning, they are unable to work with a therapeutic process. Family members facing major life changes such as redundancy, unemployment, significant health problems, marital problems, or legal problems simply cannot commit to the process. Likewise, when there is a need for chemical detoxification, the ILO is unlikely to be able to engage in the abstinence-based requirement of the systemic family intervention outside of a safe therapeutic environment.

Instead, systemic family interventions are most appropriate when people are engaged in relatively normal family life, work, or college/university. When individuals are physically or mentally still able to function, such a method is more likely to be successful. Additionally, the model may be limited to those who can afford it. Workshop meetings often require that families go away for a whole weekend. In practice, this model tends to appeal to those who are highly weekend-focused or used to going away. But it requires the time and money for engagement.

Additionally, family systems work is more complex than non-family approaches because more people are involved. A systemic family intervention will often be inappropriate when a significant family member requires treatment for codependency and chronic enabling behaviors. If the family are unable to hold boundaries, or they cannot be supported in holding boundaries, the family needs time to recover themselves. It is not strange for family members to sabotage the recovery process through lack of knowledge, distorted beliefs or fear.

The very nature of systemic family interventions accommodates irregular intervals, which allows the ILO to isolate. Some may participate in one session, grow angry about the message, and/or refuse to participate in any later sessions. This is a risk families must be willing to take.

The model also requires highly trained and experienced clinical skills in family therapy and individual counseling. Family systems take special training and skills beyond those typically required in intervention certifications. When working with communication and trauma issues, a three-day crash course in intervention will not suffice.

Finally, the systemic model poses specific challenges. Relatively little research-based information is available concerning effectiveness with subsets of the general population, such as women, minority groups, or people with serious psychiatric problems, for example, and people must be willing to spend a weekend or more in training.

### Advocates of the Systemic Model

- Judith Landau and James Garret: *A Relational Intervention Sequence for Engagement (ARISE)*.
- Ed Speare and Wayne Raitner: *ARISE*.
- Brad Lamm: *Breakthrough Interventions*.
- Dr. Louise Stanger: *Collective Intervention Strategy*.

## The Action Model

The action intervention model technique is credited to three clinicians: Jean Campbell, LCSW, Dr. Jim Tracey, and Bill Maher. The action intervention training model combines the systemic and invitational intervention models with sociometry and psychodrama. In fact, the model combines strategies from other models to warm up families to the idea of change so that they can create a treatment plan for the entire family system to recover. This model was awarded the Innovator's Award by the American Society of Group Psychotherapy and Psychodrama in 2016.

The action model teaches families in a group process over the course of a workshop. However, the model employs mapping family relationships to target the most influential member(s) of the system. Sociometry, or the study of relationships within a group of people, has shown us that when we identify key individuals for training based on network structures, such as those with the greatest numbers of ties or influence potential, we can train people to be change agents. The action model employs this strategy to foster change within the unit. For example, network attributes such as centrality can be derived for each network member, and those with the highest scores targeted for training.

What sets this model apart from systemic interventions, however, is that interventionists teach families how to adjust their behaviors and dynamics in fundamentally different ways. Specifically, the action model employs methods such as:

- action demonstrations;
- experiential techniques; and
- family sculptures.

These demonstrate just how toxic addiction and enabling are to a family.

The clinician uses a form of psychotherapy during which blocked spontaneity from earlier traumas is unblocked and reintegrated through dramatic action methods. In workshops, the action model also uses a team of skilled assistants who perform skits to explain the theory, as well as provide support for all group members. The environment is relaxed and highly conducive to learning. Then the clinicians provide specific recommendations for how families can focus on their own recovery and move forward on their own path of healing, whether the ILO is abstinent or not.

Workshops are held in a variety of settings, including treatment centers, businesses, agencies, clinics, schools, and hospitals, to facilitate staff trainings, team building, strategic planning, and crisis management.

### Efficacy of the Action Model

Currently, we do not have research that specifically targets the action model for outcomes in treatment initiation or retention. While there is research on this type of intervention directly, psychodrama and sociometry are respected modalities used in the behavioral healthcare field. Indeed, evidence from research on psychodrama in addiction treatment has shown that integrated psychodrama in substance-abusing group settings is a powerful tool for personal growth.[34] Researcher Sharon Wegscheider-Cruse effectively integrated psychodrama in the late 1980s to heal family-of-origin issues within the context of addictive behaviors.[35] She found that psychodrama offers people in addiction treatment an opportunity to:

- confront feelings that have not been dealt with;
- imaginatively change apparent problems that block progress;
- practice empathy;
- rehearse new behaviors;
- relearn forgotten skills; and
- understand past and present experiences.

During the process of acting in psychodrama, important concepts become real, internalized, and operational that might otherwise be purely theoretical. Changes experienced through acting become accessible to the psyche as part of the lived history of the individual. Some client self-reports in the early 1990s suggested the value of psychodrama for female clients in treatment for alcoholism, particularly for highly educated women and those who are inclined to be extroverted and verbally expressive.

Further, it has been generally accepted that social network interventions targeted by sociometry practices can effectively change health behaviors. Indeed, observational and longitudinal sociometric studies have documented the link between social network factors and behavior change. While these findings may not yet tell us how to best design interventions for maximum diffusion, sustainability, and behavior change, the evidence compiled points to the fact that social networks can become effective agents for individual change.

## Limitations of the Action Model

One of the major limitations of the action model is that it requires a highly specialized skill set for facilitation. Expressive therapies used in this model require highly skilled staff or outside consultants to provide these services. As such, this model takes additional time for preparation and can be costly. Further, as the trainings involve specialized training of families, limitations of time and budget can also be constraints.

Second, expressive therapies can stir up very powerful feelings and memories in group settings. Facilitators require experience and skills to recognize the signs of reactions to trauma and be able to contain emotional responses when necessary. Action model interventionists also need to know how to help clients obtain the resources they need to work through their powerful emotions. Finally, it is important to be sensitive to people's ability and willingness to participate in action model activities. Some participants may be in a vulnerable emotional state, and setting boundaries for group members' behavior is essential.

### Advocates of the Action Model

- Jean Campell, LCSW-TEP Founder and CEO of Action Institute of California.
- Dr. Jim Tracey, DDS.
- Bill Maher, Action Institute.

## References

1. Substance Abuse and Mental Health Services Administration (2014) *Projections of National Expenditures for Treatment of Mental and Substance Use Disorders, 2010–2020.* Rockville, MD: Substance Abuse and Mental Health Services Administration. Available at: https://store.samhsa.gov/shin/content/SMA14-4883/SMA14-4883.pdf (accessed March 4, 2018).
2. NASW Delegate Assembly (2017) *National Association of Social Workers Code of Ethics.* Washington, DC: NASW. Available at: https://socialwork.utexas.edu/dl/files/academic-programs/other/nasw-code-of-ethics.pdf (accessed March 4, 2018).
3. Smith PG, Morrow RH, and Ross DA, editors (2015) *Field Trials of Health Interventions: A Toolbox* (3rd edition). Oxford: Oxford University Press.
4. Center for Behavioral Health Statistics and Quality (2017) *2016 National Survey on Drug Use and Health: Detailed Tables.* Rockville, MD: U.S. Department of Health and Human Services, Substance Abuse and Mental Health Services Administration. Available at: www.samhsa.gov/data/sites/default/files/NSDUH-FFR1-2016/NSDUH-FFR1-2016.pdf (accessed March 4, 2018).
5. Park-Lee E, Lipari RN, Hedden SL, Kroutil LA, and Porter JD (2017) *Receipt of Services for Substance Use and Mental Health Issues among Adults: Results from the 2016 National Survey on Drug Use and Health.* Bethesda, MD: NSDUH Data Review. Available at: www.samhsa.gov/data/sites/default/files/NSDUH-DR-FFR2-2016/NSDUH-DR-FFR2-2016.pdf (accessed March 4, 2018).
6. Miller WR, Meyers RJ, and Tonigan J (1999) Engaging the Unmotivated in Treatment for Alcohol Problems: A Comparison of Three Strategies for Intervention through Family Members. *Journal of Consulting & Clinical Psychology.* 67(5): 688–697.
7. Liepman MR, Nirenberg TD, and Begin AM (1989) Evaluation of a Program Designed to Help Family and Significant Others to Motivate Resistant Alcoholics into Recovery. *The American Journal of Drug and Alcohol Abuse.* 15(2): 209–221.
8. Morgan OJ and Litzke CH, editors (2012) *Family Interventions in Substance Abuse: Current Best Practices.* New York: Routledge.
9. Landau J, Stanton MD, Brinkman-Sull D, Ikle D, McCormick D, Garrett J, Baciewicz G, Shea R, and Wamboldt F (2004) Outcomes with ARISE Approach to Engaging Reluctant Drug- and Alcohol-Dependent Individuals in Treatment. *The American Journal of Drug and Alcohol Abuse.* 30(4): 711–748.
10. Azrin NH (1976) Improvements in the Community-Reinforcement Approach to Alcoholism. *Behaviour Research and Therapy.* 14(5): 339–348.
11. Sisson RW and Azrin NH (1986) Family-Member Involvement to Initiate and Promote Treatment of Problem Drinkers. *Journal of Behavior Therapy and Experimental Psychiatry.* 17(1): 15–21.

12. Meyers RJ, Smith JE, and Miller EJ (1998) Working through the Concerned Significant Other (pp. 149–161). *Treating Addictive Behaviors* (2nd edition). New York: Plenum Press.
13. Szapocznik J et al. (1988) Engaging Adolescent Drug Abusers and Their Families in Treatment: A Strategic Structural Systems Approach. *Journal of Consulting and Clinical Psychology*, 56(4): 552–557. Available at: http://dx.doi.org/10.1037/0022-006X.56.4.552 (accessed March 4, 2018).
14. Walton MA, Goldstein AL, Chermack ST, et al. (2008) Brief Alcohol Intervention in the Emergency Department: Moderators of Effectiveness. *Journal of Studies on Alcohol and Drugs.* 69(4): 550–560.
15. Rollnick S, Miller WR, and Butler CC (2008) *Motivational Interviewing in Health Care Helping Patients Change Behavior.* New York and London: Guilford Press.
16. Miller WR et al. (2006) Brief Interventions for Alcohol Problems: A Review. *Addiction.* 88(3): 315–336.
17. Miller WR and Rollnick S (2002) *Motivational Interviewing: Preparing People for Change* (2nd edition). New York: Guilford Press.
18. National Council on Alcoholism and Drug Dependence (2015) *Intervention: Tips and Guidelines.* New York: NCADD. Available at: www.ncadd.org/family-friends/there-is-help/intervention-tips-and-guidelines (accessed March 4, 2018).
19. Johnson V (1972) *I'll Quit Tomorrow.* New York: Harper & Row.
20. Liepman MR, Nirenberg TD, and Begin AM (1989) Evaluation of a Program Designed to Help Family and Significant Others to Motivate Resistant Alcoholics into Recovery. *The American Journal of Drug and Alcohol Abuse.* 15(2): 209–221.
21. Substance Abuse and Mental Health Services Administration (2016) *Facing Addiction in America: The Surgeon General's Report on Alcohol, Drugs, and Health.* Washington, DC: U.S. Department of Health and Human Services, Office of the Surgeon General. Available at: www.ncbi.nlm.nih.gov/books/NBK424860/ (accessed March 4, 2018).
22. White WL and Miller WR (2007) The Use of Confrontation in Addiction Treatment: History, Science and Time for Change. *Counselor.* 8(4): 12–30.
23. Loneck B, Garrett J, and Banks S (1996) A Comparison of the Johnson Intervention with Four Other Methods of Referral to Outpatient Treatment. *The American Journal of Drug and Alcohol Abuse.* 22(2): 233–246.
24. Loneck B, Garrett J, and Banks S (1996) The Johnson Intervention and Relapse during Outpatient Treatment. *The American Journal of Drug and Alcohol Abuse.* 22(3): 363–375.
25. Pickard F (1991) *Family Intervention.* Center City, PA: Hazelden.
26. Jay J and Jay D (2008) *Love First: A Family's Guide to Intervention* (2nd edition). Center City, PA: Hazelden.
27. Finnigan C and Finnigan S (2008) *When Enough Is Enough: A Comprehensive Guide to a Successful Intervention.* New York: Penguin Group.
28. Storti E and Von Wolffradt S (1995) *Heart to Heart: The Honorable Approach to Motivational Intervention.* New York: Carlton Press Corporation.
29. Landau J and Garrett J (2006) *Invitational Intervention: A Step by Step Guide for Clinicians Helping Families Engage Resistant Substance Abusers in Treatment.* Charleston, SC: BookSurge.
30. Lamm B (2010) *How to Help the One You Love: A New Way to Intervene and Stop Someone from Self-Destructing.* New York: St. Martin's Griffin.

31. MacKinnon LK and James K (1987) The Milan Systemic Approach Theory and Practice. *Australian and New Zealand Journal of Family Therapy.* 8(2): 89–98.
32. Center for Substance Abuse Treatment (2004) *Treatment Improvement Protocol (TIP) Series, No. 39: Substance Abuse Treatment and Family Therapy.* Rockville, MD: Substance Abuse and Mental Health Services Administration. Available at: www.ncbi.nlm.nih.gov/books/NBK64269/ (accessed March 4, 2018).
33. Stanton MD, Todd TC, and Associates (1982) *The Family Therapy of Drug Abuse and Addiction.* New York: Guilford Press.
34. Loughlin N (1992) A Trial of the Use of Psychodrama for Women with Alcohol Problems. *Nursing Practice.* 5(3): 14–19.
35. Wegschedier Cruse S (1998) *Another Chance: Hope and Health for the Alcoholic Family* (2nd edition). East York: Hushion House.

# 3

# THE BASIC ANATOMY OF AN INTERVENTION

## The Collective Intervention Strategy

As a clinician and interventionist, I work directly with families and their loved ones on alcohol and other drug misuse and abuse, process disorders, mental health, and chronic pain issues. To unpack and address the complex nature of these issues, I find it helpful to use what I call a "Collective Intervention Strategy":

- *Collective*, in that we need a team of families, friends, colleagues, associates, business partners, managers, or co-workers to work together toward change.
- *Intervention*, in that we seek to move (i.e. motivate) a person to a place of change.
- *Strategy*, in that nothing is set in stone; we may adapt the process as needed.

The Collective Intervention Strategy (CIS) will offer you protocol, process, tools, and ideas. The interventions that you will facilitate will require that you think on your feet. You will need to be flexible and contextual. Therefore, the strategy that we present here – while helpful as a guide – need not be followed blindly. Instead, we encourage all clinicians willing to explore the domain of interventions to adjust the Collective Intervention Strategy to their own practice.

Plus, we know that one form of addiction bleeds into another: co-occurring mental health disorders such as depression, anxiety, and personality disorders, juxtaposed with medical problems such as chronic pain and legal or school issues. The complexity of *what's really going on* is a mystery to most families. That's why they usually call you in the first place.

In fact, you normally won't even need to perform an intervention unless someone else in the addiction treatment has not been able to "close" or gotten an ILO to a "yes." This book has been created to help clinicians understand the process, have the courage to help others, and to inspire change. Whether you facilitate the intervention or successfully refer to someone else, the strategies we outline for you can help.

## If You Learn Anything from This Book . . .

I want to impress upon the reader this point: There is no one "right process" that can guide you to a successful intervention. If you take away anything from this book, let it be this:

> No matter what you say and no matter what process you employ, the truth is that you're going to use yourself and the skills you must help move someone to change. To be successful, you're going to have to integrate your own best practices into your professional being. Knowing and being explicit about the assumptions you make about human behavior will be the key to your understanding and success.

Did you know that in the first moments of a conversation, whoever is on the end of the phone will decide if they are going to trust you or not?[1] According to scientists, even a single word such as "hello" is sufficient to yield ratings highly consistent across listeners. The way you talk has a great deal to do with this; believe it or not, a female sing-songy voice appears the most trustworthy.

This little-known evidence-based fact can propel you to get real! In the process/strategy I'm about to present, the following principles are at the foundation:

1. It's important you know what you're doing.
2. You need to make explicit your assumptions about human behavior and the persons you are engaged to help.
3. You need to be clear that your assumptions view motivation as a change agent, not an agent of coercion or shame.
4. You can use the skills to the best of your ability.
5. You are willing to engage in supervision and learn from others.
6. It's important to be willing to collaborate.
7. It's important to be willing to learn more.

## Model or Process?

People seek help from professional interventionists when other types of treatment fail. Families are desperate. They have tried absolutely everything. Nothing seems to work. Some ILOs may have already had more official invitations to change: jail, hospitals, or institutions. But nothing works!

I maintain that interventions are not a model; rather, they are a process. In fact, I posit that it doesn't even matter what model you use. No family is the same. Each will respond best to an appropriate intervention. However, in the process of an intervention, there are strategies that all clinicians have to go through no matter what theoretical background you come from. We can be trained in many different theories. In the end, you've got to use a combination of skills, methods, and modalities in order to get a person to "yes."

> *You've got to be nimble on your feet like an emergency room doctor, or the intervention is not going to work.*

## Core Intervention Skills

Before we get into the actual protocol in the next chapter, it is helpful to review the core skills that are necessary when using the Collective Intervention Strategy for substance use disorders. It is noteworthy to know that an intervention includes much advance preparation. Coaching is ongoing throughout the process as we work to develop and implement a change plan. In order to get to "yes," an interventionist must be able to facilitate and guide the following:

- team formation;
- family mapping;
- portraiture;
- retrospective biopsychosocial analysis;
- case strategy;
- treatment planning and placement;
- aftercare recommendations; and
- family engagement in the healing process.

The CIS approach uses a qualitative research methodology called "portraiture," which was developed by the Harvard-endowed scholar Sara Lawrence-Lightfoot, best known for her seminal qualitative research guide *The Art and Science of Portraiture*.[2] In addition, this process uses evidence-based approaches that includes a qualitative research interview methodology called portraiture, as well as cognitive behavioral, motivational interviewing, solution-focused, 12-step, and mindfulness modalities within an invitational team systems framework.

Further, communication skills are essential to interventions. Interviewing skills and solution-focused skills are critical. Throughout the process, the interventionist manages all team and third-party communication. They serve as a liaison. For example, individual phone interviews with prospective team members may be required, or an interventionist may need to provide safe escort or transport to the selected treatment center.

Case management is also required for the evidence-based interventionist. Treatment center matching and referrals are necessary. Likewise, follow-up and regular case management with treatment centers while clients attend rehabilitation programs is critical. Finally, consultation and coordination of aftercare, as well as solution-focused family recovery coaching for all team members, ensures lasting change.

## What Is an Intervention?

An intervention is an invitation to change. The interventionist's end goal is to get someone struggling with a substance problem, mental health issue, process disorder, and/or chronic pain to enter treatment. As such, an intervention is a critical conversation. In some cases, this is a life-or-death conversation. And in the best cases, an intervention is a life-saving conversation.

However, interventionists do not work one-on-one, as in individual counseling. Interventionists always work with groups, family systems. We do this for two reasons: first, addiction affects the entire family; second, groups provide a larger context and sphere of influence when combined. Change must take place in the context of people, places, things, thoughts, and feelings.

*A successful intervention has the potential to transform not just the identified client, but an entire family.*

Evidence states it takes much longer than most people think to change a habit: an average of 66 days.[3] Our professional goal as clinicians is to work with the whole family system while the ILO is in and out of primary treatment, so that all may change. Treatment gives people time to grow and change. The correct treatment or placement will also provide families with the help they need to disengage and rethink how they may love as well.

One additional task we face as interventionists is to help families approach their loved one in a respectful, compassionate way to seek appropriate help. We must also work with the family in a solution-focused recovery way so that they may disengage from their loved one. In other words, families are often inadvertently a part of the problem and must be included in the solution (if possible)!

Indeed, interventionists help families discover how they can improve their own quality of life and become part of the solution. Our simultaneous task is to help the family realign, seek healthy ways of loving, and connect with appropriate treatment centers. Put simply, families must have opportunities to grow alongside their loved one that is in treatment. As Krissy Prozatek, LCSW, suggests, this is a "parallel process."[4]

Interventions are transformative! So, in the weeks before, during, and after a successful intervention, people have the opportunity to rewrite their stories and to become the man, woman, husband, wife, brother, sister, partner, father, or mother they were meant to be.

## What an Intervention Is Not

A confidential, respectful, invitational intervention is very different than what you see on TV. Confidentiality and discretion are paramount. Likewise, safety is essential. In this respect, interventions are extremely difficult to conduct when a person is:

- actively psychotic;
- a danger to self or others as per "duty to warn" laws;
- extremely depressed and potentially harmful to self or others;
- in mania;
- intoxicated to the point that they need to be hospitalized;
- known to be violent;
- suffering a serious mental health disorder that makes hospitalization more appropriate; and/or
- suicidal.

If these conditions exist, then the interventionists must be trained and aware of how to handle these potentially volatile situations. This means that clinicians must understand mental health disorders, possible commitment laws, be up to date on state "duty to warn" and "duty to protect" laws, and be mindful of safety and other concerns.

> *The utmost care must be taken that the entire process is safe, caring, and beneficial for everyone involved. It is imperative that the clinician/interventionist understands family dynamics, mental health disorders, and processes.*

Additionally, extra precautions are taken when performing interventions with clients who have a history of violence. For example, if guns are in the home, the intervention needs to take place in a safe, neutral setting. Other scenarios include when a patient is addicted to cocaine, methamphetamines, or other similar stimulants, and is also in mania. Still other precautions need to be taken when a client is potentially violent or a threat to self or others. Further, when a young girl is suffering from both anorexia and depression, one must be careful in terms of assessing suicidality.

## A Word on Ethical Considerations

Ethics may be defined as the shared written beliefs a group or individual maintain about what constitutes correct and proper behavior. Think of ethics as standards of conduct that guide the choices that we as behavioral healthcare experts make, moment to moment, as we organize and provide care for clients. Ethics are individual at the micro level, group at the mezzo level, and organization/societal at the macro level.

Often, an interventionist will help identify which facilities can best provide the clinical expertise and social skill setting needed. An independent interventionist will have no fiduciary relationship with the treatment center(s) they refer. An interventionist professional aims to connect the ILO with three facilities based on the retrospective analysis and financial concerns that are best suited for the individual and their family. Further, the family must ultimately choose a specific treatment option so that they are invested in the process and have taken responsibility. See Worksheet 3.1 (Clinical Questions for Treatment Centers). Do your due diligence to help families connect with the best treatment options!

In today's world, it is important to note that not all interventionists are clinicians. One may be approved as a Certified Intervention Professional (CIP) by the Pennsylvania Certification Board, for example. This certification is based on continuing education courses designed to meet these requirements, irrespective of educational degrees (not necessarily master's degrees). The CIP does not serve as a marketer or recruiter for a treatment facility; rather, they are a frontline professional who is directly engaging an individual and family to help guide them to treatment, and is a part of the recovery team.

Clouding the issue, some persons who are CIPs do work for treatment centers. Therefore, it is always best to ask and to know if the interventionist you meet is employed by a treatment center or is independent of any particular center.

As a trusted practitioner, it is assumed that you're practicing under your license or certification and that you are following an organization code of ethics. I'd further suggest that you develop a personal or organization mission statement. Let the world know your mission, values, and ethical statements. Further, malpractice insurance is essential to the professional interventionist or behavioral healthcare provider. Be sure you have it on your website!

Also, consider:

1. engaging in continuing education that specifically deals with laws and ethics;
2. continuing to build your practice by seeking ongoing supervision and training; and
3. having an ethical decision-making process, such as the one outlined in Chapter 10.

## How Does an Intervention Begin?

An intervention usually begins with a call for help. People call for expert help when their own efforts have failed; their hearts are broken. They do not know how to help a loved one who is experiencing a mental health or substance abuse disorder. These families require outside help as the nagging, pleading, screaming, cutting off, or giving in has not worked. They are at their wits' end.

Families are often in confusion. Their lives have become centered on their loved one's disease; meanwhile, the families have become part of the problem too. They have unconsciously aligned with their loved one being ill (or being the troubled problem one themselves) and inadvertently assume roles that maintain this homeostasis. So, before we begin, families must be prepared, and need to know what to expect.

Hence, families require being taught three key components:

1.  The nature of substance abuse, process, and mental health disorders. When appropriate, we teach about chronic pain syndrome or other medical or legal conditions.
2.  The way in which an intervention is conducted.
3.  The active and instrumental part they may play in moving someone to change.

I have developed CIS to be an 11-step process with the potential to yield a total team solution. The approach is 11 steps divided into three phases. Each step is based on sound social work principles of "starting where the client is." In other words, clinicians begin at the beginning and work from a foundation of compassion and unconditional positive regard.

## How Long Does an Intervention Take?

In my experience, the most successful interventions are part of a process that unfolds over a period. Due diligence can be done thoughtfully and quickly and still be clinically sound, though your work may continue well past 90 days with the family. Ongoing work allows clinicians to be a collaborative instrument in the healing process.

When you adopt a collective perspective within an intervention, your role as a clinician is to bring together people for the common good. You are not there to diagnose and treat individual family members. Rather, you are ever mindful of conflicts and other issues to hold in abeyance.

### Case Study: The War of the Roses Enters a Ceasefire

A husband and wife called me who were divorced; their parting was "The War of the Roses." They had not been in the same room for over 15 years, and held each other with disdain. They came together for the common good of their 27-year-old daughter who was experiencing delusions, substance abuse disorder, and engaging in inappropriate relationships. Their coming together was the key, or pivot, that brought about change. This was the first time they gathered together on her behalf without other siblings or grand verbal protestation.

In truth, the intervention process is much more involved than people realize. The process is labor-intensive, especially with respect to preparation and treatment planning, interviews, team meetings, and the meetings with the ILO. At best, the in-person intervention itself may only take a couple of hours.

> *However, it may take several days or even weeks to plan and organize for a successful intervention, or it can be done quickly and effectively. It all depends on the circumstances presented.*

Planning is a critical part of the process. Planning may involve multiple meetings and counseling to prepare family and loved ones for the intervention itself. And once an intervention is completed, coaching can continue for up to 12 months. The changes take place little by little. However, when family members understand their role in the intervention process, a systemic approach can heal the entire team. Together, the opportunity for change increases. This process does not and cannot occur overnight.

## The Basic Anatomy

The basic anatomy of the Collective Intervention Strategy can be split into three main phases: agreement, research, and implementation. Throughout, the interventionist provides education, support, and guidance. In effect, the interventionist serves as a coach and a guide.

### Phase 1: Intervention Agreement and Initiative

The process begins when the client/family agrees to the terms of a working relationship or clinical engagement. Clinicians must have buy-in from the families that they work with. So, we generally work with a first caller who's going to agree to take certain actions. Then clinicians must outline and strategize what must be done. You'll need to agree on who's involved and what outcomes you'll produce. Further, you'll need to agree on the terms of your engagement, including confidentiality and payment issues.

Second, this phase of the intervention helps the clinician determine what it is they are dealing with (the nature of addiction, mental health disorders, or family dynamics) and helps set a path forward. For example, it is crucial that clinicians uncover the nature of the serious problem at hand from the beginning. The main problem may be diagnosed as a substance abuse disorder (alcohol, legal drugs, illegal drugs), or a process addiction disorder (food, Internet, sex, gambling, debt), or a mental health disorder (depression, bipolar, mania, borderline). However, you'll need to determine the exact nature of the problem before moving forward.

Additionally, clinicians need to identify the key stakeholders in the group and create an initial genogram, or family map, during this phase. The family map evolves during the process. Still, the first baseline diagram provides a clearer picture of what is happening within the family system. This is the starting point for defining the family group, the members of which we call the "accountability team."

Finally, this phase of the intervention concludes with coordination and agreement of all group members. The clinician helps move the accountability team to be united on key decisions. In determining what it takes to reach group consensus, clinicians help fashion and establish group boundaries. From there, the interventionist helps define and develop the group's motivational strategy.

## Phase 2: Education, Information Gathering, and Assessment

Then, during phase 2, clinicians share their knowledge about the brain disorder of addiction. I use the ASAM definition of addiction.[5] Clinicians may also teach about the process disorders of sex, gambling, shopping, digital, or exercised addiction. Where appropriate, clinicians can shed light on disordered eating, mental health issues, chronic pain syndrome, and how these all interface.

Then accountability team members review the overall process, ask questions, and begin to learn more about addiction. Through this practice, everyone learns more about what is going on, what the disease of addiction looks like, and how the team is going to get healthy together.

Phase 2 also includes learning more about the ILO, their lifestyle, and the most significant relationships they have. Working in collaboration, we identify the most appropriate people to be part of the intervention meeting and accountability team. Information gathering comes from a variety of sources: family members, friends, partners, employers, treatment professionals, and others. Together, everyone paints a portrait of the ILO.

The goal?

Through triangulation of data, a clinical assessment can be gleaned through a retrospective analysis. By obtaining a good biopsychosocial history and combining this with the generational map from the first phase of an intervention, a clinician can determine many complex factors, including if there is an underlying mental health disorder.

This phase also continues to evaluate different treatment options and potential aftercare programs specific to the client's needs and situation. The right approach will be determined based on the unique circumstances and mental and physical health conditions of the people you are working with.

## Phase 3: Implement, Review, and Follow Up

Finally, a plan is created in phase 3 of the process. It is during this phase that you set a date for a pre-intervention meeting and the intervention meeting. The intervention itself is a well-orchestrated event, a drama that is created and stylized. The main goal of the intervention is core to our work.

*Interventions help move the ILO to change and to accept treatment.*

It is important to note that some interventionists stop there. Some interventionists are only interested in moving or getting someone to treatment. However, dropping the case at this point can result in many negative outcomes:

- complications;
- financial problems;
- increased complexity;
- legal problems;
- relapse; and
- treatment dropout.

Indeed, what happens *after* the intervention is equally important. You'll have to help the family navigate through treatment, support group attendance (12-step work, ALANON, ACA, open AA meetings, or SMART Recovery are most often used), and possibly dealing with refusal for treatment. You'll need to continue working with families to teach them how to take care of themselves as they deal with substance abuse, process disorders, physical issues, and mental health issues in the system.

Families will need to learn to set healthy boundaries, for themselves and their loved ones. Family members may be referred out for care to family counselors, individual therapists, recovery coaches, or other behavioral/mental healthcare providers.

*The key point is this: follow up is crucial to the success of developing healthy family systems.*

Families struggling with complex substance abuse and mental health problems are behavioral systems in which the illness-related behaviors have become the central organizing structure. Over time, an identity is forged around this. The family accommodates unconsciously to the special needs of the person diagnosed with substance or mental health behavior. When recovery begins, this identification of the client as the "troubled one" must be altered to allow for success. This calls for each family member to pivot and take on a new persona and a new way of evaluating the ILO in treatment. The idea is to support systemic family health through personal behavioral change.

Meanwhile, families also contend with:

- legal issues;
- physical issues; and
- family history.

This is the reason why a true collective intervention embraces a systemic approach that includes case management and active coaching over time. From experience, it can take many months for a family to become "collective" and to operate in harmony again. For example, siblings often take a different stance when person enters treatment. They may be jealous or resentful that their brother or sister gets all the attention and that they are left to fend for themselves. In this way, the healing process and relationship renewal with a sibling may take longer to build than a mother–child relationship.

Everyone in a family accepts that possibility, and goodness is possible for the loved one in treatment at different times and ways. Indeed, each member of a family is unique and will have their own trajectory of healing. So, working with family members over time as they come to their own understandings and healing is the best way to proceed.

Furthermore, continued case management allows for motivational and solution-focused approaches with key family members so that they may express their feelings, their hopes, and their concerns with you, the clinician. This continued engagement with a professional clinician allows individuals to work on themselves. Used in this way – as solution-focused family recovery coaching – clinical involvement serves as a grand augment to a treatment center's family programming and/or family therapy offering(s).

In short, phase 3 of the CIS aims to create a three-legged stool in which the treatment center clinician, family program manager, and you as a case manager work in harmony to help the entire family heal. Just as people have different reactions to death and loss, so do family members have different reactions to a loved one's addiction and concomitant issues.

Remember, recovery begins when treatment ends. Engaging the accountability team in the recovery process leads to positive outcomes! Weekly coaching calls are a superb way to do this. Also, clinicians can liaise with the treatment facility and help with aftercare. Each plan is designed to ensure that the client's process is beneficial for all involved.

## Philosophy of the Collective Intervention Strategy

A successful intervention will uncover the tension between life, loss, and liberation. Components of inviting change share the philosophy of motivational interviewing, solution-focused therapy, CBT, and 12-step facilitation, and are in harmony with more modern methodologies such as acceptance and commitment therapy (ACT) and mindfulness training. For example, successful interventions take a directive, client-centered approach. It is, by nature, collaborative. Further, an invitation to change is a process, not a technique. The aim is to elicit clients' internal viewpoint and to promote autonomy. Finally, we learn to roll with resistance.

We might agree that all interventions should be:

- client-centered;
- collaborative;
- inclusive;
- realistic; and
- solution-focused.

But what are the defining tenets of the collective approach?

First, this invitational process is strength-based. It begins by looking for what is good and healthy. We assume that the expression of goodness will always be laced with imperfections. We know that goodness lies underneath behaviors and actions, and we look for that strength.

Second, we employ collaborative qualitative inquiry. In this way, the clinician becomes a researcher. We ask open-ended questions. We listen as objective, third-party strangers. Rather than dominate, the clinician becomes witness to the conversation and joins in to dig deeper.

Finally, this process always considers context. Where interactions take place becomes part of the portrait. Human experience is framed shaped by the setting, and we must be conscious and deliberate in our choices of environment in this approach.

## Merits of the Collective Intervention Strategy

So, what merits does the CIS approach have to its credit?

First, we advocate for interventions that are respectful. They are direct and to the point: we invite people to a meeting. An invitation to an intervention allows the ILO to decide to attend or not. In my experience, ILOs show up 90% of the time. Whether it's narcissism or curiosity, people show up! But through the invitation, we are consistent with principles of client choice and empowerment.

Further, we are consistent with cultural sensitivity: the client leads. The counselor's agenda is not imposed. Though the event is structured so that the critical conversation does take place, an interventionist needs to feel for cues and know when openings present themselves. Like an orchestra conductor, we are always looking for movement, and the ultimate crescendo note is to get to a "yes!"

Second, as a process or as a strategy, this approach allows for movements backward and forward. It accounts for the humanness of the experience of an intervention. There is an ebb and flow built into the process that allows clinicians to adapt strategies nimbly.

Third, you can move people to change when the clinician serves as a warm, empathetic, affirming, and respectful guide. It is important to note we hold meetings in the most inviting place possible, be it a boardroom, hotel conference room, or (most likely) a family environment where the identified patient (IP) is respected and vulnerable. And even though we are there to set a clear direction, the relationship is egalitarian. Therefore, as clinicians, we guide and elicit rather than instruct and persuade. We express empathy. We develop discrepancy. And we support self-efficacy. This works because we are intimately present, and we remove ourselves from the equation.

Thus, the clinician's approach is a delicate balance. To keep the client moving closer to change, we aim to be active and directive. "No" is seen as a conversation starter. Still, as we help shape behavior, our strategy must be specific and systematic.

In sum, the job of the evidence-based interventionist is to bring people together for the common good. They will identify substance abuse, mental health issues, and other problems. Once identified, the interventionist sets out a plan. In fact, I like to say that interventions can be an 11-step process for a 12-step solution.

## Who Am I? The Real Role of the Interventionist

Using the words of Sara Lawrence-Lightfoot,[6] we envision that an invitational interventionist has internalized the following monologue:

> I am the mirror who reflects back their pain, their fears, their voices. I am the inquirer who asks difficult questions, who searches for evidence and patterns. I am the companion on the journey bringing my own story to the encounter, making possible an interpretive collaboration. I am the audience who listens, laughs, weeps, and applauds. I am the spider women spinning their tales. I am the therapist who offers catharsis support and challenge . . . I am also the stage manager coordinating the intersection of three plays – the storyteller, the narrator, and the readers inviting your voice to the drama.

Now we can get to the details.

## References

1. Belin P, Boehme B, and McAleer P (2017) The Sound of Trustworthiness: Acoustic-Based Modulation of Perceived Voice Personality. *PLoS ONE*. 12(10): e0185651.
2. Lawrence-Lightfoot S and Davis JH (1997) *The Art and Science of Portraiture*. San Francisco, CA: Jossey-Bass.
3. Lally P, van Jaarsveld CHM, Potts HWW, and Wardle J (2009) How Are Habits Formed? Modelling Habit Formation in the Real World. *European Journal of Social Psychology*. 40(6): 998–1009.
4. Pozatek K (2011) *The Parallel Process: Growing alongside Your Adolescent or Young Adult Child in Treatment*. Brooklyn, NY: Lantern Books.

5. American Society of Addiction Medicine (2011) *Public Policy Statement: Definition of Addiction*. Rockville, MD: ASAM. Available at: https://asam.org/docs/default-source/public-policy-statements/1definition_of_addiction_long_4-11.pdf?sfvrsn=a8f64512_4 (accessed March 4, 2018).

6. Lawrence-Lightfoot S (1994) *I've Known Rivers: Lives of Loss and Liberation*. Cambridge: Basic Books.

# PART 2
# Clinical Skills

# 4

# HOW COLLECTIVE INTERVENTION WORKS

## Step 1: Engagement

To begin an intervention, clinicians first secure buy-in from core participants and agree to specific terms of engagement. During step 1, you will explain to the family exactly what an intervention is, the assumptions one has, and the scope of the work. At its most basic, step 1 is an outline of the necessary steps to make an invitation to change possible.

Most interventionists will give 20 to 30 minutes of complimentary time when discussing a situation with a potential client; clinicians usually don't do this. Instead, you may be used to inviting clients to attend a counseling session and charge for one session. While interventionists may consider initiating a consultation session as the industry moves toward more professionalism, just know that it is not standard now.

Most of the time, you are communicating with first callers on the phone. You're not in an office. You might be on Skype or FaceTime, but often first contact is audio-only. So, there is one thing you need to know about your voice: someone decides in the first moments of a conversation whether they like you or not, and this is often based on the tone of your voice.[1] Further, it takes just a tenth of a second for people to make judgments about you based on your facial appearance.[2] Your presence will very much influence the decision someone makes to work with you or not.

These are the key questions you ask immediately in step 1:

- What was the tipping point that caused you to call today?
- Tell me about your loved one.
- What makes your heart hurt today?

- What have you experienced in the last six months that makes you not sleep at night?
- What have you experienced in the last six months that makes you worried?
- What are your fears?
- What are your hopes?

I call these "first caller questions". See Worksheet 4.2 (Intake Questions for First Point of Contact).

Again, the first call should be no more than 30 minutes. Otherwise, the caller may move on because they have been able to share what hurts them and feels momentarily better. In terms of the stages of change, there is an art to closing. You want to move clients from precontemplation into the action stage. You want them essentially to book your services. We'll get into the stages of change more in Chapter 5.

In other words, there is a difference between talking and closing in the work of interventions. Indeed, unresolved issues are at the center of why someone calls you. In the role of interventionist, you need to keep tension present so that the client will seek help. If you let someone talk to you for a longer time, they may never book, especially if they have been able to temporarily expunge their concerns.

Hence, in moving the conversation forward, we discuss the financial terms of the intervention, outline, and agree upon services right from the start. This ensures that the payor – most commonly the first caller – knows what to expect and is committed to the intervention process. It's important for you to help the payor discover insurance benefits related to their medical insurance policies. That can be done by you if you have the capability, or you can outsource this task later to treatment centers.

At this point, you send an engagement contract to the first caller for review. We often work with those who are closest to the ILO in the initial phases of contact. In fact, the person who assumes responsibility for payment is often the one who spends the most time on the intervention planning. They will often connect directly with treatment centers that best match presenting problems. They too are the ones who first suggest who might be part of the accountability team and reach out to others so that the interventionist may converse with them.

Indeed, at this juncture, the payor is encouraged to think of who the clinician might interview. The goal is to learn more about the ILO. So, preliminary discussions are had as to who these folks might be. A time is set aside for approximately 90 minutes to consult with the first caller so that the family mapping process can begin. Finally, best practice is to have families agree that the interventionist is allowed to talk to as many people as needed.

Generally speaking, once an engagement is set, interviews can take place quickly, and a date for a pre-intervention and intervention meeting time are set. Decisions such as who will attend, can someone Skype, and location all have to be taken into account.

## Step 1 Assumptions

The probability of any type of behavior change or movement toward or against the goal will be based on participants' engagement with the process. While motivation can be intrinsic or extrinsic, it is our job to ask the question, "What is this client/family motivated to do?" Families need to be open to the process, feel heard, and listened to by the interventionist they hire. They also need to be open to novel ideas. Still, you'll need to stress to the team the importance of taking responsibility for the intervention results.

## Activity 1.1: Contracting

Independent clinicians need to have contracts and agreements in place before starting any work with clients. Standard working agreements help define your role, the amount of time you will spend, your fee, and expectations – from both you and the client. In this regard, you will need to prepare a client information sheet and service agreement. This document or series of documents explicitly specifies what you do or do not do. It's a great idea to have a lawyer review a templated agreement, as different states require different wording. Be specific! And most importantly, do not under- or overcommit to what you do!

This initial service contract can also be used as an informational guideline. You can describe the type of methodology you use and its efficacy. You can outline your legal confidentiality limitations. For example, while personal information about treatment remains confidential, some states allow clinicians to break client confidentiality if clients are in danger of hurting oneself and/or someone else, in situations of child abuse or of an elderly or legally dependent adult, and in some legal situations or by court order.

Additional engagements made after this initial engagement ends can extend to family coaching or other support services that you offer. See Worksheet 4.1 (Sample Service Agreement) for an outline for interventionists.

## Activity 1.2: Family Mapping

We learn about the ILO through a family history, which includes a snapshot of generational issues, known as the "family map" or "genogram." I usually begin a family map after an engagement contract has been signed, although I start the process on the first phone call of first contact with a concerned loved one. Families hold many secrets. Plus, when we look backward, we'll probably find generations of trauma, addiction, mental health problems, substance misuse, or process disorders.

In Chapter 8, we'll describe how to create a family map in detail. Generally, clinicians look for a multitude of variables, including (but not limited to) changes in income or migration, along with divorce, sudden death, or illness.

History of substance abuse, mental health, legal issues, and school challenges are also important. We also map learning difficulties, birth order, or other relatives' issues. Abuse, death, sudden and unexpected life events, or trauma are also key. Taking a look and learning about the family is important and helps you locate the ILO in the context of the family system. For more about the clinical features of Family Mapping, see Chapter 8. You may also refer to Worksheet 4.3 (How to Listen to Wounded Heart: Questions for Guided Conversations with Clients) and Worksheet 4.4 (Additional Interview Questions for Families).

## Step 2: Determine Key Stakeholders

*Q: What happens when you go one-on-one with someone in active addiction?*

*A: You lose!*

In contrast to many intervention styles, the Collective Intervention Strategy guides intervention teams – called "accountability teams" – through the process. The members of the accountability team are the key stakeholders in the intervention. Think of these teams as a village of potential change agents. By inviting others to join the intervention team, you expand the sphere of influence the team has.

An accountability team can consist of:

- accountants;
- business acquaintances;
- employers;
- employees;
- estate attorneys;
- executive protection employees;
- family;
- friends;
- hairstylists;
- money managers;
- nannies;
- nurses;
- personal assistants;
- household help; and
- bankers

The team can consist of anyone who has an interest in and cares for the ILO to become healthier and stronger. Key stakeholders can be immediate or extended family members, business partners, clergy, best friends, human resources or co-workers, and others.

Note here that team members may have competing wants and needs. Occasionally, team members don't even like each other. However, they must put aside their own issues and come together seeking the common good and health of their loved one. How can you help accountability team members reach out to others who are significant in the life of the ILO? Most often, a phone call does the trick. In delicate matters of estrangement, I find that people rally for a time. They can focus on the ILO and the treatment needs. If someone is incredibly unwilling to participate, it is best to allow for that choice as well.

In step 2, you will also gather data through your participant observations and by conducting semi-structured interviews. Participant observation is a method of data collection wherein a researcher participates in the action with the subjects of the study, and the interaction happens mostly on the subjects' terms. It can be helpful to keep case notes in individual team member files of your own making or to record notes on the family map. The point is that you will observe or pick up on facts in both formal and informal conversations. Don't let anything go unnoticed!

During the interviews, you'll be talking to more than one person about the ILO and the family system. This is a way of putting together more data about the family and individuals within it. Many times, the ILO feels like they are the only one with a problem. In reality, there is a long line of family members that have experienced complex problems. Helping to identify the backstories helps immensely when performing an intervention.

One-on-one interviews of 45–60+ minutes will provide you with a robust picture of the situation. As you collect and record data, you learn key insights into how the ILO functions. You can even identify other loved ones who require treatment and can see who might be a great support in the intervention process. Likewise, interviews help you understand who might inadvertently become a saboteur.

## Step 2 Assumptions

Families are experts in hurting. Families are also experts about their own lives. As behavioral healthcare professionals, it is imperative that we adopt a posture of not knowing. This is easier said than done! Our counselor expertise is called for along the way. But this is not about you. So, avoid one-upmanship and become an open vessel.

Assumptions to avoid:

- A person *ought* to change.
- A person *wants* to change.
- A person's health is the prime motivation factor.
- If they decide not to change, consultation is a failure.

- Individuals are either motivated to change or they are not.
- Now is the right time to consider change.
- A tough approach is always the best approach.
- I am the expert and I know best.
- An egalitarian approach is always best.

### Activity 2.1: Individual Interviews

To create a robust picture, clinicians should pursue multiple sources of information to be able to triangulate data. This means talking to as many people related to the client as possible. The first goal is to determine if substance abuse is primary, mental health is prominent, and which came first. This can be difficult. The second goal is to achieve a robust picture of who the identified client is, what they are doing, and where they came from.

Plan to interview each member of the accountability team for 45 to 60 minutes and get to know their perspective. If you interview people in a group, you are likely not to get as robust information as you would if you interview separately; there is more freedom for people to express their perceptions and viewpoints when they are one-on-one with a clinician.

These interviews can be conducted on the phone, via video chat, or face-to-face. Take notes. You are particularly looking for accounts of:

- car accidents;
- changes in behavior;
- hospitalization;
- major family changes;
- school records;
- trauma; and
- sudden death.

Basically, you are looking for the same things you look for in the family map. Plus, clinicians can ask people to send photos of themselves and their loved one. I like to ask my clients to show me a picture of their homes; I am looking for data in multiple ways.

It is also important to get a perspective from someone who is outside the family system. So, be sure to interview or talk to an outlier: a friend, an uncle, a best friend, a co-worker, an employee, or someone who isn't living in the house. Often, outliers know more than individual family members, especially parents.

Interviews also provide clinicians with the opportunity to make sure that everyone understands their role and is supportive in the process. During this time, we provide coaching for vocabulary and encourage patience as family members learn the right words to communicate effectively during the intervention. Coaching continues in all steps of the strategy, keeping accountability team members informed on what's going on in the here and now, on what's happening today.

See Worksheet 4.3 (How to Listen to Wounded Heart: Questions for Guided Conversations with Clients) for more ideas on how to conduct individual interviews.

## Activity 2.2: Portraiture

When clinicians embark on an intervention, our job is not to provide a client with a definitive clinical diagnosis. However, the information we gather will help differentiate between disorders so we can navigate an intervention course and choose the appropriate course of treatment and rehabilitation center. When performing an intervention, be sure to talk to every individual who is in relationship with the ILO, because everyone holds a different portrait of that loved one and they see different things.

Note here that clients seek the help of professional interventionists when they are at the end of their rope. They come loaded with feelings of trauma, shame, guilt, humiliation, embarrassment, grief, and loss. The way that they *feel* affects the stories they *tell* about themselves. Our goal is to open up/encourage/personify the possibility. We are there to motivate aspiration, to convey the message that a better life is possible.

In this light, we collect rich, meaningful data throughout the process to create a "portrait" of the ILO. We talk more about clinical features of this skill in Chapter 8. In fact, the qualitative research method of portraiture is a combination of in-depth interviews and observation. Portraiture creates a dialogue between clinician and client. It defines clinician and client as collaborators in this story. And the portrait of the individual will unfold as you go through the Collective Intervention Strategy.

## Step 3: Define Client Guidelines and Confidentiality

This step requires great clinical skill. It is critical that every member of the accountability team agrees with the expectations, commitments, timelines, ground rules, goals, and objectives. So, after discussion and agreement, it's best to get this in print. At the same time, you'll also want to outline your personal commitment to fostering a trusting, purposeful, and confidential relationship. Trust is a two-way street.

During step 3, you'll also begin coordinating options with the most appropriate treatment centers. During the vetting process, you'll share profile data with the treatment center, looking for a therapeutic match. Your end goal is to provide the family/client with three viable, appropriate treatment centers.

Note here that no two treatment centers are alike. Further, your treatment referral may change over time. You may need to change facilities as you gather more information and continue through the process. Remain flexible and communicate all changes to all parties at all times so that they can make an informed choice about where they'd like to send the ILO.

You'll also note that folks are usually in a state of crisis when they start calling treatment centers. It can be extremely challenging to distinguish a top-rated treatment center from one with little services and a great website. Depending on what the problem is, whether drugs, alcohol, sex, gambling, shopping, obesity, food, codependency, Internet addiction, etc., the general public may have a difficult time discerning one treatment center from the other based on the resources they are given.

See Chapter 10 for more on ethical practices in referral.

## Step 3 Assumptions

Simply stated, there are several goals that clinicians work toward or look for during an intervention. First, the payor or first caller has defined that they are at their wits' end; they do not know how to move their loved one to change, and they see professional intervention as the correct method to bring about change. Second, in reaching client consensus, the assumption is that all will work toward the common good, put disagreements aside, and help the loved one accept treatment. Third, the clinician assumes that help is possible and that they have the skills necessary to move all to change.

## Activity 3.1: Legal Agreements

Clinicians ensure that all individuals in the family sign legal documents in step 3, including confidentiality agreements. This will include a nondisclosure agreement, which confirms each person has permission to talk with you and are bound by their own confidentiality agreement(s). Participants receive copies of privacy practices and HIPAA information as well.

Clinicians who are mandated reporters (such as myself) must give "duty to warn" disclosures to clients and must report to the appropriate regulatory agency. "Duty to warn" is among the few exceptions to a client's right to confidentiality and the therapist's ethical obligation to maintain confidential information related in the context of the therapeutic relationship. In other words, there are specific cases in which I may break confidentiality and alert a likely victim of harm or call the police. If this is the case in your clinical practice, it is important that clients are assured that their confidentiality and that of their loved one is honored for trust to ensue.

In the case of the high-profile client, all must be guaranteed that the information gleaned will not be shared with the media and the privacy of the identified client is kept intact. To do anything else is a breach of ethics and trust.

## Activity 3.2: Initial Treatment Matching

Selecting appropriate treatment options for clients is at the center of our work. However, not all treatment centers are alike. As licensed professionals, we have a professional and ethical obligation to help clients navigate the world of addiction treatment and help them choose the right treatment center based on their loved ones' presenting problem and the financial resources they have. In fact, you'll need to verify that an addiction treatment center does what they say they'll do.

The job of the clinician-interventionist is to take one step at a time, be mindful of a client's financial resources and insurance needs, and do due diligence with suggested placements. Note here that you must be engaged as an interventionist to refer clients to addiction treatment. Otherwise, you face malpractice.

Some general guidelines to follow when preparing three initial treatment centers for referral:

1. Know the qualities of a good treatment center.
2. Be aware of red flags and avoid unethical businesses.
3. Visit treatment centers personally.
4. Use your network to gather more information.
5. Ensure a financial match.
6. Ensure a therapeutic match.
7. Communicate options with the payor.

## 1. Know the Qualities of a Good Treatment Center

To learn if a treatment center is a good match, it's important to understand the landscape of addiction treatment. Over time, you'll become acquainted with dozens of top-quality, reputable addiction treatment centers. At the beginning, you'll need to invest time into knowing who's who.

> *If you don't make a good referral, you're the one who will ultimately be left with a bad reputation.*

The reality is this: the addiction treatment industry is a $35 billion a year industry. Websites are very deceiving. Marketing programs don't always tell the truth. For example, treatment centers may offer services that they cannot provide: golf, horses, swimming pools, or a spa-like environment. Some treatment centers operate on a for-profit-only basis; the revolving door model suits their desire for higher profit, and clients are often churned in and out.

See Worksheet 3.1 (Clinical Questions for Treatment Centers) and Worksheet 4.5 (Questions for Treatment Centers for Families) for more specific questions designed to help you complete due diligence of good addiction treatment and to guide families in discussions with treatment centers.

## 2. Be Aware of Red Flags and Avoid Unethical Businesses

To avoid referring clients to centers that are subpar, place particular weight on mission and ethics statements. Verify that the center publishes both, and talk with staff about the treatment center's vision for mental healthcare.

Red flags that signal unethical treatment practices include:

- offering to pay patient airfare;
- non-credentialed staff;
- no joint commission accreditation;
- no Commission on Accreditation of Rehabilitation Facilities (CARF) accreditation;
- no listing of staff on the website;
- no description of their business' length of existence; and
- claiming to take insurance in full – what does that really mean?

## 3. Visit Treatment Centers Personally

If at all possible, visit any center you refer and meet the clinical team. Know the staff. See a group running in action. See how clients are treated or sit down and talk with staff to have a better understanding on what the setting is like. Get educated about the facilities and their general demographics. At the very least, talk with the business development director, admissions director, or clinical services director. Finally, become familiar with treatment center intake processes. This will help ease the process of treatment initiation when it begins.

## 4. Use Your Network to Gather More Information

If you are not familiar with a particular center, you can also reach out to your colleagues and ask for guidance or feedback. You can also seek referrals from members of NII or AIS. Talk about their experiences with clinical staff. What is the turnover? What is the treatment philosophy?

## 5. Ensure a Financial Match

Know your clients' finances and the resources they have to spend. Then match accordingly.

## 6. Ensure a Therapeutic Match

When required, make sure you are referring to a center that can handle substance abuse, mental health, co-occurring disorders, and/or trauma with PTSD. The treatment center must have experience in handling cases of dual diagnosis if and when indicated.

Further, you need to be sure that amenities are appropriate for clients. If the ILO is a celebrity, you need to anticipate what type of concierge services or escort security you'll need to put together. If they are an executive or a high-wealth client, you'll need to think about how their leadership roles need to continue during treatment.

Know too that length of stay and residence options can affect treatment outcomes. When clinicians refer to treatment centers, we must be realistic in that 30 days of treatment is often not enough. If a person has been using drugs or alcohol for one-half to one-third of their life, a one-month stay just begins to stabilize the body. Instead, a community integration approach of 90 days inpatient, followed by structured sober living, and then five days a week of outpatient treatment, connected with meetings and individual therapy for nine months to one year, may be the best option. In my experience, this is a more successful treatment plan than "28 days in rehab."

If a treatment center refers a client to you, and after you complete a full assessment you feel that a therapeutic match exists, great! You are working ethically when you select the treatment center in your list of top three treatment options. Let them know that. If the ILO does not fit the treatment culture, call the treatment center that gave the referral and report your findings. Ask the treatment center staff, "What do you think about that?" And listen to their feedback.

## 7. Communicate Options with the Payor

While you are vetting programs, offer the payor contact details for your top three preferences and connect them with the top three centers. Always respect the client and follow up with their own preference(s). If you don't know about the center, do due diligence. In fact, you have an ethical obligation to check it out. However, if a client's preferences do not ensure a therapeutic match, guide the payor into considering other treatment options and explain exactly why you have misgivings.

Final Thoughts on Treatment Matching

> *As you are matching people to addiction treatment, always be asking yourself, "If this was my relative, what would be the best three places in the country to send this person?"*

In a perfect world, a clinician or interventionist can recommend the three best treatment centers in the United States for the ILO based on personal knowledge. This requires many years in the industry. If you are well versed and positioned in the community, perhaps you can do this.

More likely, what is most often involved is a lot of phone-calling. It is helpful to have a list of strategic partners that provide consultation and can help with decision-making. Indeed, working with colleagues on case consultation is rewarding and builds your network. Still, you need to come from a place of sincerity, honesty, and ethics any time you refer to addiction treatment.

There are times when you will receive a referral directly from a treatment center. In this case, you must decide if this is the best possible center for the ILO after you have done due diligence. I always thank a center for referring, get back to them after I have done due diligence, and ask if they think it's the best match. Sometimes it is not, and I explain why. I always give my clients three options in terms of treatment facilities, even when a center has referred.

## Step 4: Educate About Addiction

Once the intervention agreement is finalized, focus can shift to the accountability team. While team members are open to review the overall process and ask questions, they also begin to learn more about addiction (and other co-occurring diseases). Through this practice, everyone learns more about what is going on, what the disease of addiction looks like, and how the team is going to get healthy together.

It is important to note here that everyone involved needs to learn about substance abuse, mental health, process disorders, chronic pain, and trauma. Think of short, concise ways to teach on these subjects. Accountability team members may be world-renowned experts in their field and know nothing of ours. Look to have resources that are meaningful to individuals and the group as a whole. Again, focus on a customized curriculum. See Worksheet 4.6 (Sample Addiction Curriculum for Families).

This phase is still "pre-intervention." While it's imperative to focus on addiction, you also want to educate them about the intervention process itself. In fact, it's a great time to teach families more about what the process looks like. You can provide worksheets, brochures, or descriptions to clients, or you can simply talk them through what will happen. Note here, it's imperative to always keep your clinician's hat on through any interaction. While you are a good listener, you should also be a good observer; clinicians are continually gathering information.

As a side note, I stay in a concierge mode during this time. This means that I am on call to answer accountability team member questions day or night. If the situation is volatile and the crisis is directive, it's really a matter of being able to tell them what to do. This will not appeal to every clinician. You have to be able to think on your feet and respond at a moment's notice. Clients might need to call 911 if a situation gets out of control.

## Step 4 Assumptions

Educating the intervention accountability team is a must. People need to learn that addiction is not a moral failing. Indeed, many clients learn the appropriate ways of separating one's behavior from one's experience, so they might have an opportunity to develop compassion and empathy in the face of grave sorrow.

Further, the words we use have great power in the intervention process. Teaching loved ones how to convey and communicate their ideas in thoughtful, nonjudgmental ways is imperative. The group is attempting to break down the denial system of the individual, and as the old saying goes, "One can catch more bees with honey than with vinegar."

## Activity 4.1: Develop a Custom Curriculum on Addiction

Families must have opportunities to grow alongside their loved one that is in treatment. Families work best when they learn about the following:

- What is addiction?
- What is mental health?
- What are process addictions?
- What is chronic pain syndrome?
- What is trauma?
- How are trauma and addiction intertwined?
- What is codependency or enmeshment?
- How to establish healthy boundaries.
- How to invite their loved ones to change.
- How to begin to take care of themselves.
- What constitutes good treatment?

Each family requires a custom program. Some of this can be taught verbally. When on the phone, for instance, you talk about their experiences and get a feel for their gaps in knowledge. You understand more about what they allow. Initially, most families need to learn about addiction as a disease. And you use the conversations as a starting point. Often one discussion will lead to a new need.

Then use multiple media to communicate ideas and to share information. For example, SlideShare works well when teaching families directly. Sometimes you can educate via email, personalized messages, and attached documents. Sometimes we learn about these issues by going into a lived experience.

The point is that you'll need to develop a custom curriculum based on clients' needs. The key to knowing what they need? Listen to your client first. You have to start where they are.

## Step 5: Retrospective Analysis

In the Collective Intervention Strategy, clinicians complete a retrospective analysis of the ILO *and* key stakeholders of the accountability team. Why?

A biopsychosocial analysis assumes that disease processes such as addiction require that treatment address biological, psychological, and social influences upon a client's functioning. Philosophically, this means that we agree that the workings of the body or environment can affect the mind, and vice versa. Indeed, the biopsychosocial model posits that it is important to handle the three together!

Due to the complex nature of addiction, recovery requires a broad approach to the disease. Rather than relying on strictly medical or biological models, recent research indicates a need for incorporating social and psychological influences as well.

> *Client perceptions of health, threat of disease, and barriers to treatment are rooted in their social or cultural environment.*

In this way, we can better identify barriers to treatment – including denial – via specialized interviewing skills. Indeed, the collective, biopsychosocial approach examines addiction as the product of more than just one influence. That's why a successful intervention involves interviewing multiple sources and looking at multiple pieces of information.

By looking at a robust picture of a client, what they are doing, and where they came from, clinicians can create a colorful map that illuminates which problem to tackle first. It's critical to create this picture from multiple sources of information. Thus, more than one person is interviewed so that the data are triangulated and verified. In doing this, clinicians build a collective intervention strategy that is mindful of who the clients are, as well as their strengths, weaknesses, and resiliencies. When we identify strengths, this gives families a prescription for action and heals everyone involved.

Finally, the role of a comprehensive retrospective analysis becomes a key component of the intervention process; it helps you determine the skills and strategies you need to intervene with respect, compassion, and success. It is a guidepost in helping determine what might be the three best treatment centers in the country for the ILO or patient to enter so that health and wellness may be achieved. Let's take a look at the particulars.

### *Biological Analysis for Physical Health*

A robust physical history must be completed in order for a good retrospective analysis to take place. Often family members develop somatic complaints as a result of substance use disorders: their stomachs hurt, their necks ache, they have difficulty sleeping, and they may over- or under-eat as they are worried about their loved ones. Likewise, those who experience a substance abuse disorder may also develop physical symptoms related to the disease.

For example, alcoholism can result in a distended liver, a bloated stomach, bloodshot eyes, and in some cases early-onset dementia or Korsakoff's syndrome. Methamphetamine or cocaine users may develop grave dental problems, while those who abuse THC may have black tar in their lungs.

## Psychological Analysis for Mental Health

Mental health disorders (anxiety, depression, bipolar, mania, or personality disorders) may co-occur alongside an addiction. They become tightly entwined, and one can trigger or worsen the other. By completing a robust retrospective analysis, clinicians can fetter out which came first.

Trauma is another important factor to consider when completing a retrospective analysis. Trauma causes intense feelings of discomfort, and mind-altering substances are often used to numb feelings and memories. Trauma is both subjective, based on what a person feels, and objective (i.e. based on what external event happened – my child died, I was in the war, I had a terrible accident, I was raped, beaten, verbally abused, etc.). Often people are asked to remember what was important to them at different stages of their lives. What they remember versus what was actually going on in the outside world is a way of taking a gentle look at how trauma may have played a part in their growth and development.

## Sociological Analysis for Family Systems Health

Clinicians must also take a look at family or origin issues, as well as outside community influences. For an effective intervention, it's essential to have a comprehensive view of family history. This includes a robust history of brothers, sisters, aunts, uncles, grandparents, and even pets. It includes not just disorders, but also marriages, deaths, cultural background, religion norms and rituals, and sexual behaviors. Questions go beyond just addictions, and marriages, divorces, deaths, work, school, legal, religion, moves, relationships to sex, money, food, and even digital devices are considered. Families are as complex and unique as the issues they face. Hence, one must consider lifestyle factors and cultural factors such as preferred treatment approaches.

## Retrospective Analysis during an Intervention

The truth is we are working all the time on a retrospective analysis when we are in contact with clients. Any phone call that you have with a family member will provide you with more information on the family system and the ILO. Any meeting. Any conversation. For this reason, it can help to take notes any time you speak with clients. Then add what you have learned to the growing body of evidence of the family map or to the individual's biopsychosocial assessment.

### Step 5 Assumptions

Clinicians must adopt a posture of inquiry, of not knowing, in order to gather the most objective data possible. When using an open posture of inquiry, one has the ability to learn from strangers in a way that allows the assessment to unfold in a naturalistic setting and allows for serendipity.

### Activity 5.1: Complete a Retrospective Analysis of the ILO and Key Stakeholders

To apply a biopsychosocial approach to interventions, clinicians must elicit a client's history in the context of life circumstances. Then we decide which aspects of biological, psychological, and social domains are most important to understanding and promoting the person's health. Finally, we recommend or provide multidimensional treatment that addresses each of these areas.

Biological components of treatment might focus on:

- the effects of substance use on the body itself;
- the importance of nutrition, sleep, and exercise; and
- the genetic and inherited components of substance use.

Psychological components of treatment might focus on:

- the thoughts, feelings, and behaviors surrounding and generated by substance use;
- difficulties regulating emotions; and
- issues related to trauma.

Social components of treatment might focus on:

- a client's relationships with a partner, parents, children, friends, or close loved ones;
- disconnection from home or school; and
- underdeveloped social competencies.

This skill of performing a biopsychosocial assessment is taught in most master's-level courses in social work. Guidelines for conducting biopsychosocial assessments can be found in continuing education courses offered by the Society of Behavioral Medicine and in schools of social work or psychology.

Clinical principles underlying these skills are outlined in the landmark book *Learning from Strangers*[3] by Robert S. Weiss. Other books that are helpful include Kathy Charmaz's second edition of *Constructing Grounded Theory*.[4] *Narrative Inquiry*,[5] written by D. Jean Clandinin and F. Michael Connelly, or *Narrative Research*,[6] from Amia Lieblich, Rivka Tuval-Mashiach, and Tamar Zilber, are also excellent reads.

## Step 6: Teach and Survey the Accountability Team

In step 6, clinicians continue to work with the accountability team members as they address the pain of living with addiction or mental health disorder. Often families need extensive counseling and coaching. So, clinicians help each member of the team develop and practice self-care, setting clear boundaries. Often we can refer to the curriculum outlined in step 4. Families continue to learn about substance abuse, process disorders, mental health, and chronic pain.

We teach families in a family setting. This way, they are more relaxed. In a compassionate way, you start to examine what is helpful and what is not helpful for each member of the team. On the timeline of events, we introduce concepts in step 6. Then we continue to gather information. Not much teaching occurs until the ILO is in treatment; families are burned out! They are typically:

- hypervigilant;
- traumatized; and
- living in upset.

One way to look at it is that treatment gives family a "time out." In fact, much time spent in education peaks after the loved one is in treatment. Once the ILO accepts help, you can begin to change shift the focus from the "trouble" to the personal. This way, accountability team members can start to see the part that they play in the disease cycle.

*Still, you break into the system of denial as you go.*

Families struggling with substance abuse and mental health problems are behavioral systems in which the illness-related behaviors have become the central organizing structure. Over time, an identity is forged around this. The family accommodates to the special needs of the person diagnosed with substance or mental health behavior.

But it's not just the central issue that affects the unit. Families also contend with:

- legal issues;
- physical issues; and
- family history.

Daily rituals reflect this new identity and can alter the balance that exists between growth and regulation in the family. Families begin to count on this new identity – consciously or unconsciously – and are somewhat resistant to change. In other words, addiction is actually maintained by the family. Hence, the introduction of change most often appears as emphasis on short-term stability at the expense of long-term growth.

Family distortions occur as a result. This can manifest as "family fusion" and lack of boundaries such as:

- lack of personal space;
- being over-controlling;
- blurred lines;
- blaming;
- power;
- denying;
- rescuing; and
- faulty reasoning.

Before treatment, families are frequently attached to the problem. They typically deny the issue or minimize mental health problems. Feelings families have include anger, sadness, and love. Families also report feeling confused or bewildered.

So, accountability teams typically describe feeling a combination of any of the following descriptors:

- angry;
- ashamed;
- at wits' end;
- controlling;
- disgusted;
- depressed;
- embarrassed;
- frustrated;
- loving;
- mad;
- resentful;
- sad;
- shocked;
- terrified; and
- worried.

The bottom line? They want the pain to go away.

But, paradoxically, they are stuck in a cycle of behavioral reinforcement. They don't know how else to live. They continue the same dysfunctional patterns without an end in sight. Their resistance can be summarized as an "immunity to change."

Note here that managing family members or friends in the accountability team can be as complicated as distinguishing between disorders. Group dynamics can be extremely difficult. This is one reason it is helpful to work with a teammate.

Continuing the process, we teach families how to shift perspective. Accountability team members need to be reminded that they do not need to be part of the problem – they learn to be part of the solution! In doing so, clinicians can teach the seven C's taught by the National Association for Children of Alcoholics as a guidepost for new ways of being:

1. You did not *cause* your loved one's addiction.
2. You alone cannot *cure* the addiction.
3. You alone cannot *control* your loved one's addiction.
4. You can take better *care* of yourself.
5. You can learn to *communicate* your feelings.
6. You can make healthier *choices*.
7. You can *celebrate* yourself and your growth.

The third aspect of step 6 is defining and creating healthy boundaries. Accountability teams must be able to wake up each morning, look themselves in the mirror, and know that they are worthy and that they can stick to the boundaries they have set. To this effect, clinicians help families define their boundaries and then write behavioral change agreements (see Activities 6.1 and 6.2 for more on this).

It is of paramount importance that accountability team members begin to take care of themselves, physically and emotionally. Families need to turn to their own personal values to find strength. This may come in the form of spirituality or a connection with a higher power. Al-Anon, other support groups, meditation, mindfulness, exercise, and social bonding aid in the healing process.

This discussion might begin with families considering solutions in a perfect-world scenario. To do this, it is helpful to ask the question:

> *When you wake up tomorrow, what would an ideal world look like to you? What would you want to do to take care of yourself?*

This work is getting family members to take care of themselves. Another route is to be totally pragmatic: you're getting homework assignments, they're giving suggestions, and helping people moved toward whatever their perfect world is.

Finally, step 6 helps determine the final involvement of accountability team members in the actual intervention. Upon education about the process, addiction as a disease, setting boundaries, and self-care principles, team members may elect to participate or not. It's not always an easy decision, as interventions are incredibly emotionally taxing. The team members are faced with the choice of progress and some hard work, or stagnation and further decline.

Note here that another type of boundary might be to set limits with a problem member within the group. When a family member directly works *against the long-term health* of the ILO, they hinder the process and can sabotage the plan. These individuals are best identified and then excluded from an intervention. Therefore, if a family member is not ready to change the system, or is dependent upon the continued substance use of the ILO, they may need to be "disinvited" from the process. Exclusions such as this do occur sometimes, and may be required.

## Case Study: The Race Car Driver

I once worked with a family who were concerned about a talented young man, a racing driver. He was taking stimulants, getting in his car, and driving at speeds of 180 mph or more. Most of his loved ones were on board with the action plan, intervention meeting, and his need for treatment. In fact, his mother and wife were desperate to get him help. However, his father had different interests. His father agreed for the need to get his son help, but insisted that he run one last race. The intervention was planned for just before this big race; the father insisted that he compete. I had to gently but directly "disinvite" this gentleman from participating in the intervention. When the father was removed from the process, a significant barrier to treatment was also removed. The young man accepted help.

## A Word about Letter-Writing

Many intervention strategies suggest that loved ones write a letter to the ILO expressing their relationship and their experiences, hopes, and fears. These have been traditionally sent with the loved one to the treatment center. Instead, as a clinician interventionist, I coach folks to speak their truth during the intervention. Then I practice and coach them based on what they want to say; the goal is that a person become one with the emotion they express through narrative.

> In the moment of a loving intervention, I have found that people speaking from their heart works best.

I have no issue with this practice. However, over the years, my own practice has evolved and changed to where I do not see this as a requirement. My experience has been that people sometimes lose the intensity of the moment when they do a rehearsal and write letters. Instead, a collective intervention can make use of letters reaffirming family positions later in the process. Or I teach them to work on change agreements.

As you develop your own style, feel free to try what you are most comfortable with. For example, if someone cannot attend an intervention meeting and is critical to the process, then, yes, I encourage them to write, and I integrate that into the meeting. Still, letter-writing varies by case. Remember, you will develop your own style based on sound principles and practices.

## Step 6 Assumptions

During an intervention, family or friends are in crisis. Someone is engaging in behaviors that are antithetical to the good person they are. Your job is to get that person to a "yes."

The best way to do this is to gather and harness the power of the group. When you focus on how to get to the common good and show empathy at how people's lives have changed, you motivate hope for change. You spark a new growth. This is often a turning point for loved ones. Participants often discover hope and optimism at this stage. They begin to see that it is possible to laugh again.

## Activity 6.1: Define Boundaries

Here are questions that need to be asked related to building honest and healthy boundaries:

- What is OK behavior and what is not OK?
- What was OK before treatment, and how has that changed?
- What was not OK before treatment, and how can you make it better this time?
- What gets confusing?

The key notion is that healthy boundaries are critical for personal health and happiness. Once a loved one experiencing addiction seeks treatment, all family members, friends, and colleagues and business associates must take a hard look at their own behaviors and redraw these boundary lines to find change.

## Activity 6.2: Change Agreements

In step 6, clinicians help families develop behavioral change agreements (BCAs). These agreements are a written document in which stakeholders clearly articulate what they are willing to do to support their loved one in recovery. They are not actually delivered unless the ILO refuses help or says, "I'm not going to treatment."

Through a BCA, we get to define ways in which family members are going to take care of themselves. For example, these agreements often include family members attending Al-Anon and other support groups and/or professional counseling. We also recommend setting firm limits for financial and other types of support that will build on recovery.

Change agreements also define ways in which team members are going to take care of themselves. Change agreements often include family members attending Al-Anon and other support groups and/or professional counseling, as well as setting firm limits in what their financial and other types of support they will render that supports recovery. Expectations are concisely articulated.

For example, the ILO may engage in treatment as outlined by a professional. This usually includes:

- attending intensive outpatient treatment;
- attending meetings; and
- randomized drug testing.

See Worksheet 5.5 (Sample Behavioral Change Agreement (General)), Worksheet 5.6 (Sample Behavioral Change Agreement (Mental Health)), and Worksheet 5.7 (Sample Behavioral Change Agreement (Medical Chronic Pain)).

## Activity 6.3: Introduce Key Concepts of Self-Care

### Brainstorm and Map Self-Care Activities

When we talk about self-care, we ask accountability team members to start to take care of themselves! To illustrate, we first draw a horizontal line and place the days of the week. Then we create a vertical line and outline the next 90 days into 12 weeks. Then we ask clients:

> *How are you going to take care of yourself physically, emotionally, and spiritually (consistent with your values)? What activities will you engage in each of these domains at least three times per week?*

Sometimes team members have no idea of where to begin. A simple way to get a conversation started is by using the alphabet to define activities within each category, from A to Z. There are at least 26 ways to engage in physical, emotional, or spiritual fitness!

Have accountability team members brainstorm and list activities A to Z by category on a whiteboard, easel, or large piece of paper together in a group. Then each person can complete their own personalized self-care calendar for the next 30 days. You'll refer to this calendar in coaching phone calls and personal conversations in later steps.

## Practice Gratitude

We also like to include a soft introduction to gratitude at this time. You can give accountability team members each a homework assignment to practice gratitude. It can be this simple:

*When you wake up in the morning, write down five things you are grateful for.*

## Step 7: Develop a Measurable Action Plan

After the above information is gathered, step 7 consists of evaluation through careful investigation. Then the best treatment center is chosen and a date is set for the intervention. In step 7, we work to set a strategy that defines the action plan:

- *Where* the intervention will be held.
- *When* the intervention will take place.
- *Who* will attend.
- *How* the intervention will be introduced.
- *What* we are going to do in the meantime.

The actual place and time of the intervention is set and transportation is arranged. Special consideration is given to the timing of the intervention to avoid intervening when the ILO could possibly be under the influence. Also consider the help of clinical colleagues for the intervention meeting. Can you benefit from having a pain specialist, specialized trauma counselor, or other medical expert on hand? What about a lawyer or the family financial advisor? What about including a representative from the selected treatment center?

Further, participants also anticipate objections to treatment that the ILO may bring up: childcare, employment, school, or other plans that they see as too important to miss. A plan is developed to address, minimize, and eliminate objections. Likewise, accountability team members explore reasons that the ILO might accept and embrace treatment. Members prepare to share their experiences, their fears, and their hopes with their loved one.

### Step 7 Assumptions

Accountability family members experience relief when they are doing something, and are no longer inert or passive. There is hope and inspiration. You are inspiring change.

Picture someone with a backpack full of rocks, walking around with a load of rocks on their back, but they don't know exactly what to do with it. Now that an intervention is possible and the right people will be there (clinical psychologist or pain specialist, for example), they can take that backpack off.

## Activity 7.1: Choose a Treatment Center

Initial treatment options defined in Activity 3.2 are now sorted into the top three preferences by clinical and financial match. Beginning with treatment center 1, you call and communicate with intake teams to arrange for treatment initiation. Once you have secured or reserved a space for the ILO, you can communicate the availability to the client(s) and a final decision can be made.

Indeed, clinicians planning an intervention should be prepared to make multiple phone calls until the intervention meeting takes place. Again, I work in a concierge style and answer my telephone myself. Other interventionists choose to delegate this task to someone else. There are big houses with multiple people working for them. But if Johnny upsets the family, mom can reach out and talk about it.

## Activity 7.2: Define and Communicate the Action Plan

Like planning any life-changing event, you take a look ahead. The action plan will consist of a pre-intervention meeting, the intervention itself, and necessary follow-up. You need to know your schedule and that of other teammates, attendees, or clinicians who will attend the pre-intervention and/or intervention meetings. Plus, you need to coordinate with accountability team members. In sum, you need to consider every person's needs and then coordinate these events.

Ninety percent of this time is spent on the phone. Sometimes you may meet people in person, but many are worldwide. Via Skype, FaceTime, and online apps, be prepared to spend an amazing amount of time talking with strangers!

## Step 8: Pre-Intervention

Before holding the actual intervention, accountability team members meet in person or via the Internet to finalize the action plan and to process their own emotions. Family interventions are difficult and delicate matters. Anger and profound sorrow often result when someone is forced to look at their own behavior. Family members often experience mournful rage, deep sadness, and powerful guilt over previous failed efforts. So, meeting *before* the intervention helps people process and prepare.

In step 8, accountability team members gather to communicate openly in a pre-intervention meeting. During the meeting, clinicians guide specific discussions. We set up the scenario. We plan where to sit. We discuss the order of events. We finalize operational details. You might also decide that a specific person should not be present for the intervention itself.

Further, the pre-intervention meeting defines all mitigating factors. Most importantly, team members revisit potential objections of the ILO and problem-solve answers to their arguments. Together, we anticipate objections to treatment and come up with counter-objections. Even more, clinicians coach members on:

- how to deliver the invitation to the intervention meeting;
- what to say during the intervention itself;
- how to speak from the heart in nonjudgmental ways; and
- defining consequences for worst-case scenarios.

To avoid the Brady Bunch Syndrome (where everything is always great), you don't go around the room and practice exactly what each person is going to say at the intervention. This could actually deflate the emotional intensity of the delivery. In fact, you stand a chance of losing emotional affect when the actual intervention takes place if members rehearse what they're going to say in front of one another. Instead, you offer general guidelines and offer to do role play individually with people one-on-one. Employing a bit of psychodrama at this stage is often helpful.

Coaching is key here; clinicians should consistently be available to speak with individuals and assuage their anxieties. It is also necessary to set boundaries or to refocus in cases of extreme conflict. Life is messy. Relationships are messy. So, we continue to reframe conversations around the original purpose of the intervention: we hold the ILO in the center of the family and come together for the good of this person. Participants may also attend support groups or continue seeing their own counselors during this period.

During this time, family members are gently asked to look at their own behaviors and explore the intricacies of relationships and behaviors that have been built around the addiction. It is imperative for a clinician to be present to help coach everyone along the way. A safe, comfortable, and respectful atmosphere is essential for success.

This is an emotional time for the accountability team. Together, they learn there are "no more secrets." Communication opens up the possible ways in which each member may have enabled their loved one's addiction in the past. Oftentimes, the behavior was inadvertent and done out of love, such as:

- covering up work absences;
- excusing missed school; and
- ignoring missing money.

However, clinicians need to guide families away from blame and shame. With clinical skill, you can use the past to motivate present change. Movement starts with a willingness to change, sprinkled with fierce love and commitment, coupled with the tools necessary to change. When those are in place, family members no longer have to travel down a pity path that leads to cajoling and bargaining. No longer will they mortgage homes or blame others in an effort to have their loved one stop using drugs or alcohol. Instead, they focus on themselves and what they can control.

You can help families tell the truth without shame, guilt, fear, humiliation, fear of recrimination, and a lifetime sentence that each is the eternally bad sister, mother, father, brother, husband, wife, partner, lover, grandparent, business manager, or personal assistant. Because they don't have to have all the answers. Instead, you help guide family members to take positive action to become their own best selves.

## Step 8 Assumptions

### Activity 8.1: Pre-Intervention Meeting

During a pre-intervention meeting, you gather members of the accountability team together in a comfortable setting. The setting should be relaxed and comfortable. For example, a warm space with ample furniture works well. As for my practice, I don't have a traditional office. Sometimes we meet in my home. Know this: whatever space you choose should be neutral. You want to create a compassionate space that allows for talking. I prefer round tables as opposed to rectangular ones.

Teach members how you're going to talk during the intervention itself. People need to learn how to:

- express how much they care about the ILO (express love);
- express how much they have missed their loved one and watched them continue to engage in self-defeating behaviors (express hurt); and
- express that there is a solution (express hope).

Also, discuss what the intervention will look like. How might people be sitting, for example? I tend to sit below others. Sometimes I walk around. Like an orchestra conductor, the interventionist is conducting. When you move around, the real stars are the loved ones who inspire the person they care about to stop, pause, reflect, and take the help that is offered. In fact, when working outside a clinical setting, we need to be fluid and flexible, especially when people are very uncomfortable. You will need to be an active participant, both in the pre-intervention meeting and during the intervention itself, so consider the room dynamics.

Further, it's sometimes helpful to assign a person(s) to be with the ILO. This person may walk outside of the room for a smoke break or walk with the ILO during the intervention. This person needs to be prepped with instructions for containment to be sure that the ILO does not flee the scene.

Keep in mind that clinical skills are extremely helpful during any meeting involving accountability team members. Emotions run high. Blame, shame, and judgment are present. For more on the skills any clinician needs to navigate families in crisis, we review clinical skills and therapeutic strategies for interventions in Chapter 5. Also, see Worksheet 4.9 (Easy Meditation Practice), which you can teach clients and use yourself.

Suffice it to say that clinicians require empathy, communication skills, and experience in group facilitations. To summarize briefly, we use open-ended questions, affirmations, reflections, and summaries when working with families.

Some specific traps to avoid that originate in motivational interviewing include:

- becoming the expert;
- blaming others – who is to blame is not as important as to the concern we have;
- a labeling trap based on diagnosis codes;
- premature focus trap – start with the clients' concern, not yours;
- taking sides; and
- question–answer trap.

## Activity 8.2: Invite the ILO to the Intervention

From the time we start working together, I suggest that the accountability team (primarily the first caller) inform the ILO that the process of getting help has begun by saying, "Our family problems/our business problems have gotten so big that I am working with professionals and we will find a solution." However, actually delivering the invitation to the intervention meeting is postponed until after the pre-intervention meeting.

Furthermore, if you disclose that an intervention is coming, expect resistance. To avoid major pitfalls, families need direct coaching. Coaching on how to invite an ILO occurs during the pre-intervention meeting.

Here are some main principles:

1. *Face to face is best.* An intervention invitation or discussion is best when it is a face-to-face meeting between two individuals.
2. *Choose your family representative based on reception.* The accountability team member with the most meaning to the ILO should deliver the invitation to the intervention meeting. This should be the individual who will be best received by the ILO. Sometimes this person is an outlier.
3. *Language training is key.* I tell team members from the get-go, "It's OK to say, 'I've started to see someone. Our family has too many problems. We're going to find a solution, including all the problems you're having.'" In other words, families need to:
   - confidently state the facts;
   - take ownership of decisions; and
   - include the ILO in the solution.
4. *Role-play this conversation.* During the pre-intervention meeting, spend additional time with the person who will deliver the invitation. Spend extra time coaching on language and tone. Talk about objections and how to take care of them. Go through the conversation a few times and field questions.

## Step 9: The Intervention Meeting

Interventions are highly stylized conversations. So, only after careful coaching, planning, and wise deliberation is the intervention conducted. Emphasis is on speaking to the ILO in a respectful, loving, caring manner in which all participants come together for a common cause – helping the individual get treatment. In doing so, accountability team members strengthen their bond and respect for one another.

The role of the clinical interventionist varies with each intervention team. Most often, the accountability team is coached along as they address their loved one. When necessary, clinicians accompany the ILO to a quiet place to calm them down so that they are more able to listen to their friends and family. The attention is always on being in the moment – making sure they are respected, valued, and cared for.

Still, the main goal of an intervention is to get the ILO into treatment. To this end, an interventionist needs to be prepared. Earlier steps provide clinicians with opportunities to get to know the ILO from multiple perspectives. To direct conversations toward health, be sure to review Worksheet 4.7 (Common Objections to Addiction Treatment and Their Counter-Objections). This worksheet is a compilation of the most common resistance points and the responses that have worked for me in my own practice. Please feel free to add to this worksheet or connect with me to share what's worked for you!

From a safety standpoint, if an intervention has the potential to be volatile or become violent, threatening harm to the loved one or someone on the team, it is critical to have two professionals present. See Chapter 5 on therapeutic skills used with families during an intervention for more on how and why to work in a team with colleagues during an intervention. Worksheet 4.8 (Will You Need Executive Protection? Safety Checklist) is a safety checklist that can help you prepare as well.

This system also gives the loved one the opportunity to relate to more than one professionally unbiased person. It also allows someone to stay with the intervention team after your loved one is escorted to treatment to process the events of the intervention, providing closure and reassurance, and answering questions and concerns that come up.

After the ILO agrees to go into a treatment program, in most instances a team member accompanies them and gets them registered and settled in. In certain circumstances, transportation can be arranged when necessary.

### *Step 9 Assumptions*

### *Activity 9.1: The Intervention Meeting*

The intervention meeting is the event that attempts to move the ILO to change. We've talked about it. We've planned it. Now it is here. Your clinical skills will be challenged. This is the time when your own best practices come to light. Your professional being will be stretched to the limit.

During the intervention, the accountability team gathers. Each member is invited to share – in compassionate ways – why their hearts are hurting. They share what is special about the ILO. They share what they have experienced firsthand. In other words, team members communicate why their hearts are breaking and what their hope or invitation is: that the ILO will accept this offer of help.

In a perfect world, boundaries or bottom lines are not used. Instead, it is the power of the group, the transparency, honesty, vulnerability, and wholeheartedness of the group, that brings a person change. This is the time when family members find their voice of love. When accountability team members will not settle for anything less but safe passage to health and wellness, the opening can happen.

For a full checklist when planning the intervention meeting, see Worksheet 4.10 (Intervention Planning Checklist).

## Activity 9.2: Forward Clinical Notes to the Treatment Center

At this point, when the ILO is on the way to the admissions department of the treatment center, you can forward your clinical notes to the treatment center staff. This can be done in electronic form by email or in hard copy with your transport specialist. Passing on clinical notes is highly important, as you can help addiction treatment get a footing in a case before they begin their own assessments.

## Activity 9.3: Forward Family Letters to the Treatment Center

In some cases, you may have worked with families on special letters that reaffirm their position on treatment adherence during the pre-intervention meeting. Some family member may have brought a hard copy of a letter with them to the intervention meeting. Give family letters to the transport specialist to deliver to treatment center clinicians and to use as motivation during the treatment stay.

## Step 10: Intervention Progress Review and Feedback

Following the intervention and its outcome, clinicians offer time together with the accountability team to review this life-altering process. Together, the team reflects on the event. Immediately following the intervention, they are given the opportunity to process their feelings.

Second, clinicians can return to education. Many families want the clinician to put together "the solution." They need to believe that they can get through the episode and start to repair themselves. However, they see themselves as victims. You can take this opportunity to begin to teach about victim, martyr, and traitor.

Finally, the accountability team is challenged to take care of themselves, physically, emotionally, and in a way that is spiritually consistent with their values. We look at how each team member can take care of themselves – be it a support group, therapy, a fun activity, or simply having a good night's sleep because their loved one is in a safe place. Finally, the team is given instruction on the best ways to communicate with the ILO while in treatment.

## Step 10 Assumptions

Often family members obsess about the ILO. Their thoughts are cycled into patterns of anxiety, rumination, and hopelessness. Assigning people tasks is a helpful way to draw them out of their own heads. There is also a certain amount of comfort people feel in having a small task and collaborating for a larger goal. Be sure, however, to not overwhelm them.

In essence, the homework that you assign is getting families ready for systemic change. You're connecting them to feel 100% good about the treatment they've picked, and you're helping them shift focus from ILO to self. It is a gradual change, but one that accelerates once the ILO is in treatment.

## Activity 10.1: Client Homework

Client homework is assigned according to where family members are in the process of an intervention. Essentially, you give homework assignments dependent on who you're talking to and what stage of the process you're in. High-risk times include any transitional times: initial intervention phone calls, moving a client into treatment, family week, and ending treatment. During these times, your contact with clients should increase, as will any "assignments."

The main milestones for client homework include:

- first caller assignments;
- pre-intervention planning;
- treatment initiation;
- family week at the treatment center; and
- post-treatment aftercare transition.

During step 10, we also return to the education begun in step 6. It is helpful to have family members commit to self-help activity calendars and activities. We also assign homework related to gratitude. We work with behavioral change agreements. And, when possible, we deliver educational content about personal transformation. In sum, client homework is customized and adaptable.

See Worksheet 5.1 (Client Homework Assignments) for a complete list of suggested homework activities by stage of process.

## Step 11: Post-Intervention Follow-Up

In this step, the clinician also works closely with treatment centers. At this time, clinicians serve as the buffer between the treatment center and the family; we work to coordinate services and collaborate with the clinical team on aftercare or post-treatment recommendations. Main considerations include:

- ongoing counseling for the ILO;
- ongoing counseling for the family;
- options for outpatient treatment;
- sober housing arrangements; and
- mutual support group attendance.

We talk with treatment clinic staff about the family's progress as support for treatment, as well as the ILO's progress at the treatment center. The goal is to make treatment recommendations as necessary. We also work to be a collaborative ally.

Further, it is helpful to provide solution-focused coaching for accountability team members as they navigate new ways of caring for themselves. Together, the team talks once a week and receives advice on family programs from the treatment center, local self-help groups, and mental health groups. Weekly team meetings can consist of face-to-face meetings or video chat. The whole team may attend or any individual members of the team are invited to call in. Video chat software, online meeting, or telephone applications can facilitate communication. Services such as WebEx, Skype, or Viber are convenient and low-cost.

Regular weekly meeting takes the focus off the loved one in treatment and places focus on how accountability members may change their behaviors so that they experience appropriate detachment and develop constructive boundaries. Then periodic check-ins are scheduled to build on the team's success and to create a healthy, positive change for the family and the ILO that lasts.

Indeed, offering a full range of solution-focused coaching to the accountability team helps family members follow through with their own behavioral change. This can consist of offering concierge services in addition to weekly team meetings. Concierge services consist of quick response to individual concerns; team members may call you at any time and you respond within 24 hours. Finally, clinicians can also offer case management services as along as consent forms are in place.

### *Step 11 Assumptions*

Behavioral change takes 90 days or more. This change is as important to family members as it is to the ILO in addiction treatment.

Evidenced-based studies have shown that that it takes much longer than 30 days to institute change or for a new action to become a habit; the range is more like a few weeks to many months, with an average of 66 days.[7] The assumption is that families or accountability teams have previously identified their loved one as "troubled." Unconsciously, the family is coalesced around the loved one being the troubled one. Everyone must learn how to reframe this perception and see hope and possibility. This takes practice, trust-building, and reframing of thoughts through actions.

## Activity 11.1: Weekly Phone Calls

Weekly phone calls are a part of solution-focused recovery coaching that you can offer in the weeks and months that follow an intervention. We'll cover the exact nature and clinical features of solution-focused coaching in Chapter 5. What's important to know is that weekly phone calls help clinicians facilitate a pragmatic, here-and-now approach to solving problems. The immediate goal is to try to find solutions to current circumstances.

During weekly phone calls, it is best to keep a straightforward agenda. Anxiety tends to escalate around family weekends and with transitions, whether to transitional living or to going home. Knowing how to address these is important. A typical phone call looks like:

1. *Check in with callers.* This can be a series of open-ended questions ("How are you? How is your heart doing? Where are you today?") as you ask about general well-being.
2. *Clinical update.* You need to know what relationship (if any) the callers have with the treatment center and take the lead. If you have access to medical records via consent form, callers always want to know how the ILO is doing in treatment. Be brief and to the point. Statements such as, "They are still not allowed to use phones" or, "It appears they are participating in all of the program and making progress" are helpful.

   Callers might ask lots of questions such as, "Can we send something? What can we send?" Or they may lament they have not heard from the ILO, or that a consent form has been rescinded. There are so many variations on this theme that one must be prepared and knowledgeable. Expect clinical and operational questions and have answers at the ready.
3. *Start where the client is.* Ask if there are any burning desires or pressing issues they want to talk about. Remember, we need to start where our clients are.
4. *Review last week's assignments,* including, but not limited to, how are they taking care of themselves, how was their experience at a 12-step group, gratitude list, meditation or mindfulness practice, etc. See Worksheet 5.1 (Client Homework Assignments) for a full list of homework assignments.

5. *Then discuss a particular coaching issue.* You might pick a curriculum to discuss, such as boundaries, early recovery, or how to prepare for a person coming home. Depending on where the ILO is in the treatment process, help the family prepare for family week for phone calls. Keep the discussion limited to a set time frame.
6. *Summarize the call and plan for next steps.*

## Activity 11.2: Periodic Check-Ins

Periodic check-ins can also be offered in the months following treatment initiation or completion. The number of times that you call varies depending on the nature of your original contract or arrangement with the family. Still, you may choose to do a periodic check-in to see how someone is doing or to check on accountability team member progress. You might even ask the family if they might talk with another family, especially in success cases.

During these informal calls, you are generally interested in how everyone is doing and want to know about the state of the situation. You also want to affirm them for the courageous action they have taken. Finally, you show your respect and gratitude during these phone calls. While less intense than the initial solution-focused coaching, you remain open to helping, answering questions, or clarifying issues.

## References

1. Belin P, Boehme B, and McAleer P (2017) The Sound of Trustworthiness: Acoustic-Based Modulation of Perceived Voice Personality. *PLoS ONE.* 12(10): e0185651.
2. Willis J and Todorov A (2006) First Impressions: Making Up Your Mind after a 100-ms Exposure to a Face. *Association for Psychological Science.* 17(7): 592–598.
3. Weiss R (1994) *Learning from Strangers: The Art and Method of Qualitative Interview Studies.* New York: Free Press.
4. Charmaz K (2014) *Constructing Grounded Theory* (2nd edition). London: Sage.
5. Clandinin DJ and Connelly FM (2000) *Narrative Inquiry: Experience and Story in Qualitative Research.* San Francisco, CA: Jossey-Bass.
6. Lieblich A, Tuval-Mashiach R, and Zilber T (1998) *Narrative Research: Reading, Analysis, and Interpretation (Applied Social Research Methods).* Thousand Oaks, CA: Sage.
7. Lally P, van Jaarsveld CHM, Potts HWW, and Wardle J (2009) How Are Habits Formed? Modelling Habit Formation in the Real World. *European Journal of Social Psychology.* 40(6): 998–1009.

# 5

# THERAPEUTIC STRATEGIES USED IN INTERVENTIONS

## Evidenced-Based Strategies for Interventions

Helping clients and their families begin the process of behavioral change can be exceptionally challenging. In this chapter, we'll take a look at the evidence-based practices used in clinical settings that can be applied directly to addiction interventions. Indeed, some of the skills we review here are essential to successful outcomes. Our aim? To bridge the gap between the theory and practice of successful intervention.

First, we'll look at the main theoretical concepts of what it means to help someone "change." Then we'll see how each specific evidence-based strategy can be applied to communication and relationship-building. We'll break down these strategies as they apply to families first, and then to the ILO. In fact, much of our work centers around the family. We only get real face-to-face time with the ILO during the intervention meeting itself.

So, first we address the accountability team. We get to know them and the ILO through their eyes. Then we apply our clinical skills to the ILO during the intervention meeting. So, while the techniques differ according to who we're talking to, our main concern remains the same in both cases:

*How do we move a person to a place of "yes"?*

Finally, you can expect to understand more about the benefits of adapting these strategies to your own clinical practice and the foundational principles for doing so. The main strategies we will cover include:

- 12-step facilitation;
- boundary-setting;
- cognitive behavioral therapy (CBT);
- motivational interviewing (MI);
- solution-focused coaching; and
- values clarification.

## Stages of Change during an Intervention

Washing faces, brushing teeth, making beds, taking showers. These are all common, daily habits. But if you stop to think about it, these habits didn't appear out of thin air. We learned them, just as clients and their families have learned to live in complex systems of dysregulation and dysfunction.

Because alcohol and other drug use and codependent relationships are a combination of physical, emotional, and social patterns, these behaviors become repetitive, entrenched, and bring a certain amount of comfort in the discomfort. In fact, I would bet that each of us encounter resistance to change every day of our professional lives.

So, how can we, as clinicians, help clients move to a place of change, especially knowing that change is incredibly difficult? How do we begin to cope with denial, resistance, and lack of motivation?

> *The first thing we must do before helping clients "change" is to understand where clients are coming from, to frame clients within a continuum of change. Only then can we intervene effectively.*

To begin, what do we mean by "change"?

Simply put, change is to make or become something different. In my experience, change is a process that gradually unfolds over time. Change is not an event that suddenly occurs. As this process begins to unfold, a person's motivation changes. Mapping exactly where a client and their family is along the cycle of change is the first step to identifying places where intervention can be most effective. For this, the stages of change model is extremely helpful.

Developed by James Prochaska, PhD, and Carlo DiClemente, PhD, the stages of change model was first adapted to help people quit smoking.[1] The model theorizes that there are certain stages of change a person goes through when they want something to be different; individuals change behaviors gradually in a cyclical series of phases. Each stage defines a person's readiness and motivation for change. See Figure 5.1 for a diagram of the typical cycle in a client's readiness for change.

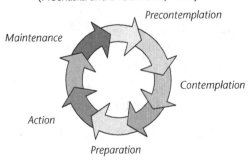

**Stages of Change Readiness**
(Prochaska and DiClemente, 1992)

FIGURE 5.1 Prochaska and DiClemente's stages of change model

## The Stages of Change Model

Prochaska and DiClemente determined that intentional change is key to changing habitual behaviors; in other words, individuals must want to change their behavior and be ready to do so. In the addiction field, this means that drug or alcohol users need to *want to stop using* before they can get to a place of "yes." In the case of addiction intervention, we hope to move clients from using substances to abstinence or reduced harm actions.

So, what are the stages of change and the clinical task associated with each?

1. *Precontemplation.* In this stage, the ILO (and possibly some family members) do not see the need for a lifestyle change. Indeed, the client believes there is no problem present. They may feel forced into treatment. Estimates put 80% of people either in the precontemplative or contemplative stage of change.[2]

    When someone is precontemplative, they may say, "Dad is just that way," or, "But he just graduated college with honors," or, "There is no problem, she gets her work done." Furthermore, they may point to someone else's symptoms: "I don't have a drink problem; do you see how much Molly smokes weed?" In other words, there is a huge discrepancy between the truth of the problem that someone is experiencing and the reality.

    *Clinical Task:* To raise doubt. To increase the person's perception of risks and problems with current behavior by using actual examples of things that have happened in a person's life.

2. *Contemplation.* In this stage, the ILO is considering making a change and has not decided yet. They are not fully convinced that treatment is the right change needed, or that they have the ability to change. This stage is summarized by the statement, "Maybe I will."

    *Clinical Task:* Work with the ambivalence that is present with both family and client. Tip the balance. Strengthen self-efficacy.

3. *Preparation.* In the preparation stage, the family has chosen to move forward with an intervention and is preparing for a meeting with a love one. In this stage, obstacles and boundaries are illuminated.

    There are beginning signs that the ILO is willing to go to treatment; they may have decided to change and/or are considering how to make changes. Motivation fluctuates, as does ambivalence. In this stage, the loved one may try negotiation and say things such as, "I will go to treatment *but* I can't go until I finish this work project," or, "I need to be assured that I can do important business work there." Others say, "I can't go to treatment, as I have children/a dog/a pet to take care of."

    *Clinical Task:* Motivational interviewing can help elicit change. Therefore, you are exploring ambivalence and rolling with the resistance the client presents. Plus, you can explore objections and their counters. See Worksheet 4.7 (Common Objections to Addiction Treatment and Their Counter-Objections). Oftentimes, the objections have already been removed. Other times, you may need to us use a decision-making tree to define: (a) what's the best thing about treatment; and (b) what's the worst thing about treatment to remove the objections. Also, if one has questions about the treatment center, you might have a representative of the center present for the actual intervention, so the client can begin alignment and questions can be answered.

4. *Action.* The ILO is actively doing something to change. They may experience setbacks.

    *Clinical Task:* Encourage action, set examples, and give homework.

5. *Maintenance.* In the maintenance stage, the person is maintaining activity over time. Change has existed over six months or more. Some temptation to return to former behavior or small lapses are still present, especially regarding triggers to use. Relapse is common.

    *Clinical Task:* Help the person renew the process of contemplation, determination, and action without getting stuck in Shameville!

In sum, it is the clinician's role to encourage our clients to take care of themselves physically, emotionally, and spiritually in ways that are consistent with their values so they form new habits and break old ones.

Forming new habits is neither instantaneous nor easy. Truth be told, it takes 90 days of hard concentrated practice to institute a new behavior or habit. New habits are added through learned behavior and can be taken away. This is how change is possible.

Still, we need to face our traditional assumptions of motivation and change before we even begin to engage with clients. Take a look at the following assumptions. Where and how do your beliefs affect your practice?

- Symptoms are weaknesses that need to be fixed.
- The client is damaged, and the counselor fixes the client.
- Doctor knows best.
- Only the client has control over motivation.
- A client must hit "rock bottom."
- Change is linear and static, much like an "on/off" switch.
- No motivation = no treatment.

## Starting with Yourself: A Precaution

I am a fierce advocate for systemic change on the micro (individual), mezzo (family), and macro (community) levels. In order to bring change to a system, we need to be able to listen, observe, and record. We need to give people the equivalent of "no-fault" insurance. In other words, when we work with addiction, we leave our personal judgments at the curb.

When we talk about substance abuse, we often say, "I have never met anyone who said they want to become an alcoholic or addict when they grow up." If you agree with this statement, you can begin to view addiction as a condition that pops up more like a survival instinct to numb painful memories than a need to get high.

The places clients have been, the things they have witnessed, the abuse – physical or emotional – among other experiences, shape who they are and may awaken an addiction as a means of coping. Addiction becomes a friend, a good intention that goes bad. As behavioral health clinicians, our first question must not be, "What is wrong with this person?"

*Instead, we must ask: "What happened to this person?"*

Second, we turn ourselves and aim the questions internally. We ask ourselves, as clinicians:

- Am I generous in my interpretation of self and others?
- Am I nonjudgmental?
- Am I reliable?
- Do I do what I say I will do?
- Do I hold myself accountable to the ethics and professional standards of my industry?
- Do I seek collaboration when necessary?
- Do I keep confidentiality?

Only when we can clear our heads from assumptions and preference can we begin to work with families or ILOs in a way that does them justice.

See Worksheet 2.1 (Self-Assessment of Your Clinical Style) to record your thoughts, beliefs, and assumptions about clinical work with addictions. We invite you to explore your own personal principles of practice in depth as you grow as a clinician.

## Working in a Team

As for myself, I do not conduct interventions alone. I always work with a teammate and often partner with board-certified addiction medicine psychiatrists, psychologists, private detectives, and security as needed. Why team up during an intervention? Teaming provides a more robust service and gives families and ILOs a more comprehensive perspective to treatment options, motivations, and outcomes.

As professionals, we are often expected to have all the answers. But this is simply not possible. What I have learned is that partnering provides clients and families with more options to the myriad challenges that are presented during an intervention.

There are several reasons for teaming, which include:

1. *Broader scope.* Combining skill sets leads to a synergistic response. Working with another clinician or physician during an intervention gives you the ability to encompass areas of expertise that you are not familiar with. It allows you to combine skill sets. This broader scope allows for the intervention team to have a larger "toolbox" to better assist their clients. For example, working with an interventionist who is also an experienced attorney opens access to the courts, probation, and other strategic partners.

   Conversely, partnering with an experienced clinician provides input and diagnostic perspective. Many interventionists may have strong recovery backgrounds but no clinical training or family expertise. Finding a teammate adds a necessary clinical and familial system dimension. Bringing in an additional expert such as a board-certified psychologist with psychiatric hospital-admitting privileges, a trained nurse, or a trained retired police officer for security and safety may be essential! In other words, bringing in those resources that you do not have can benefit the family. Together, we have comprehensive access and strength, more than either of us can offer alone.

2. *Building rapport.* When working with groups, having two co-facilitators works well because it gives clinicians an opportunity to relate to different clients. Viewing it in this light, we all have people we relate to better than others. There is no order of importance in matters of the heart or a way to predict who will reach that resistant loved one or help a struggling family member find their voice. Collaboration produces many more moments of possibility and breakthrough when talents are blended. Miller and Rollnick,

the founders of motivational interviewing, further demonstrated, when they combined the talents of a soft-spoken professional with a pragmatic active professional, that a movement toward health and wellness takes place, outlined in their book *Helping People Change.*[3]

3. *Multiple data points.* A clinical perspective alone, however informed, is often not going to be sufficient to obtain the best and most useful information. The landscape of an intervention is ever-shifting and elusive in the chaos of a family system in crisis. For as we know, only through the triangulation of data sources can we obtain truly precise, honest, and transparent results.

4. *Post-intervention processing.* Too often interventionists overlook the physical logistics and limitations working as a single interventionist. In these cases, the family may be left behind while the loved one is transported to treatment. From a clinical standpoint, the post-intervention time with the accountability team is just as important as the intervention meeting itself. This is a missed opportunity to process and work on systemic family change. So, the collective interventionist plans for a period of debriefing to conclude the intervention successfully and satisfactorily.

When you work in a pair, one person can stay back with the accountability team to "process" what just occurred. This may be the only opportunity left to speak to the intervention team as a group and in person. In my experience, 95% of the time I will stay back and process with family and friends, who are often in amazement their loved one has chosen to go to treatment. This is a perfect time to teach accountability team members what is expected of them while their loved one is in rehab. It's also a great time for them to talk about the emotions of what just happened and what will happen next. Shifting the focus from the ILO to personal self-help is critical. Staying behind allows for this process to begin.

5. *Safety and security.* Ensuring that at least two seasoned professionals are present during a collective intervention gives clinicians an advantage in terms of safety. I have experienced several situations in which two people were necessary to calm a situation. For example, when an ILO indicated he was going to kill himself, as a mandated reporter I needed to work with the police department and emergency response unit until help arrived 15 minutes later. My teammate was able to contain the loved one (a large 6-foot gentleman), who eventually fell down in a closet while I spoke with family until the police arrived. Another time, when a mother clearly was neglecting her children due to her substance abuse disorder, and was "non-intentionally emotionally unavailable," my partner calmed the group while I called child protection services.

Further, providing safe passage to treatment is an integral part of the intervention process. The person who transports needs to be as skilled as the person or persons performing the intervention. On the other hand, my teammate is developing a rapport with the loved one and is rolling with whatever resistance may appear. Anyone who has taken an ILO on an airplane knows that there must be expert care and nourishing of a loved one as they leave. Oftentimes they are frightened and resistant to care. Making sure the admissions process is handled smoothly, and that the treatment center is there to welcome their new patient and have them gain entrance smoothly into a new place and new surrounding, is important work requiring motivational skills.

6. *Division of attention.* I can think of quite a few interventions that involved sidebar discussions and some degree of caucusing. So much of what we do involves shuttle diplomacy; the process should not grind to a halt when family members or ILOs need to have private conversations. Some of my proudest breakthrough moments have come when I have been alone with the ILO, outside the intervention meeting, on the patio where something intimate gets shared or a phone call gets made that changes everything.

In these cases of divided attention, the family is not held in suspense. They are directed to other work and stay engaged with the business of moving forward. It is erroneous to think you can be all things to all people. With the demand for divided attention, it's imperative to have a partner who is present and aware during a collective intervention.

## What Types of Families Will You Encounter?

There is hardly a family that has not been affected by addiction. As mentioned in the eResource accompaniment to Chapter 1, the statistics on the matter of opioids, alcohol, and marijuana are alarming. Not to put too fine a point on it, but as estimated by the advocacy group Facing Addiction, one in three American families are affected by addiction.[4] These families are consciously and unconsciously motivated to keep the status quo of the organizing structure of their dysfunction.

Before we can address the usual ways of relating, categorizing, and thinking, we have to unpack the history of the families. The secrets. The lies. The shame.

I usually come across certain types of families in performing addiction interventions. The common thread among them is that they have become hurting experts. While they are currently motivated and seeking solutions, the family of origin has been wounded. Further, family leaders or dominant influencers have been unsuccessful in finding proper solutions. So, they may not see their part in the problem. In sum, most families want you to "fix" their loved one.

Here's a description of how some families or their member(s) tend to operate:

- *The agreeable family.* Does everything you ask.
- *The complainer.* Nothing is ever good enough.
- *The helicopter.* Hovers and is overly involved in a child's life.

- *The invisible family.* Always in the background.
- *The know-it-all.* Knows everything about everything.
- *The micromanager.* Everything has to be their way.
- *The questioner.* Calls and emails all the time.
- *The Saran Wrap.* Smothers the loved one and often tries to smother you, the clinician.
- *The steamroller.* Rolls right over you and others.
- *The submarine.* Comes up and attacks from down under.
- *The talker.* Talks and talks and talks.
- *The worrier.* Worries to the point of inertia.

## Therapeutic Strategies Used with Families

You can't be everything to all people. Instead, you move and motivate members of a group toward health and wellness. You're selling a solution, albeit health and wellness. However, you're principally going into a family system in a coaching fashion. Note here that this is a wounded system.

As you talk with families and accountability teams, you hopefully have people in the action stage of change readiness. In fact, the action stage is a short window in which people are not in denial. So, in order to make the most of this stage working with families, you focus on two skills: you need to be good at communicating and relationship-building.

1. *Communication.* To get to the root of the addiction problem, you talk with family members individually. You find out who they are and what their problems are. You are privy to insider information. Ask them what's important. You'll learn ahead of time – before the actual intervention – what obstacles exist and what the objections are, so skills are necessary for interviewing.

   Teaching is also very important. You'll need to communicate what an intervention is. You'll need to provide information about what addiction is. You'll ask them to practice what to say. You'll teach them to talk with a hand over their heart. But more than this, you'll be modeling the boundaries that you teach. Family members obviously have their own issues. So, you also need to identify to what extent their issues will impede or not impede the process.

   The bottom line is this: You're not there to treat the family. You're there to get an ILO into treatment. You offer a highly solution-focused way of being. "No" is just a conversation starter. You're there to show families: Yes, this person will go to treatment. Yes, hope is possible. Yes, you can all live a better, more satisfying life!

2. *Relationship-building.* An intervention is not a free-floating discussion. You are directly and purposefully bringing people together for the common good, to make change, to help someone get help. But family systems are

broken and wounded. So, your role as clinician is to help families start to build trust again. You set the ground rules for how everyone is going to talk. You affirm everyone. You use positive, strength-based skills.

Again, the focus or locus of change is the person who is identified as the person who needs help. As clinicians, we will be acutely aware of other family members' issues, problems in living, or mental health, but we hold off. If a member is an impediment to the process, however, we invite them not to participate. If a person can be a part of the solution, they are invited back into the process.

In talking with families, you'll be having critical conversations. These will be life-saving conversations. So, to be best prepared for communication, here are some guiding principles to keep in mind:

1. The client is always right.
2. Agree with the client's goal – it's about choice.
3. Use the client's language.
4. Develop compliments to support change. Compliments can be direct and use a positive verb, attribute, or reaction to the client. Or compliments can be indirect, something that implies a positive.
5. Provide a bridging statement and rationale for suggestions.
6. Assign tasks based on relationships. These tasks should also be weighed based on readiness to change. Focus on attainable goals and design tasks in small steps. Proceed slowly.
7. Seek solutions.

The skills and strategies outlined below are not cookie-cutter solutions to the complex systemic problems of addiction. Instead, the following strategies are guidelines for talking and engaging with families. They will help you truly understand your clients better so that you can get their ILO into appropriate treatment. You're going to use these strategies when you need them, as you go.

## 12-Step Facilitation

People get really nervous about attending a 12-step group. They see the need for a support group as outside of themselves. They don't see that they have a problem – that's their ILO. Plus, the 12-step world has developed a culture and language of its own. So, if you just tell them, "Go to Al-Anon. You'll learn more about addiction there," they're confused. And if you as a clinician have never attended a 12-step group, it is very, very hard to make a good referral; you know not what you speak about.

In reality, clinicians need to bridge people to self-support groups in a thoughtful way. We first teach them what a 12-step group is and define the language that is used in the culture. We also affirm whatever 12-step work they've done so far. Then we anticipate and provide answers to common questions, such as:

- What is a 12-step program?
- How does it work?
- Do I have to talk?
- Are all meetings the same?
- How do I find a meeting?
- What do sponsors do?
- How do I pick a sponsor?
- Are there any alternatives to 12-step programs?

As you bridge family members into 12-step groups, you initially ask them to attend six different groups and report back to you. If they do not like any of the initial groups, you ask that they try another six groups or meetings. Note here that support group attendance exists outside the 12-step model. Popular and successful models include:

- Secular Organizations for Sobriety;
- SMART Recovery;
- Women for Sobriety;
- Jewish Alcoholics, Chemically Dependent Persons, and Significant Others; and
- Celebrate Recovery.

Furthermore, community-based spiritual fellowships can help people clarify their values and change their lives. What's important is that you offer options, explain the protocol, and remain available to family questions about attendance.

Here are some common definitions of types of meetings that can be helpful when talking about 12-step groups:

- *Closed meetings.* These group meetings are for members only, or for those who identify as a member of a specific group and have a desire to live differently. Participation is voluntary but encouraged.
- *Open meetings.* These are available to anyone interested in the program of recovery, although attendance is conditional to remaining an observer, and not a participant.
- *12-step or 12-tradition meetings.* These feature discussions on one of the 12 steps or 12 traditions, sometimes using a reference book.
- *Book study meetings.* These focus on reading a chapter from the main text of the 12-step group (for AA, this is the *Big Book*; for NA, the *Basic Text*). After reading, participants discuss personal experience or a topic related to the reading.

- *Speaker meetings.* These feature a person telling a story of past or present experience, strength, and hope.
- *Topic meetings.* These feature a discussion on a specific topic such as fellowship, honesty, acceptance, or patience. Everyone is given a chance to talk, but no one is forced.

Other questions you might ask include:

- Have you ever been to a 12-step meeting? If so, what was your experience?
- Do you plan to attend any 12-step meetings? Where? When?
- How might you make best use of 12-step meetings?
- Are there alternatives to 12-step meetings that you might consider attending?

## Boundary-Setting

The practice of boundary-setting is critical during an addiction intervention. Many families need to learn to set boundaries – and keep them firm. In truth, many families experience "family fusion," a condition that manifests as:

- blurred lines;
- blaming;
- denying;
- faulty reasoning;
- finishing others' sentences;
- lack of personal space;
- taking over, especially with controlling member(s); and
- rescuing.

What is a boundary? In relationships, boundaries define our interaction with others; a good boundary will define where you begin and where you end. In fact, boundaries help define all our interactions with others. Boundaries are made up of the following considerations:

- *Physical boundaries.* Closeness, touching, clothes, shelter, physical differences, sexuality, privacy (mail, bathroom, telephone), as well as the time and energy you spend on others or by yourself.
- *Emotional boundaries.* Personal beliefs, thoughts, and actions about your emotional life, including secrets, rules, and related consequences.
- *Spiritual boundaries.* These define the personal experience with the higher self. Sometimes people do not like the concept of spirituality, so one talks about being consistent with values.

Boundaries are about limits; we ask ourselves, "How far can we go comfortably in a relationship?"

> *This research has taught me that if we really want to start practicing compassion, we have to start by setting boundaries and holding people accountable for their behavior.*[5]

Judeo-Christian beliefs stress the importance of living life as your true self, connected to God and to all living things. In these terms, our cultural message is clear: you do not have to stay with people who mistreat you. Often addiction spurs on the opposite. In fact, in family systems where addiction is present, relationships and interactions with others tend toward codependency.

Codependent relationships are identified by excessive emotional or psychological reliance on a partner, typically one with an illness or addiction who requires support. However, codependence does not manifest in family systems alone. Codependence can be present in relationships with:

- friends;
- work colleagues;
- romantic partners; and
- family.

Worksheet 5.3 (Self-Assessment for Codependency) and Worksheet 5.4 (Ways to Address Codependency) can help family members identify and start to work on issues that are rooted in codependence.

Families I work with are absolutely powerless. Oftentimes weary from worry and overly focused on other matters, I have met many a parent or spouse, brother or sister who has lost their way in their worry about their loved one. They have forgotten their hopes and dreams and locked them in a trunk, waiting until their loved one improves.

> *Families need a combination of compassionate discipline when dealing with the ILO and letting go of the role as hostages and hostage-takers.*

While in treatment, it is imperative for the ILO to learn new ways of being. It is equally important for loved ones to get help. Sometimes loved ones are sicker than the ILO. There is a saying: "Nothing changes till someone changes." Waiting just for the IP to change may be pure folly if those around them do not change!

Systemic, long-term change is the goal when setting new boundaries. But most families consider change to be a one-way street. Many think that change is restricted to the ILO. In truth, many families tend to look a bit miffed and ask, "How can we form new habits?"

Families first define:

- What is OK?
- What is not OK?
- What was OK before treatment?
- What was not OK before treatment?

In truth, boundary-setting is highly personal. They look directly at issues that feel confusing and declare for themselves, "Some of my boundaries today are . . ." See Worksheet 5.2 (Boundary-Setting Questions for Families).

## Examples of Healthy Boundaries

Appropriate boundaries vary from culture to culture. However, in the context of addiction intervention, boundaries can be solution-focused and tied to treatment acceptance or adherence. If an ILO is resistant to seeking help for addiction, a family member can:

- ask them to move out of the house;
- stop paying for the phone; and
- stop giving them a credit card.

Simply put, people define boundaries when they describe what they can or cannot support. When one of my clients wakes up in the morning and looks themselves in the mirror, I want them to know what they are willing to say "yes" or "no" to. Families need to commit to what will they do to support health and wellness. While this is often seen as contradictory to love, it is the beginning of change.

See Worksheet 5.5 (Sample Behavioral Change Agreement (General)), Worksheet 5.6 (Sample Behavioral Change Agreement (Mental Health)), and Worksheet 5.7 (Sample Behavioral Change Agreement (Medical Chronic Pain)) for examples of behavioral change agreements that can come from setting boundaries. Worksheet 5.8 (Personal Change Worksheet) can also be useful; it is a personal change worksheet to be used in cases of self-evaluation and behavioral modification, whether clinical or personal. Finally, in this context, Worksheet 5.11 (Finding Joy Worksheet) can be helpful as an exercise in evoking change. These worksheets can be used for both families and the ILO.

## Setting Boundaries between Families and Treatment Providers

When loved ones are in treatment, families are often anxious. They may want instant results, 24/7 communication with treatment providers, and get angry when they do not get instantaneous results. Some families prefer that their loved one has a mental health or physical illness rather than a substance abuse or process disorder. Believe me, they get mighty angry if professionals disagree. Sometimes, in an attempt to control information, a loved one might take a clinical professional off the consent form as a way to exert control over them.

> *When family members remove clinicians from a medical consent form, a healthy boundary is required. Letting families know that it this not acceptable behavior and explaining how it hampers the treatment team's ability to help is necessary.*

Getting mad at the treatment provider is not the answer. Rather, setting and holding firm boundaries is the answer. Families need to allow the ILO to gain experience making their own bed; they need to stop ordering others around. The frustration families feel may not be rational. It's not that the treatment provider has failed, but rather how long will it take for the ILO to join up their own dots and seek health and wellness for themselves?

Sometimes doing nothing is the answer. The family has to trust that they have entrusted their loved one into safe and capable hands, as they themselves know they have not been successful for years. In truth, treatment centers you refer to should have such excellent reputations and do such great work that they do not need the client unless it really is the right mutually aligned match. So, encourage families to let it go. Stand back, pause, and let the center do the work!

## Signs of Healthy Boundaries

Families experience recovery in stages. We can characterize these stages as early, middle, and advanced recovery. The basic idea is that members move from patterns of codependence to interdependence. During this process, families practice self-care and begin to find new identities as they move closer to their authentic selves.

It is important to note that the parallel process of addiction treatment and family growth is imperative to the overall health of the entire family system. Families need to grow alongside their loved ones. Why? The truth is that all parents fail their children. All partners fail one another. The task lies in growing to find unique ways of loving and to live from a connected but separate "self."

In the process of rebuilding family, members necessarily need to grieve. Grieving helps clients identify past and present losses, especially the consequences of neglecting one's own needs. Then family members start to realize the validity of their own needs and begin to get those needs met.

In truth, getting personal needs met is at the foundation of the parallel process of recovery for families affected by addiction. Tendencies to be over-responsible are replaced by becoming responsible for the self. Clear boundaries and setting limits result in increased self-esteem and improved self-efficacy. With boundaries comes a sense of control. Family members learn to identify what is "theirs" and let go of what is not. All-or-none thinking is replaced as families learn that there are choices: a multicolored worldview can be better than a "black-and-white" perspective. And when families set boundaries, they start being real, becoming authentic.

Clinicians can jump-start the process by developing a three-week calendar for families. This allows them to put in the things they will do each week to take care of themselves, emotionally, physically, and consistent with their values. This can range from doing a morning grateful list and meditation to taking a walk in the park, dipping into a bubble bath, or going out. The idea is to integrate wellness activities into one's daily living. Accountability teams are required to do nine activities each week to take care of themselves.

Then we provide feedback. When folks are asked to show up and do new things – even when they do not want to – the results are astonishing. Instead of wallowing, families begin to celebrate new skills, to practice new habits.

## Cognitive Behavioral Therapy

Cognitive behavioral therapy (CBT) is perhaps the most popular of the "talking therapies" in the world of psychotherapy. The goal of CBT is to help people manage their problems by changing the way they think and behave to become more positive. Used in addiction interventions, CBT creates a therapeutic alliance with families. We work together to discover goals and values, then we join up and come alongside clients to help them implement and track their change.

The main tenets of this type of psychotherapy applied to addiction interventions are that CBT:[6]

- assumes the client is motivated;
- seeks to modify maladaptive cognitions;
- provides specific coping strategies via treatment;
- teaches through instruction, modeling practice, and feedback; and
- teaches specific problem-solving strategies.

When thinking about applying CBT to interventions, think homework assignments. We give families assignments so that family members can participate in the solution. However, we are also addressing cognitive formulation.

The context of the task changes by individual. We might ask someone to list self-care activities and commit to one or two per week, for example. Another person may be asked to explore their heart and report back on what is special about the ILO. Still another person may be challenged to set new, inner boundaries for themselves. Other times, showing a journal or daily gratitude list is called for. In most cases, I invite (with their permission) accountability teams to start each day writing down three to five things they are grateful for. Then

I propose that they engage in a morning reflection or meditation. Tools that I provide for them include Worksheet 4.9 (Easy Meditation Practice), as well as referrals to apps and online content.

The main idea is that CBT applied to interventions should change thinking patterns. Thinking patterns keep families stuck. So, we aim to address automatic thoughts to adapt newer, healthier ways of thinking. See Worksheet 5.1 (Client Homework Assignments) for an entire curriculum of homework assignments related to the Collective Intervention Strategy.

## Motivational Interviewing to Elicit Change Talk

"Change talk" is a type of cue that clients give about their own readiness and motivation for change. As clinicians, we need to first attune our ears to change talk, and then to recognize and affirm it when we hear it.

In motivational interviewing, the main principles of change talk are captured in the acronym DARN, which reminds us to assess a person's desire, ability, reasons, and need for change.

> When you evoke a person's own desire, ability, reasons, and need for change, you are fueling the human engines of change.

People first talk about what they want to do (desire), why they would change (reasons), how they could do it (ability), and how important it is (need). As DARN motivations are voiced, commitment gradually strengthens. The person may take initial steps toward change.

Desire statements:

- I'd like to take care of myself if I could.
- I wish I could make my make my life better.
- I want to . . .
- Getting in shape would make me feel . . .

Ability statements:

- I think I can do that.
- That might be possible.
- I'm thinking I might be able to . . .
- If I had someone to help me, I probably could . . .

Need statements:

- It's really important to my health to change my diet.
- Something has to change or my marriage will break up.
- I will die if I keep going on like this.

Reason statements:

- I have to quit acting like this because it is not healthy.
- To keep my grandkids around, I need to quit drinking.
- My kids may be taken from me if I keep reacting like this.
- I don't like my kids to see me this way.

*Note:* When people talk about change themselves, they are more likely to change than if someone else (such as the clinician, a friend, or family member) talks about it. In this way, change talk is self-advocacy.

Eliciting change talk can be extremely powerful. The idea is that clinicians ask guiding, leading questions to bring ideas to the surface of the conscience mind. When families state the solution themselves, it is more powerful than when the listener does so. So, learning to recognize change talk when you hear it, and then reinforcing it, is key to Motivational Interviewing during a collective intervention.

## DARN Worksheet and Questions to Elicit Change Talk

The main way to elicit "change talk" is to be aware of a person's motivation for change. You can also have clients complete a DARN worksheet. See Worksheet 5.9 (Change Talk, DARN Principles, Motivational Interviewing, and Solution-Focused Therapy Strategies for Evoking Change). Questions we ask include:

- What do you think you will do?
- What does this mean about your habit?
- What are your options?
- What's the next step for you?
- What are some good things about making a change?
- Where does this leave you?

## Examples of Change Talk

- I accept . . .
- I agree to . . .
- I aim . . .
- I am devoted . . .
- I am predisposed . . .
- I am ready to . . .
- I anticipate . . .
- I aspire . . .
- I assume . . .
- I believe . . .

- I bet . . .
- I concede to . . .
- I consent to . . .
- I declare my intention to . . .
- I dedicate myself . . .
- I endorse . . .
- I envisage . . .
- I expect to . . .
- I favor . . .
- I foresee . . .
- I give my word . . .
- I guarantee . . .
- I guess . . .
- I hope so . . .
- I imagine . . .
- I intend to . . .
- I know . . .
- I look forward to . . .
- I mean to . . .
- I plan to . . .
- I pledge to . . .
- I predict . . .
- I presume . . .
- I promise . . .
- I propose . . .
- I resolve to . . .
- I shall . . .
- I suppose . . .
- I think I will . . .
- I volunteer . . .
- I vow . . .
- I will . . .
- I will try . . .

## Ten Strategies for Evoking Change

1. Ask evocative questions.

   - Why would you want to make this change? (desire)
   - How might you go about that? (ability)
   - What are the three best reasons for doing that? (reasons)
   - How important is it for you to make this change? (need)
   - So, what do you think you will do? (commitment)

2. Ask for elaboration.

   • When change talk emerges, ask for more detail. In what ways?
   • Tell me what you did. When was the last time that happened?
   • Was there ever a time that things were good? What was that like for you?

3. Ask for examples.

   • When was the last time that happened? Give me an example.

4. Look back.

   • Ask about a time before current concern emerged.
   • How were things better?
   • How were things different?

5. Look forward.

   • What would happen if things stay the same?
   • If you are 100% successful in making changes you want, what would life look like?

6. Extremes.

   • What is the worst thing that could happen?
   • What is the best thing that could happen?

7. Use change rulers.

   • On a scale of 1 to 10, how motivated are you?
   • On a scale of 1 to 10, how confident are you?
   • You picked the number X. Why wasn't this a lower/higher score?

8. Explore goals and values.

   • What are the person's values and goals?

9. Join up; come alongside.
10. Respond to change talk by exploring, affirming, and summarizing.

## Nonjudgmental Speaking

When we talk, we are often inadvertently judgmental. Teaching families how to speak in "I" terms coupled with feelings is most important. This can be effectively taught by providing families with a robust feeling chart and with some interactive teaching. Examples include:

- I felt scared, baffled, and confused yesterday when I came home and found our young son playing by himself while you had passed out on the couch.
- Last week, when school called and said they found you wandering around the campus, I felt bewildered, worried, and concerned. Together, we can find a solution.
- Yesterday, when you screamed at me and told me to leave as you continued to rage and throw things, I felt angry, disgruntled, worried, and scared. There has to be a better solution, and we will find one.
- Yesterday, when I found pills and other drug paraphernalia tucked away in your backpack and spoons and silver paper wrapped tightly in your room, I felt upset, worried, and concerned. This problem has gotten bigger than the both of us. Together, we will find a solution.

Substituting the word "I" for "it" is powerful. Often someone will say "It hurts so much." They are actually saying, "I hurt so much." Changing "it" to "I" allows family members to take responsibility for what they say and to examine their own behaviors. In short, using "I" terms coupled with feelings allows one to express how they feel in a nonjudgmental way.

Also, teach your clients to watch their "buts." Using "but" in a sentence negates the first half of the sentence: "I love you, but . . ." Instead, teach clients to replace "but" with "and." For example, "I love you, and I am no longer going to engage in unhealthy behaviors. We will find a solution."

## Solution-Focused Coaching

Peter Berg and Insoo Young, two social workers, developed the term "solution-focused therapy." The principles of the strategy are outlined in their 1999 book *Solutions Step by Step*.[7]

*Solution-focused coaching can be summarized in one statement: "Focus on the yes!"*

This is really where the art of working with an accountability team comes into play. Teams are often scared; after all, they have to ask their loved one to change. They've yelled at them, they've screamed at them, they've nagged at them, they've pleaded, they've given, they've taken away, they've argued, they've jumped up and down, but they haven't followed through. (I call this building a fence, where theirs has been a rubber fence bending in all different directions.)

In my practice, coaching services are usually offered as weekly scheduled phone calls or meetings. Some coaches offer services 24/7. This allows clients to reach out in a moment's notice. Regular, scheduled meetings, however, are the basis of coaching, and allow clinicians to work in a pragmatic, solution-focused way, building on each team member's strength and their ability to choose new ways to relate with loved ones.

It is critical that anyone who participates in coaching agrees with the expectations, commitments, timelines, ground rules, goals, and objectives. This synthesis of personal objectives into a larger team effort requires great clinical skill. Interested persons may have competing wants and needs. Occasionally, team members don't even like each other. However, they must put aside their own issues and come together seeking the common good and health of their loved one.

Most family members haven't been consistent not because they don't know how to change, but because they're so scared. Also, there's the unconscious payoff that "If I keep you sick, I'm terrific. I can be a martyr/victim. I can be a winner. I can look good. I can be perfect. You will always need me, and you will never leave." There are so many unconscious dynamics at play. While people do not consciously set out to do this, they need guidance on how to evolve.

I use the concept of the "perfect world" to help narrow the focus and to propose solutions. Further, I talk about the possibility of a "miracle." The idea is that we are pragmatic and we are present. Instead of imposing what we think might work, we use our client's motivation to change and help instill confidence about that change.

So, a recovery coach plays many roles, from teaching basic life skills to providing more specific mental health counseling. Clinicians who work with ILOs and their families as coaches help everyone within the family system create healthy lifestyles and boundaries. Indeed, coaching helps move individuals who are in or considering recovery from addiction to produce extraordinary results in their lives, careers, businesses, or organizations – while advancing their recovery from addiction.

*Solution-focused coaching targets both ILO and family member(s) to create and sustain great and meaningful lives. Through this process, clients deepen their learning, improve their performance, and enhance their quality of life.*

The clinician who is also coaching needs to align family members with strategies needed to get a loved one into treatment. Confidence is related to tools, tools that people don't have. Your job as a clinician is to teach them the tools they need to help families get to "yes," and to do the best job they can with the resources they have.

Any component of solution-focused coaching must teach accountability team members to:

- set healthy boundaries;
- take care of themselves;
- only advocate for the health and wellness of the one they love; and
- address clinical or reverse interventions.

A word here on clinical or reverse interventions. It's helpful to know that during an addiction intervention, there can be more going on. Actually, you can expect it. Recovery is messy. Sometimes the ILO wants to leave treatment (a clinical intervention). This usually happens after detox or when the person needs more treatment, a deeper level of treatment. In other cases, an IP may want to stay in treatment but parents want them to go home (a reverse intervention).

Clinical and reverse interventions often happen in a treatment center setting. In these cases, solution-focused coaching is really an extension of the skills used to negotiate treatment initiation. However, the focus is on treatment adherence, and "no" is simply a conversation starter. For more on clinical and reverse interventions, see Chapter 7.

Still, coaching also has its limits. Collaboration with other licensed professionals is key here. In other words, know when to refer challenging families to family therapy. It is possible for a recovery coach to work hand in hand with other professionals, physicians, therapists, and treatment centers to ensure success.

Some tenets of coaching include:

1.  When coaching, it is not necessary to understand deeper cause or meaning.
2.  Goals are defined by the client, focusing on the possible and changeable; honor client choice.
3.  Small change is often all that is possible.
4.  When the goal is defined by client, you have a cooperative client.
5.  Clinicians need to adopt a posture of inquiry, of not knowing.

## Solution-Focused Coaching vs. Motivational Interviewing

The biggest difference between motivational interviewing and solution-focused coaching is in evaluating readiness and confidence for change. During solution-focused coaching, we ask the parent or family member questions about importance and confidence for change. We ask:

> On a scale of 1 to 10, how important is it to you to get your child/family member to treatment?

> On a scale of 1 to 10, how confident are you that you could really do that?

While importance (motivation) may rate at a 10, confidence (if said truthfully) might be a 7 or an 8. A confidence level is usually lower than motivation level, and speaks to the tools we need to give to someone so they can make it happen.

When we talk about the family member who is scared that their loved one is never going to talk to them again, family members often fear they're going to run away or will hate them forever if they send them to treatment. These people may say things such as, "They really don't have a substance abuse problem, it's all mental health," etc.

Whatever the perception, we're going to uncover the difference between their personal levels of importance for treatment and confidence in making it happen. What we're doing is finding out, on a scale of 1 to 10, how important it is to that person to actually get their loved one help. They may think they are an 8 or a 9 but their confidence level is a 3. The reason? "My loved one will hate me." "I can't take away their phone, because I'll never know how or where they are." "She'll run away again." So, in solution-focused coaching, we provide the family members with skills so they can gradually move from a 3 to a 5, and from a 5 to a 7, until they are confident that the only solution is a "yes!" to treatment.

## Values Clarification

Values are deep-seated, personal standards that influence every aspect of our lives. They define what is important to each of us. Values clarification is a popular therapeutic exercise that can help family members become more aware of their foundational beliefs. Additionally, they can explore ways in which they are or are not living up to them. Examples of common values to explore during addiction intervention include spirituality, integrity, relationship, family, honesty, harmony, and loyalty.

Values clarification encourages change. When family members see where value and behaviors may not be aligned, they can make positive changes to their lifestyle to better live up to their values. This exercise is completed by ranking value. We're asking families to say what's important. We generally ask:

*On a scale of 1 to 20, how important is this to you?*

Discussion should be focused on which values are being met, and which are not. When a value is not being met, what changes would need to happen?

Before practicing this skill, however, clinicians should be trained in values clarification. I don't give families a worksheet, but I teach the concept in family settings and then assign value clarification homework.

Remember, every person has a unique set of values; there are no right or wrong answers. Your values will almost certainly be different from those of your clients. Age, culture, family, and individual differences all have a major impact on what we hold as most important.

Worksheet 5.10 (Values Clarification Worksheet) can help guide clinicians and clients in helping to make personal values more clear.

## Therapeutic Strategies Used with the ILO

The clinician's only real face time with the ILO is during the intervention meeting itself. Interventionists may also need to escort the ILO to treatment. Your goal is to have them willingly enter treatment. However, no matter what methodology or theory of human behavior you subscribe to, or what technique you use:

*It's your use of self that's important. You are you own best clinical ally.*

During collective interventions, we are always looking for goodness and strength. It's all about rising to your best possible self. You need to have acute listening skills. You need to have empathy. That is not often teachable. You have to try to understand the person. You can't just use a modality. If you look to a technique alone, you're going to miss the critical elements that can drive change.

What I mean is this: when we work with clients, we need to come from a place of authenticity. So, when you ask, "How are you?" be sincere. Be sure that is really what you want to know.

Remember that we are still human beings, not just a human doing. We are more than just a machine, checking off items from a to-do list. When we place ourselves in the moment, get grounded, and give our clients our full attention, we can have that conversation, that glance, that touch. We can transform our talk into healing conversation, one filled with grace and presence.

The dialogue can become this:

> *I want to know how your heart is doing today. I want to know how your heart is doing at this very moment. Tell me. Tell me your heart is joyous, tell me your heart is aching, tell me your heart is sad, tell me your heart craves a human touch. Examine your own heart, explore your soul, and then tell me something about your heart and your soul.*

How are you present for the person in front of you? What strategy will you use? What do you bring to the table? The answer is: your presence. In fact, you've got to be your own person. You cannot be someone else. You have to take what you like from everyone you've learned and use it, with supervision.

For me, it's the work of Brené Brown, Sara Lawrence-Lightfoot, Sheldon Koop, Brad Lamm, and Ed Storti. Whatever model you use, do so with guidance. All different modalities require supervision from an experienced professional.

## Escort and Transport

Your clinical skills are critical during the intervention meeting itself. A lot of skill is involved. However, an equally difficult time is the time between the "yes" and the initiation of treatment; it's about safe escort. See Worksheet 4.8 (Will You Need Executive Protection? Safety Checklist) when considering escort needs.

There's a real art to transporting an ILO to a treatment center. You need to alternately be very fragile but firm. Safe transport includes continual motivation. A person might buck and refuse to go to treatment, for example. Or you might need to get rid of drugs before a flight. They might want to run. And when a person agrees to go to treatment, all kinds of decisions need to be made.

Before you escort a client, however, you give them some time for packing their bag. Allow them the dignity to select what they will bring, the clothes they will wear. This allows for the process to be more accepted, to be less of a "punishment." Imagine, on the other hand, that your family decides you're going to rehab and then packs a bag for you. How would you feel? Childish? Powerless?

Likewise, you have to join up with clients who you accompany to addiction treatment. You can laugh. This is a person, after all. You have to connect with them on a deeper level.

> *You are constantly intervening during the travel. Motivation for change fluctuates, and the ILO may want to flee the situation.*

Further, you'll need to be well versed with safety and security during transport. For example, you need to care for physical health during transport. Truth be told, depending on their drugs of choice, you cannot have them stop and go cold turkey across the country. You are not medically equipped for detox. Still, they cannot be so high that they cannot get on an airplane. However, your job is not to trigger a medical problem.

> *If needed, you can travel with a nurse who is skilled in medical detoxification.*

You don't ask families to take a person to treatment because sometimes this becomes a visit or a tour as opposed to accepting treatment. If you're driving, it's best to turn on child lock and to have the client sit in the back seat with one or two people. Sometimes two people escort a person the entire time. When there is a female, a female escort is desirable. Escorts will go into the bathroom and be sure that no additional drug use occurs.

The demands of transport highlight the importance of working with another colleague. It's important and vital to work as a team. In this way, one person stays with the family to help them process and the other person can accompany the IP or ILO to treatment.

## Motivational Interviewing with the ILO

Motivational interviewing (MI) is a directive client-centered approach for eliciting change behavior and for reducing ambivalence developed by Miller and Rollnick.[8] It is a Rogerian approach that is coupled with setting direction. In other words, the approach involves guiding and eliciting vs. instructing and persuading. Motivational interviewing has a robust history in hospital, college, prison, and religious settings related to addiction and its treatment.

Further, MI is a process and not a technique. The goal is evocation; we aim to elicit a client's internal viewpoint and work as collaborators to help individuals create change in their lives. The client remains autonomous as clinicians roll with resistance. Central to the process is an assumption that the therapeutic relationship is egalitarian. The clinician is active and directive, but the outcomes are consistent with principles of client choice. As such, clinicians aim to be warm, empathetic, affirming, and respectful.

Motivation is a reason or reasons for acting or behaving in a particular way. We've found in addiction interventions that the probability of behavior change or movement toward or against the goal of treatment is heavily depending upon whether the motivation to attend is extrinsic or intrinsic. Again, you need to be trained in motivational interviewing before practicing it. This is a strategy, not a recipe. The concepts are not difficult, but we're talking about modalities that are worthwhile for you to take a look at.

## Motivational Interviewing Strategies

The practice of MI is a specific and systematic strategy used to empower clients. Because the focus of MI is on evoking a client's inner perspective, clinicians practice MI with a certain cultural sensitivity. In these terms, the client leads and the clinician's agenda is not imposed. Instead, we are there to express empathy, help the client develop discrepancy, and to support self-efficacy. Our main role is to help clients get unstuck from ambivalent feelings so that they can move forward to change.

In this way, clinicians take on the role of an explorer. We are there to explore motivation, situation, and possibility. In fact, it is imperative that clinicians are able to suspend judgment and fear. Instead, the focus is on affirming; MI practitioners actively use affirmations throughout the process.

In the meantime, this strategy requires that you learn to roll with resistance. In fact, the ability to facilitate the process but to simultaneously "get out of the way" is a difficult feat. MI helps motivate people to change because we build on the capacity of a person to believe they can carry out a specific act or behavior.

## What Motivational Interviewing Is Not

- based on a transtheoretical model;
- trickery;
- a specific technique;
- decisional balance (equally exploring pros and cons);
- assessment feedback;
- CBT;
- just client-centered;
- easy to learn;
- what you are already doing; or
- a panacea for every clinical challenge.

## Strategy #1: How to Express Empathy

To express empathy with clients, it is critical to master a few communication skills used in MI. These include asking open-ended questions, using affirmations, reflecting, and summarizing.

### Open-Ended Questions

Questions can be either "open-" or "closed-" ended. Closed-ended questions are those that can be answered by a simple "yes" or "no." Open-ended questions are those that require more thought and more than a simple one-word answer. Some good conversation starters we use in MI during addiction interventions include:

- What types of things do you want to talk about?
- Tell me about . . .
- What brings you here today?
- How long have you been concerned about . . .?
- Are there good things about your drug use?
- How do you think smoking pot is related to the problems you talk about in your marriage?
- Don't you think your wife and kids are hurt enough by your drinking?
- Isn't your friend's idea that you quit?

### Affirmations

Use specific language to affirm your client and their character as related to the goal(s) they are exploring. Some examples of ways to affirm clients during an intervention include:

- I appreciate your honesty.
- I can see that caring for your children is important to you.
- It shows courage and commitment to come back to meetings.
- You have good ideas.

### Reflections

Used strategically, reflections can emphasize a client's view, feelings, ambivalence, emotional change, or change talk. This skill can truly move a person closer to change! An example of simple reflection might be:

*Client:* She is driving me crazy trying to get me to quit.
*Counselor:* Her methods are really bothering you.
*Client:* I don't have anything to say.
*Counselor:* You are not feeling talkative today.

In order to listen reflectively, clinicians must first be able to be quiet and engage in active listening. We must listen with emotional attunement. We do not react. Instead, we respond with a statement that accurately reflects the essence of what the client meant. You might also think in terms of forming a hypotheses, or best guess, at what the client is saying. Some examples of a reflection include:

- Do you mean . . .?
- What I think you're saying is . . .
- Is it correct to say that you think . . .?

Furthermore, to be good at reflection, you have to *differentiate between a question and a statement*, both during listening and talking. The main difference between the two is that the voice goes down at the end of the statement, rather than up with a question. In this light, the sentence "You're angry with your mother . . ." could be either a statement or a question. (*Note:* A statement does not require an answer.)

Likewise, the level of reflection is important during MI for addiction intervention. Some of the more common types of reflection include:

- *Repeating*, during which you repeat what someone has just said.
- *Rephrasing*, or substituting a few different words.
- *Paraphrasing*, making a fairly major restatement inferring what you think a person has said.
- *Reflecting feeling*, a special kind of paraphrase where you are not necessarily reflecting content, but trying to capture the feeling behind the communication.

Other types of reflections can be used when called for. For example, an *amplified reflection* exaggerates what the client says. As a communication device, we exaggerate so as to get someone's attention.

When using this reflection, be careful to avoid sarcasm:

Client:     All my friends smoke weed, and I don't see giving it up.
Counselor:  So, you are likely to keep smoking forever.

Or, *doubled-sided reflection* can be used to capture both sides of an issue:

Client:     It would stink to lose my job over a dumb policy because I have been using, but do I want to quit partying just because of that?
Counselor:  On the one hand, you value your job because it allows to live comfortably, and on the other hand you also enjoy using drugs with your friends.

## Provide Summaries

Summaries communicate and track what clients say so that you have an understanding of what is being said. Further, a summary helps structure the conversation, so you do not get sidetracked and provide clinical opportunities to emphasize statements about change talk. When we summarize, the summary gives clients another opportunity to hear what they have said in context provided by the counsellor:

*Counselor:*   So, Sally, let me know if I heard you correctly. You care about your children and you are hoping social services does not intervene. You believe you need to change your relationships that involve using, and aren't quite sure how to do that? Or what else would you add?

*Counselor:*   Jonathan, it sounds like you have made the choice to seek continuing care. If I heard you correctly, you said it feels like the right thing, though a scary thing to do. You have started to look at some structured living situations that include monitoring and help getting a job.

## Strategy #2: How to Explore Ambivalence

Ambivalence can be defined as:

> *Conflicting emotions or thoughts about a person, thought, object, or idea.*

We face ambivalence frequently during addiction interventions. Often ambivalence about change – even change that promises to bring positive consequences – is present in both ILOs and their family members. Our goal as clinicians is to reduce ambivalence in clients so that they might accept change more readily:

*Counselor:*   So, one the one hand, you want to stop smoking, and on the other hand you do not.

*Counselor:*   So, on the one hand, you say you are angry, and yet you have little emotion.

*Counselor:*   On the one hand, you want to be able to leave the children with your wife, but you are afraid to.

*Counselor:*   On the one hand, you want Mark to get well and be a part of the family, and on the other you never want him to return to your home.

## Decisional Balance Worksheets

To explore ambivalence, clinicians principally ask about what is good or not so good about changing a certain behavior. While the discussion may seem to center around the "pros" and "cons" of behavioral change, what is actually happening is that we guide clients toward resolution of the ambivalence.

As clients consider what they would like to change, they list the good things about changing a certain behavior and the not so good things about changing that behavior. The process is that of completing a decisional balance sheet listing pros and cons. What is good about going to treatment, for example? What is not good about going? What do I have to give up? And what are the associated consequences?

So, as one works with the ILO to figure out what are the benefits of going to treatment vs. what's not good, herein lies the heart of objections. If you are prepared, you will learn these in advance and have sorted through solutions.

### Strategy #3: How to Roll with Resistance

When clinicians meet resistance in traditional counseling sessions, we often make the assumption that the client is "not getting it." The MI view holds that the counselor may not be getting it. In fact, we may hold subconscious assumptions about the counseling process that block us from accepting resistance.

Some assumptions to avoid include:

- This person *ought* to change.
- This person *wants* to change.
- A person's health is their prime motivating factor.
- If they decide not to change, the consultation is a failure.
- Individuals are either motivated to change or they are not.
- Now is the right time to consider change.
- A tough approach is always the best approach.
- A negotiation approach is always best.
- An egalitarian approach is always best.
- I am the expert and I know best.

### Signs of Resistance

During the practice of motivational interviewing during an intervention, you'll need to be particularly aware of signs of resistance. The following are all signs of resistance:

- arguing;
- blaming;
- catastrophizing;
- challenging;
- claiming impunity;
- cutting off;

- demanding;
- denying;
- disagreeing;
- discounting;
- discouraging;
- excuses;
- filibustering;
- hostility;
- ignoring;
- inattention;
- interrupting;
- minimizing;
- pessimism;
- reluctance;
- sidestepping;
- taking over; and
- unwillingness to change.

You can address these signs of resistance by turning the conversation back to change. As you continue the conversation, you are always rephrasing or re-summarizing ideas.

*Note:* When you find yourself arguing for change and the client defending status quo, you know you're off course. Evoking change in the conversation is a difficult clinical skill. See the 10 strategies listed earlier in this chapter for more ideas on evoking change.

## Strategy #4: Brief Negotiation

The brief negotiated interview (BNI) is a specialized intervention originally developed by Steven Rollnick for emergency department work.[9] The BNI has been used to help healthcare providers explore behavior change with patients in a respectful, nonjudgmental way within a finite time period. Since its development, the BNI has been demonstrated in multiple peer-reviewed studies to be effective at facilitating a variety of positive health behavior changes.

> *During brief negotiated interviews with your clients, you are selling health and wellness. To do so, there has to be some play in the interaction.*

The foundations of BNI are firmly rooted in motivational interviewing. In fact, practitioners recommend speaking respectfully with the patient and asking questions, instead of telling the patient what to do. The idea is that you are trying to increase the patient's motivation to change, and their autonomy to carry out those changes. So, instead of telling the patient what changes they should make, the BNI is intentionally designed to elicit reasons for change and action steps from the patient. It gives the patient voice and choice, making any potential behavior changes all the more empowering to the patient.

At its most basic, good BNI techniques remain in the form of an algorithm, or "script," that guides providers through the health intervention with carefully phrased key questions and responses, all at the providers' fingertips. In dealing with addiction, negotiation skills are effectively outlined in the bestselling business book *Crucial Conversations*.[10]

## References

1. DiClemente CC and Prochaska JO (1982) Self-Change and Therapy Change of Smoking Behavior: A Comparison of Processes of Change in Cessation and Maintenance. *Addictive Behaviors*. 7: 133–142.
2. DiClemente CC and Prochaska JO (1998) Toward a Comprehensive Transtheoretical Model of Change: Stages of Change and Addictive Behaviors (pp. 3–24). *Treating Addictive Behaviors* (2nd edition). New York: Plenum Press.
3. Miller WR and Rollnick S (2012) *Motivational Interviewing Third Edition: Helping People Change*. New York and London: Guilford Press.
4. Facing Addiction (2016) *The Facing Addiction Action Plan*. Washington, DC: Facing Addiction. Available at: www.facingaddiction.org/wp-content/uploads/2015/08/Action-Plan-10-28-16.pdf (accessed March 4, 2018).
5. Brown B (2010) *The Gifts of Imperfection*. Center City, PA: Hazelden.
6. Center for Substance Abuse Treatment (1999) *Brief Interventions and Brief Therapies for Substance Abuse: Treatment Improvement Protocol (TIP) Series, No. 34*. Rockville, MD: Substance Abuse and Mental Health Services Administration. Available at: www.ncbi.nlm.nih.gov/books/NBK64948/ (accessed March 4, 2018).
7. Berg IK and Reuss NH (1997) *Solutions Step by Step: A Substance Abuse Treatment Manual*. New York: W.W. Norton & Company.
8. Miller WR and Rose GS (2009). Toward a Theory of Motivational Interviewing. *The American Psychologist*. 64(6): 527–537.
9. D'Onofrio G, Bernstein E, and Rollnick S (1996) Motivating Patients for Change: A Brief Strategy for Negotiation (pp. 295–303). *Case Studies in Emergency Medicine and the Health of the Public*. Boston, MA: Jones & Bartlett.
10. Patterson K et al. (2012) *Crucial Conversations: Tools for Talking When Stakes Are High* (2nd edition). United States: New York: McGraw-Hill.

# 6

# HOW TO ADJUST INTERVENTIONS BY POPULATION

## Objections to Treatment

Let's be honest: most people don't want to go into treatment. However, many people will have some level of inner ambivalence about their substance use. Maybe they've been arrested for driving under the influence. Perhaps their children have been taken away, or a spouse has left. In other cases, an ILO may be self-aware enough to want to address their inner despair or to air out trauma.

> *To get a person to "yes," we're going identify internal motivation for change and build on that. Further, thoughtful and detailed responses to objections to treatment can increase client readiness to change.*

In fact, clinicians can greatly benefit from expecting certain objections from clients and planning counter-objections in advance. Accountability team members will identify specific known arguments against treatment during interviews, and again in the pre-intervention meeting in step 8 of the Collective Intervention Strategy. Worksheet 4.7 (Common Objections to Addiction Treatment and Their Counter-Objections) can also be very helpful. Indeed, knowing the common barriers to treatment and common objections will help you respond accordingly, rather than react.

Regardless of how well motivated or how poorly motivated someone may appear, there is almost always an opening that can be discovered in their armor. While an ILO's motivation is likely to waver repeatedly over time, clinicians must remain mindful of soft spots. When we know what our clients care about, we can break through the hollow walls of denial.

## Expect Confabulations (aka Denial)

People who experience substance abuse disorder and their families always look to other reasons to explain what is going on. In fact, they confabulate or make up stories. Technically, the response is called a "defense mechanism." The way that we see this manifest during interventions is as denial. The defense mechanism of denial is defined as:

> *The refusal to accept reality or fact, acting as if a painful event, thought, or feeling did not exist.*

Denial is considered to be one of the most primitive of the defense mechanisms because it is characteristic of early childhood development. Initially, denial comes into play as a protective factor; the information that we are getting is too painful, so our brain shields us from the truth. With addiction, denial runs wild. Every excuse other than the disorder is blamed for the aberrant behavior.

It is important to note that both the person who experiences the disorder and the people around them fall prey to the denial. I like to call this the "confabulation dilemma." Think about the fable of the emperor's new clothes. People pretend that the emperor is wearing the finest of garments although he has nothing on, just like the mother or father of a son or daughter wo has flunked out of school, does not come home, or has stopped working because of the use of mind-altering substances.

The purpose of an intervention is to break into this honeycomb of denial. To do so, we use compassionate words and actual experiences. For example, parents are coached to say:

> *John, I love and care about you with all my heart. I remember when I held you in my arms as a baby. You were my firstborn. I remember the first time you ran across a soccer field, kicked a football, and when we went fishing together (positive recollection). Over the last six months, since you entered school, I am baffled and confused by your behavior. Last week, when you locked yourself in your room and I entered, I was scared as you tried to punch me and hid silver wrappers in your room. When you took the car and did not bring it back, I was worried for your safety. Then the police called, and I had to come and get you as you crashed the car and left it.*

The purpose of an intervention is to open up and break into the loved one's denial. We only have a short window of time – an opening in between the spaces of despair – to do so. Indeed, the purpose of intervention is to break into denial. However, know this:

> *No one ever likes to admit anything.*

Even more, it is a challenging task to try to help a person or a group of people who may not want to be helped at all. The ILO often fails to recognize that there is a problem; trying to have a simple heart-to-heart conversation may sometimes seem offensive to the person in trouble. So, how can you get beyond the walls of defense?

A talented clinician or practitioner must be flexible. We teach participants to be flexible and nimble. We roll with objections to always be focused on getting the loved one into much-needed treatment. In doing so, a strength-based approach focuses on "what is," not "what is wrong." Shame is often their middle name.

> *The clinician who works toward emotional fitness in an invitational way and has taught others to do so is working from a place of power and empathy, which allows others to move to change.*

Following, we'll cover some of the ways that clinicians can address counter-objections. Before we dig into customized considerations "by population," we must look more deeply at denial. Because denial is systemic. And when you dig deeper, you uncover the secrets and the lies that families hold – as individuals or in a group.

Therefore, here are some of the foundational principles I stand firmly behind when approaching individual and families who struggle with addiction. The idea is that we clinicians are looking for the truth. As clinicians, we bring light into the situation. In this way:

1. Seeking truth demands uncovering, not covering up.
2. Seeking truth demands introspection, not accusing or blaming.
3. Seeking truth demands rigorous honesty from multiple data points.
4. Seeking truth requires a stillness.
5. Seeking truth requires curiosity.
6. Seeking truth demands a commitment to change.

## How to Create Opening in Denial

The overall purpose of an intervention is to create an opening in the denial system of the ILO *and their family and friends.* The work of a successful intervention does not end when the ILO seeks treatment; the end goal of an intervention is to help families learn new ways of relating to one another and taking care of themselves. This is accomplished by helping everyone involved accept the difficult reality of the current situation.

How do we begin? We start by asking questions as outlined in Worksheet 4.2 (Intake Questions for First Point of Contact) and Worksheet 4.3 (How to Listen to Wounded Heart: Questions for Guided Conversations with Clients):

1. Tell me about your loved one.
2. What was the tipping point that made you call?
3. Tell me what is special about your loved one.
4. What makes your heart hurt?
5. What have you experienced in the last six months or year that causes you pain?
6. What are your loved one's strengths?
7. What have you done in the last six months or year to help them out?

Indeed, family interventions are difficult and delicate matters. Anger and profound sorrow often result when someone is forced to look at their own behavior. Family members often experience mournful rage, deep sadness, and guilt over failed efforts. While all persons in a family share traits and mannerisms, each person is different; each is unique, and each requires different tools and strategies to help the ILO and themselves heal.

Working with families who want to move a loved one, a co-worker, or even a celebrity to health and wellness, we begin to uncover much pain and sorrow. How do we do this? We invite all the participants to be curious, to look at their own behaviors, identify, and focus on what they *can change*.

This is done first through family mapping, where you can view the situation like a kaleidoscope: one's life, trials, tribulations – as well as resiliency – swirl together in stories. Then triangulation of data through individual interviews and participant observation helps us to create a portrait of unique individuals. Little by little, we see a way through.

In our work as clinicians performing interventions, we uncover lies and secrets. In fact, the ideas that clients hold as truth are slowly destroyed as they grow from a place of guilt, shame, confabulation (the stories we tell ourselves), or denial to a place of authenticity and transparency. Rather than see these stories as shameful, clinicians must redirect clients to the possibility of opening up to healing through self-understanding. Brené Brown calls this a "rewriting of their story" in *Rising Strong*.[1]

When clients take on an attitude of curiosity about themselves, the healing process quickens. It is the act of viewing these memories with curiosity and openness that creates something new: false truths are revealed. With growth and renewal, we become more authentic and our "shame shields," or armor, give way.

## How to Adjust an Intervention by Population

Each family intervention you facilitate will be unique. No matter how many interventions you facilitate, each will have a special flavor and character. In this way, every intervention must start where your clients are, not where the methodology proclaims you should start.

Still, there are some factors related to the demographic of the ILO that can help you. For example, knowing the common objections to treatment and their counters can help move clients from a "no" to a "yes" with more ease. Additionally, individual or family dysregulation are present in any demographic. Knowing and planning for these difficulties is part of setting up reasonable expectations for the work ahead.

Following are the most common populations and a common set of problems, barriers, and considerations for each. Of course, this demographic snapshot is not perfect. This is a starting point. I invite you to examine and to add to this based on further research and your own experiences.

**TABLE 6.1** Adolescents

| | |
|---|---|
| Characteristics | Adolescents under 18 years old. They are developmentally within the maturation process into self-awareness and identity formation. Many adolescents who abuse drugs have a history of physical, emotional, and/or sexual abuse or other trauma. Learning disability or ADHD can be present. Often experience anxiety and depression. Suicide ideation is also frequent. |
| Common signs of a problem | Impressionable. Instant gratification. Fickle. Follow the opinion of peers. Need to impress and fit in. |
| Common objections to treatment | Treatment is less important than school. I'll miss out on sports, extracurricular activities, or important events. Parental fear. "It's just a phase." |
| Counter-objections | At a young age, the personality and body are still developing. Drugs have long-lasting effects on brain development. Further, the development of good habits will be taken into adulthood. You don't want these behaviors to continue into adulthood. |
| Other barriers to treatment | Cost. Family objection. Family shame. Peer pressure. School pressure. |
| Special considerations | Sensitive issues such as violence and child abuse or risk of suicide should be identified and addressed. If abuse is suspected, referrals should be made to social and protective services, following local regulations and reporting requirements. Adolescents rarely feel they need treatment, and almost never seek it on their own.[1] Legal interventions and sanctions or family pressure can play an important role in getting adolescents to enter, stay in, and complete treatment. Further, adolescents can benefit from a drug abuse intervention even if they are not yet addicted to a drug. Substance use disorders range from problematic use to addiction, and can be treated successfully at any stage, and at any age. |

*(continued)*

**TABLE 6.1** *(continued)*

Relapses occur, so more than one episode of treatment may be necessary. Many adolescents also benefit from continuing care following treatment, including drug use monitoring, follow-up visits at home, and linking the family to other needed services. Internet and online culture, gaming, Snapchat, Facebook, and digital devices (phones and tablets) may require monitoring, limitation, or intervention.

1. National Institute on Drug Abuse (2014) *Principles of Adolescent Substance Use Disorder Treatment: A Research-Based Guide*. Bethesda, MD: National Institutes of Health. Available at: www. drugabuse.gov/publications/principles-adolescent-substance-use-disorder-treatment-research-based-guide (accessed March 4, 2018).

**TABLE 6.2** Failure to launch

| | |
|---|---|
| Characteristics | This demographic is characterized by the inability or desire or lack of preparation to leave home and begin the journey toward a self-supported life. The population ranges from young adult to adult children. In fact, this group is not isolated to youth; there are more and more cases of adult children living with greying parent(s). |
| | This group has been increasing as a result of the need for more education in a technology-driven world coincides with fewer entry-level jobs. Additionally, there may be parental pressure to "follow your dreams." Further, adult brain maturation is typically reached by age 25. |
| Common signs of a problem | Attachment disorder. |
| | Dependency on parents for financial support. |
| | Entitlement. |
| | Less rush to marry. |
| | Little desire to transition to the next stage of life. |
| | Tendency toward premarital sex with a corresponding dependency on birth control and contraceptive technologies. |
| | An average of seven job changes in their twenties. |
| | Unable to sustain a job; starts and stops working. |
| | Dual diagnosis issues. |
| | Takes little responsibility for their own well-being. |
| | Isolates. |
| | May drop out of school. |
| | Explosive and argumentative. |
| | Takes money. |
| | Stays out all night. |
| | Does not focus. |
| | Oppositional. |
| | Legal issues. |

**TABLE 6.3** *(continued)*

| | |
|---|---|
| Common signs of a problem | Missing work.<br>Nodding off.<br>Not being present for family.<br>Driving under the influence.<br>Not performing household tasks.<br>Spending lots of money.<br>Having extramarital affairs.<br>Going to lots of doctors.<br>Multiple operations. |
| Common objections to treatment | I have responsibilities of work, children, or other responsibilities; I cannot leave these.<br>I have to take care of my aging parents.<br>Family does not see the problem. |
| Counter-objections | Childcare can be provided.<br>One can take a medical leave of absence.<br>One does not get fired for getting help; rather, one will lose a job because of nonperformance.<br>Arrangements can be made to see children.<br>Other health issues can be exacerbated if not addressed; substance use puts adults at risk for injury, illness, and other negative outcomes. |
| Other barriers to treatment | Belief that substance use is a private matter and won't talk to family or healthcare providers.<br>Costs.<br>Low index of suspicion among healthcare providers.<br>Negative attitudes and beliefs about substances; this age group views substance abuse very negatively and may hide use in extreme secrecy. |
| Special considerations | Because of beliefs and assumptions about this age group, misdiagnosis can be a problem that causes other health problems and may worsen the issue. Multiple appointments and hurried doctor visits can complicate diagnosis.<br>Secrecy is important to this population. Substance use is seen as highly shameful. In fact, many relatives of middle-aged individuals with substance use disorders, particularly their adult children, are also ashamed of the problem and choose not to address it. |

**TABLE 6.4** Aged 65+

| | |
|---|---|
| Characteristics | Late-onset refers to substance use disorders that occur relatively late in life. Baby boomers, aged 50 years and up, fall into this category. The U.S. Census Bureau estimates that by the year 2050, one out of four Americans over age 65 will be 85 and older.[1] |

| | |
|---|---|
| Common objections to treatment | Denial; always someone else's fault.<br>Parents feel like they failed their children.<br>On a slower time frame/taking their time.<br>Overly protective parents.<br>Shame and guilt.<br>Trust funds and access to their own money. |
| Counter-objections | Allow the young adult independence and room to grow.<br>The hula hoop of addiction and abuse; it always comes back.<br>Toxic parent–child relationship. |
| Other barriers to treatment | Codependent relationship between parent and child.<br>Family history of alcohol or drug dependency.<br>Family wealth and legacy. |
| Special considerations | The demographic, economic, and cultural shifts in America normalize "boomerang" young adults who leave then return home. So, professionals must be trained in the complexity of these cases. Treatment centers should be built to accommodate the population's special needs for young adults and older adults, including the difficulties young adults face when transitioning into the next phase of development, a stage that involves greater independence and accountability. There must be multiple entry points for intervention for this target.<br>Additionally, parents (helicopter, steamroller, Saran Wrap, submarine) who bail children out of problems require their own forms of intervention. They need to deal with their own emotional intensity and unhealthy lack of boundaries in order for the children to begin recovery. |

**TABLE 6.3** Middle-aged

| | |
|---|---|
| Characteristics | Middle-aged people typically may begin to experience mental health problems in their forties or fifties. Drugs and/or alcohol are used to treat symptoms. Reports of loneliness and lower quality of life have been documented among the age group, for example. However, because of the age group, many assume substance abuse does not/would not occur (ageism).<br>Additionally, some people who are middle-aged begin to experience lowered resilience. Life events, loss, illness, or mental health problems may trigger substance use. Or past experiences (this population grew up with a normalized, destigmatized drug culture) allow for habits to continue in this age group. Further, aging brings on persistence in the use of prescription drugs; increased ailments/injuries/surgeries means access to pills such as opioids. |

(continued)

Aging adults experience life changes, sudden and otherwise, such as children growing up and moving away, the death and loss of spouses, partners, loved ones, and friends, retirement or loss of job, change of environment, physical health issues, reduced income, and social isolation.[2] Notably, chronic pain is one of the leading factors in late-onset substance use.[3] Grandparents, typically at an age when the body is more susceptible to disease and ailments, turn to drug treatments to ease the pain.

These multiple issues tend to compound over time. Like middle-aged individuals, late-onset users are exposed to mind-altering substances via prescription drugs. Individuals often self-medicate for both physical and mental issues; for example, most people over the age of 70 who experience a substance abuse or alcohol addiction use either alcohol or prescription drugs.[1] Also, it is important to rule out any medical illness in this population, such as dementia, Alzheimer's, or other debilitating problems.

| | |
|---|---|
| Common signs of a problem | Isolated.<br>Lonely.<br>Prideful.<br>Stubborn.<br>Stuck in their ways.<br>Depression.<br>Divorce or widowhood. |
| Common objections to treatment | Ageism; the belief that older people have a different quality of life standard and do not need treatment and care.<br>Denial or secrecy.<br>"Grandmother's cocktails are the only thing that makes her happy."<br>"That's just how she is."<br>"It's too late."<br>The family does not believe it's a problem.<br>"What difference does it make; he won't be around much longer anyway." |
| Counter-objections | Quality of life should be upheld for all age groups.<br>Other health issues can be exacerbated if not addressed.<br>Substance use puts older adults at risk for injury, illness, and other negative outcomes. |
| Other barriers to treatment | Ageism; negative attitudes and beliefs about this population.<br>Family not wanting to do anything.<br>Lack of diagnosis.<br>Comorbidity; Alzheimer's, depression, lack of mobility, or multi-infarct dementia.<br>Cost.<br>Lack of awareness; this age group views substance use very negatively and may hide/use secrecy. Most believe it is a private matter and won't talk to family/healthcare providers about the issue. |

*(continued)*

**TABLE 6.4** *(continued)*

|  | Lack of expertise; few programs have specialists in geriatrics, treat many older adults, or are designed to accommodate functional disabilities. |
|---|---|
|  | Lack of insurance coverage. |
|  | Lack of resources; not enough available retirement homes to accommodate this growing population. |
|  | Lack of time due to care for spouse, relative, friend, or grandchildren. |
|  | Shrinking social support network. |
|  | Limited benefits from social security. |
|  | Transportation. |
| Special considerations | Strategies for intervention in late-onset substance use requires putting together the right team, often a combination of doctors, clinicians, and treatment centers. Try to partner with clinicians with experience in normal, non-pathological depression following the death of a spouse and experience about aging, and with clinicians who understand the difference between divorce and loss experienced by widowers/widows. Essentially, this group responds well to both team and one-on-one conversations. |
|  | Because of the seniority of the age group, many family members and medical professionals overlook substance abuse disorders as cause for behaviors. Substance abuse often ends up at the bottom of the list or is not considered at all when a patient presents with many medical or personal problems. Providers often do not look beyond the presenting problem for which the patient is seeking care. Additionally, the amount of time physicians typically spend with a patient tends to decrease as the age of the patient increases. The result is misdiagnosis. |
|  | Further, shame and stigma also play a role in lack of treatment; relatives of aging individuals with a substance abuse disorder often avoid the issue or dismiss it with a different quality of life standard for older individuals. Elder neglect and abuse may occur. |
|  | Additionally, the structure of insurance policies can be a barrier to treatment. The carving out of mental health services from physical health services under managed care can prevent older adults from receiving inpatient substance abuse treatment. |

1. Ortman JM, Velkoff VA, and Hogan H (2014) *An Aging Nation: The Older Population in the United States.* Washington, DC: U.S. Census Bureau. Available at: www.census.gov/prod/2014pubs/p25-1140.pdf (accessed March 4, 2018).

2. Center for Substance Abuse Treatment (1998) *Substance Abuse among Older Adults: Treatment Improvement Protocol (TIP) Series, No. 26.* Rockville, MD: Substance Abuse and Mental Health Services Administration. Available at: www.ncbi.nlm.nih.gov/books/NBK64419/ (accessed March 4, 2018).

3. Center for Substance Abuse Treatment (2012) *Treatment Improvement Protocol (TIP) Series, No. 54: Managing Chronic Pain in Adults with or in Recovery from Substance Use Disorders.* Rockville, MD: Substance Abuse and Mental Health Services Administration. Available at: https://store.samhsa.gov/shin/content//SMA13-4671/SMA13-4671.pdf (accessed March 4, 2018).

**TABLE 6.5** Men

| | |
|---|---|
| Characteristics | Men are more likely to use all types of drugs than women.[1] In fact, men tend to use alcohol and drugs as problem-solving strategies. Substance use may be considered a more masculine way to deal with stress than self-disclosure and dialogue. Further, men experience higher rates of antisocial personality disorder than women. |
| | In this population, gender role socialization has influenced stereotypical attitudes and behaviors that can complicate family problems, although these vary with age, culture, ethnicity, social class, and sexual orientation.[2] It is important to note that gay, bisexual, or transgender men generally have higher rates of substance use and substance use disorders than heterosexual men. |
| | Men are generally more reluctant to seek substance abuse treatment or counseling than women, and also tend to end treatment earlier.[3] Motivations that typically bring men to treatment include criminal justice system involvement, referrals from other behavioral health resources, and family or work-related pressures. Still, most clients in substance abuse treatment are male. |
| Common signs of a problem | Notions of masculinity; social expectations to be independent, self-sufficient, stoic, and invulnerable. |
| | Notions of strength. |
| | Power and dominance are important. |
| | Pressure to take control, be the breadwinner, and/or to be successful in family and career. |
| | Varied tolerance of sexual orientation. |
| Common objections to treatment | "I am strong and resilient." |
| | "I do not need help." |
| | Denial. |
| | Family/friends pressure to "be a man." |
| Counter-objections | Address how substance use relates to a man's self-concept as a man; being a man means taking responsibility for one's actions. |
| | Consider the impact on friends/family. |
| | There is strength in admitting a substance use problem. |
| | You'll make decisions about your treatment options, be directly involved, and provide input. |
| Other barriers to treatment | Ambivalent about seeking help for behavioral health problems. |
| | Career responsibilities. |
| | Culture of hazing/peer pressure begins at a young age, and habits may continue into adulthood. |
| | Normalized substance use in the work environment. |
| | Tendencies to intellectualize and to avoid intimacy. |
| | Time; may not have time for treatment if sole breadwinner. |
| Special considerations | Men may choose a specific career path that brings with it different norms/customs/cultures that exacerbate a substance use problem. |
| | Long work hours, multiple projects, and little to no vacation time make it difficult to seek treatment. |

*(continued)*

**TABLE 6.5** *(continued)*

Men also have concerns about privacy; they need reassurance that treatment will pose no threat to their image or standing. It is helpful to seek clinical alliance by directly asking about client preferences regarding types of treatment (many men prefer more instrumental approaches, such as cognitive behavioral therapy). Treatment should be gender-responsive, examine the role of masculinity, and target the emotional/behavioral issues of most men.

Men can experience trouble analyzing their own problems, particularly feelings related to those problems. This can be a reflection of men's stoicism. Counseling style and approach can hinder or enhance a man's motivation. For example, an authoritarian, adversarial, or confrontational style may prove less effective than more client-centered, reflective approaches. Additionally, the need to be self-sufficient may result in a false sense of accomplishment or security in a man's recovery, which may manifest as unwillingness to follow through with continuing care or attend mutual help meetings.

The sexual orientation of the client and counselor should be considered when planning substance abuse treatment. Gay male clients may feel more comfortable working with a woman or a gay male counselor.

1. Center for Behavioral Health Statistics and Quality (2016) *The TEDS Report: Gender Differences in Primary Substance of Abuse across Age Groups*. Rockville, MD: Substance Abuse and Mental Health Services Administration. Available at: www.samhsa.gov/data/sites/default/files/sr077-gender-differences-2014.pdf (accessed March 4, 2018).
2. Center for Substance Abuse Treatment (2013) *Treatment Improvement Protocol (TIP) Series, No. 56: Addressing the Specific Behavioral Health Needs of Men*. Rockville, MD: Substance Abuse and Mental Health Services Administration. Available at: www.ncbi.nlm.nih.gov/books/NBK144286 (accessed March 4, 2018).
3. Green C (2006) *Gender and Use of Substance Abuse Treatment Services*. Rockville, MD: National Institute on Alcohol Abuse and Alcoholism. Available at: https://pubs.niaaa.nih.gov/publications/arh291/55-62.htm (accessed March 4, 2018).

**TABLE 6.6** LGBTQ

| | |
|---|---|
| Characteristics | LGBTQ individuals are those who identify as lesbian, gay, bisexual, transgender, and/or queer. While sexual orientation is identified and developed through the maturation process, the process is substantially complicated by issues of family rejection and lack of social support, stigma, and minority stress, as well as abuse and harassment.[1] Indeed, this demographic often faces social stigma, discrimination, and other significant challenges not encountered by people who identify as heterosexual.<br><br>This group faces a greater risk of harassment and violence. As a result of these stressors, sexual minorities are at increased risk for |

various behavioral health issues. In fact, lesbian, gay, and bisexual adolescents are 190% more likely to use substances compared to their heterosexual peers.[2]

We include here gender-nonconforming individuals, or transgender people, people whose binary sex assigned at birth and gender does not match their inner identity. Some elect to transition and undergo surgical correction to transition from male to female anatomy or female to male. Of critical clinical importance is sensitivity to gender fluidity, gender expression, and intersex identifications (mixing of genes and blending of sexual anatomy). Drugs of choice include stimulants and alcohol.

| | |
|---|---|
| Common signs of a problem | Anxiety. |
| | Confusion. |
| | Culture of partying and drug/alcohol abuse; pressure to assimilate into mainstream LGBTQ culture. |
| | Depression. |
| | Does not conform to traditional male/female societal norms and stereotypes. |
| | Internalized homophobia or transphobia. |
| | Thoughts of suicide related to forming identity. |
| Common objections to treatment | Denial or refusal to accept identity. |
| | Familial rejection. |
| | Fear of isolation and abandonment. |
| | Lack of community-specific resources and access to specialized treatment in suburbs/rural areas. |
| | Lack of education and understanding from family/friends/religious affiliations. |
| Counter-objections | Allied resources such as PFLAG, Pride rallies/marches/festivals. |
| | Available resources in urban centers. |
| | Legislative/political/economic gains and achievements. |
| | Progress in macro- and micro-acceptance and belonging. |
| | Specialized LGBTQ centers and treatment clinics. |
| Other barriers to treatment | Familial denial or refusal to financially support. |
| | Homophobia or transphobia. |
| | Kicked out of home. |
| | Lack of resources/education/healthcare for LGBTQ community. |
| Special considerations | LGBTQ persons have a greater likelihood than non-LGBTQ persons of experiencing a substance use disorder in their lifetime, often entering treatment with more severe addictions.[3] They are also more likely to have additional comorbid or co-occurring psychiatric disorders such as mental distress and depression.[4] It is particularly important that this population be screened for other psychiatric problems, and all identifiable conditions should be treated concurrently. This population faces significant discrimination, stereotyping, and social prejudice. |

One big barrier to treatment is clinician training in this area. In my experience, there is a real need for trained professionals and treatment centers who are well versed in this population. Initial and

(continued)

**TABLE 6.6** *(continued)*

ongoing assessment should include questions about the "coming out" process, and specific experiences – both positive and negative – with regard to sexual minority identity. A greater understanding of these issues will contribute to a more operative treatment plan.[5]

Current research suggests that treatment should address unique factors in these patients' lives that may include homophobia/transphobia, family problems, violence, and social isolation. Further, addiction treatment programs offering specialized groups for gay and bisexual men showed better outcomes for those clients compared to gay and bisexual men in non-specialized programs.[6]

LGBTQ people are also at increased risks for the human immunodeficiency virus (HIV) due to both intravenous drug use and risky sexual behaviors.[7] HIV infection is particularly prevalent among gay and bisexual men and transgender women who have sex with men, and substance use treatment can be effective in HIV transmission prevention and treatment.

1. Meyer IH (2013) Prejudice, Social Stress, and Mental Health in Lesbian, Gay, and Bisexual Populations: Conceptual Issues and Research Evidence. *Psychological Bulletin.* 129(5): 674–697.
2. Marshal MP, Friedman MS, Stall R, King KM, Miles J, Gold MA, et al. (2008) Sexual Orientation and Adolescent Substance Use: A Meta-Analysis and Methodological Review. *Addiction.* 103(4): 546–556. http://doi.org/10.1111/j.1360-0443.2008.02149.x
3. Green KE and Feinstein BA (2012) Substance Use in Lesbian, Gay, and Bisexual Populations: An Update on Empirical Research and Implications for Treatment. *Psychology of Addictive Behaviors.* 26(2): 265–278. doi:10.1037/a0025424
4. Cochran SD, Sullivan JG, and Mays VM (2003) Prevalence of Mental Disorders, Psychological Distress, and Mental Health Services Use among Lesbian, Gay, and Bisexual Adults in the United States. *Journal of Consulting and Clinical Psychology.* 71(1): 53–61.
5. Center for Substance Abuse Treatment (2012) *A Provider's Introduction to Substance Abuse Treatment for Lesbian, Gay, Bisexual, and Transgender Individuals.* Rockville, MD: Substance Abuse and Mental Health Services Administration. Available at: https://store.samhsa.gov/shin/content/SMA12-4104/SMA12-4104.pdf (accessed March 4, 2018).
6. Senreich E (2010) Are Specialized LGBT Program Components Helpful for Gay and Bisexual Men in Substance Abuse Treatment? *Substance Use & Misuse.* 45(7–8): 1077–1096.
7. HIV.gov (2017) Who Is at Risk for HIV? Washington, DC: U.S. Department of Health & Human Services. Available at: www.hiv.gov/hiv-basics/overview/about-hiv-and-aids/who-is-at-risk-for-hiv (accessed March 4, 2018).

**TABLE 6.7** Women

| Characteristics | Women face more barriers than men to treatment. In fact, while women are just as likely as men to develop addiction to substances, they are less likely to seek treatment than their male counterparts.[1] Substance use disorder also interferes in more areas of a woman's life than a man's.[2] Research also shows that women experience higher sensitivity to substances.[3] This manifests as a greater risk for a variety of medical and psychosocial consequences. |
| --- | --- |

It is thought that women respond to drugs in physiological ways; for example, hormonal fluctuations during menstruation cause different effects from substance use. Even more, women report more severe problems and experience more health-related consequences from substance use.[4] For example, when women do develop substance abuse problems, they tend to develop them faster than men.[5] In other words, women advance more than men in their progression from initial to regular use to abuse to first treatment (termed "telescoping").

Divorce, loss of child custody, or death of a partner or child can often trigger substance use in women. Further, women who are victims of domestic violence are at increased risk of substance abuse; addiction has been estimated to occur in 40–60% of cases of intimate partner violence.[6] Further, women experience higher rates of victims of sexual assault and domestic violence than men. In fact, many women who abuse substances were raised in families where there was chemical abuse, sexual abuse, violence, and other relational disconnections.[7] These family relationships form a basic model for the relationships women later develop with others. This is why significant consideration is also given to trauma, trauma-informed services, and integrated treatment for women with substance use disorders.

Drug use in women may also be associated with managing weight and physical appearance.[5] Indeed, several co-occurring disorders (eating disorders, anxiety, and depression) are comorbid with addiction and require attention during treatment. Other comorbid issues are shopping, hoarding, and gambling.

| | |
|---|---|
| Common signs of a problem | Caretaker. |
| | Acting on societal norms and pressures to remain quiet, thin, and pretty. |
| | Feel unheard or unknown. |
| | Lack of assertiveness. |
| | Lack of self-confidence. |
| | Powerlessness. |
| | Notions of femininity; meek and mild stereotypes. |
| | Homelessness. |
| | Relationships are central to identity. |
| | Relationships are the source of self-esteem. |
| | Seek emotional intimacy provided by shared drug use with a partner. |
| | Submissive. |
| | Women who use are more likely to be with a sexual partner who also uses. |
| Common objections to treatment | Can't take time away from the family or the children. |
| | Children need their mother. |
| | Single mothers who are breadwinners/caretakers are needed at home. |

(continued)

**TABLE 6.7** *(continued)*

| | |
|---|---|
| Counter-objections | Accepting treatment is an act of care for children.<br>Think of the impact it will have on the entire family, including the children.<br>You can begin to learn who you really are.<br>You can be the best mother/spouse/friend/colleague you can be.<br>You can finally feel peace. |
| Other barriers to treatment | Access to health insurance coverage.<br>Access to women-focused programs.<br>Lack of treatment centers specially equipped to allow children to live with mother while in treatment.<br>Cost.<br>Education; women with a high school education are more likely to stay in treatment.<br>Fear of dealing with past abuse.<br>Lack of childcare.<br>Histories of trauma and geographic, economic, and relationship/family.<br>Intrapersonal issues; individual factors, including health problems, psychological issues, cognitive functioning, motivational status, or treatment readiness, can be barriers to treatment.<br>Interpersonal, relational issues, including significant relationships, family dynamics, and support systems.<br>Sociocultural; social factors include cultural differences, the role of stigma, bias, and racism; societal attitudes; disparity in health services, or attitudes of healthcare providers toward women. |
| Special considerations | Because women are at greater risk for a variety of medical and psychosocial consequences, they may benefit from pharmacological and/or behavioral therapies that differ from those most beneficial for men.[8] For example, skills related to improving the quality of relationships – such as communication, stress management, assertiveness, problem-solving, and parenting – can be an important part of treatment. Additionally, many women will need to explore the connections between substance abuse and sexuality, body image, sexual identity, sexual abuse, and the fear of sex when they are alcohol- and drug-free.<br>Women-focused treatments for addiction can have positive outcomes.[9] Individual patient preferences or services for women that are provided by women should be considered. The idea is to provide an environment of comfort and support, which may be especially important for women who have a history of trauma. Adjunctive services, including parenting and family-related services, mental health and general medical services, comprehensive case management, and employment and economic supports, are also essential. |

The extended family often functions as a safety net that provides women with childcare, financial support, and emotional and spiritual guidance. Therefore, family therapy is an essential approach in substance abuse treatment for women. Treatment can alternatively help women connect with supports in the community: friends, work colleagues, and significant others that make up a "family of choice."

Finally, women mandated by the criminal justice system to enter treatment and who also had custody of their children are more likely to stay in treatment longer.[8] Conversely, pregnant women are more likely to spend less time in treatment; pregnancy interrupts treatment.[8]

1. Greenfield SF, Brooks AJ, Gordon SM, et al. (2007) Substance Abuse Treatment Entry, Retention, and Outcome in Women: A Review of the Literature. *Drug and Alcohol Dependence.* 86(1): 1–21.
2. Green C (2006) *Gender and Use of Substance Abuse Treatment Services.* Rockville, MD: National Institute on Alcohol Abuse and Alcoholism. Available at: https://pubs.niaaa.nih.gov/publications/arh291/55-62.htm (accessed March 4, 2018).
3. Hecksher D and Hesse M (2007) Women and Substance Use Disorders. *Mens Sana Monographs.* 7(1): 50–62.
4. United Nations (2004) *Substance Abuse Treatment and Care for Women: Case Studies and Lessons Learned.* Vienna: UN Office on Drugs and Crime. Available at: www.unodc.org/pdf/report_2004-08-30_1.pdf (accessed March 4, 2018).
5. Greenfield SF, Back SE, Lawson K, and Brady KT (2010) Substance Abuse in Women. *Psychiatric Clinics of North America.* 33(2): 339–355.
6. Soper RG (2014) Intimate Partner Violence and Co-Occurring Substance Abuse/Addiction. Rockville, MD: ASAM. Available at: www.asam.org/resources/publications/magazine/read/article/2014/10/06/intimate-partner-violence-and-co-occurring-substance-abuse-addiction (accessed March 4, 2018).
7. Center for Substance Abuse Treatment (2009) *Treatment Improvement Protocol (TIP) Series, No. 51. Substance Abuse Treatment: Addressing the Specific Needs of Women.* Rockville, MD: Substance Abuse and Mental Health Services Administration. Available at: www.ncbi.nlm.nih.gov/books/NBK83257/ (accessed March 4, 2018).
8. Polak K, Haug NA, Drachenberg HE, and Svikis DS (2015) Gender Considerations in Addiction: Implications for Treatment. *Current Treatment Options in Psychiatry.* 2(3): 326–338.
9. Greenfield SF and Grella CE (2009) What Is "Women-Focused" Treatment for Substance Use Disorders? *Psychiatric Services.* 60(7): 880–882.

**TABLE 6.8** Young women

| Characteristics | This demographic can be defined as 18 to 25 years old. There may be some minor discrepancy in this age group, as research trends standardize age groups differently. These women experience higher rates of poverty than male counterparts.[1] In fact, clinicians report greater medical, psychiatric, and social consequences from alcohol use compared to men.[2] Young women advance more quickly than men in their progression from initial to regular use to abuse to first treatment (termed "telescoping").[3] |
|---|---|

*(continued)*

TABLE 6.8 *(continued)*

A history of traumatic events particularly affecting this group, including sexual and physical assaults, childhood sexual and physical abuse,[4] and domestic violence, are significantly associated with initiation of substance use and the development of substance use disorders among women. Substance use occurs at higher rates because women with these disorders turn to substances to cope (self-medicate) with the depression or anxiety that results from the abuse. Conversely, substance use disorders increase a woman's vulnerability to additional trauma, decrease her ability to defend herself, alter her judgment, and draw her into unsafe environments.[1]

In comparison to men, women are more likely to have multiple comorbidity (three or more psychiatric diagnoses) in addition to substance use disorder.[5] This can include anxiety disorders, panic disorders, major depression, PTSD, and eating disorders. Specifically, the behavioral pattern of purging (not bingeing) appears to be associated more strongly with substance use in young women.[6]

Finally, women may experience varied levels of discrimination – based on gender, race, ethnicity, language, culture, socioeconomic status, sexual orientation, age, and disability – that affect their substance use.[1] When women experience more than one type of discrimination, the effect can be compounded. So, for some women, substance abuse may become a way of coping with the additional stresses of discrimination.

| | |
|---|---|
| Common signs of a problem | Anxious.<br>Difficulty in regulating affect and behavior (temper tantrums or frequent tearfulness).<br>History of over-responsibility with their family of origin.<br>Low self-worth.<br>Negative self-perception of physical attractiveness.<br>Novelty-seeking.<br>Obsessiveness.<br>Prone to depression.<br>Relationship with a significant other is a strong factor influencing a woman's introduction to alcohol and drugs.<br>Risk-taking behavior, especially regarding sex.<br>Sensation-seeking. |
| Common objections to treatment | Family responsibilities.<br>Fear of rejection.<br>Perceived lack of emotional and social support.<br>Stigma of weakness when considering entering treatment. |
| Counter-objections | Continued use makes you at risk and vulnerable to harm.<br>Treatment will positively affect emotional and psychological well-being. |
| Other barriers to treatment | Gender-responsive treatment requires understanding the biological, psychological, and social factors influencing women's substance use and recovery.<br>Age; women under 21 are less likely to successfully engage with and complete treatment.[1] |

| Special considerations | Like men, most women who have substance use disorders never receive treatment.[7] Self-referral, social service agencies, and the criminal justice system are the primary sources of referral to treatment for women.[1] In comparison to men, women are more likely to be identified with a substance use disorder through child protective services.[8] |
| --- | --- |
| | Depending on the specific drug class, some women may have considerable concerns regarding potential weight gain if they enter treatment and establish abstinence. Education regarding the disease of addiction, and its impact on physical, mental, and spiritual health, must be provided. |
| | Young women benefit from relationships with other women in recovery.[9] More often than not, women generally will underestimate the risks associated with past relationships, denying that these relationships are a current risk factor to relapse. A partner's substance use and attitudes toward substance use can influence a woman's substance use. So, each person close to her needs to develop attitudes and behaviors that will be supportive of the client's recovery. Likewise, clinicians can tap into their ability to be other-focused as a tool in developing motivation for recovery. |
| | Trauma is both a risk factor for and a consequence of substance abuse. Young women with histories of trauma may be using substances to self-medicate symptoms. Subsequently, interventions should be immediately put into place to help build coping strategies to manage strong affect, including relaxation training and other anxiety management skills. |

1. Center for Substance Abuse Treatment (2009) *Treatment Improvement Protocol (TIP) Series, No. 51. Substance Abuse Treatment: Addressing the Specific Needs of Women.* Rockville, MD: Substance Abuse and Mental Health Services Administration. Available at: www.ncbi.nlm.nih.gov/books/NBK83257/ (accessed March 4, 2018).

2. Bradley KA, Badrinath S, Bush K, et al. (1998) Medical Risks for Women Who Drink Alcohol. *Journal of General Internal Medicine.* 13: 627–639.

3. Greenfield SF, Back SE, Lawson K, and Brady KT (2010) Substance Abuse in Women. *Psychiatric Clinics of North America.* 33(2): 339–355.

4. Liebschutz J, Savetsky JB, Saitz R, Horton NJ, Lloyd-Travaglini C, and Samet JH (2002) The Relationship between Sexual and Physical Abuse and Substance Abuse Consequences. *Journal of Substance Abuse Treatment.* 22(3): 121–128.

5. Zilberman ML, Tavares H, Blume SB, and el-Guebaly N (2003) Substance Use Disorders: Sex Differences and Psychiatric Comorbidities. *Canadian Journal of Psychiatry.* 48(1): 5–13. Available at: http://journals.sagepub.com/doi/pdf/10.1177/070674370304800103 (accessed March 4, 2018).

6. Mann AP, Accurso EC, Stiles-Shields C, et al. (2014) Factors Associated with Substance Use in Adolescents with Eating Disorders. *Journal of Adolescent Health.* 55(2): 182–187.

7. Center for Behavioral Health Statistics and Quality (2017) *2016 National Survey on Drug Use and Health: Detailed Tables.* Rockville, MD: U.S. Department of Health and Human Services, Substance Abuse and Mental Health Services Administration. Available at: www.samhsa.gov/data/sites/default/files/NSDUH-FFR1-2016/NSDUH-FFR1-2016.pdf (accessed March 4, 2018).

8. Green C (2006) *Gender and Use of Substance Abuse Treatment Services.* Rockville, MD: National Institute on Alcohol Abuse and Alcoholism. Available at: https://pubs.niaaa.nih.gov/publications/arh291/55-62.htm (accessed March 4, 2018).

9. Hunter BA, Jason LA, and Keys CB (2013) Factors of Empowerment for Women in Recovery from Substance Use. *American Journal of Community Psychology.* 51(0): 91–102.

**TABLE 6.9** Pregnant women

| | |
|---|---|
| Characteristics | Women are more stigmatized by alcohol and illicit drug use than men, especially pregnant women. They are characterized as selfish, morally lax, sexually promiscuous, and neglectful. Substance use is associated with delayed prenatal care in pregnant women, a result of fears pertaining to potential legal consequences.[1] For example, pregnant women often fear that admitting a substance use problem will cause them to lose custody of their child/children. In addition, some women report that they use stimulants to help meet expectations associated with family responsibilities. These fears and stereotypes compound a woman's shame and guilt about substance use and interfere with help-seeking behavior. |
| | Continued substance abuse during pregnancy is a major risk factor for fetal distress, developmental abnormalities, and negative birth effects. First, substance abuse by a mother during pregnancy can cause dependence and withdrawal symptoms in newborns. Further, risk of stillbirth, miscarriage, congenital abnormalities, preterm delivery, low birth weight, and reduced gestational age for babies of women who use substances while pregnant is higher.[2] Postpartum depression – which is already common in women – can exacerbate or trigger drug use, as can hormonal imbalance during the pregnancy.[3] |
| | Additionally, pregnant women themselves who use drugs can experience adverse effects. For example, they can experience negative effects on the heart or blood vessels. Pregnant women are also highly influenced by high levels of hormones in the body. As a result, they are prone to not only migraines or fibromyalgia, but also to mood disorders which they may try to self-medicate through substances.[4] |
| | Women with substance use problems tend to have less money – and thereby less resources available to them – than men.[5] A pregnant woman may already have children; another is on the way. They may be victims of sexual assault; women who are victims of domestic violence are at increased risk of substance abuse.[6] Further, divorce, loss of child custody, or death of a partner or child can trigger substance abuse or mental health disorders. |
| Common signs of a problem | Fear prosecution or incarceration for substance use. |
| | Frequent or severe changes in mood due to pregnancy sex hormones. |
| | Possible victims of domestic violence. |
| Common objections to treatment | Boyfriend/partner/spouse may leave. |
| | Cost. |
| | Don't want to think about substance use. |
| | Don't want to leave family or children. |
| | Family denial. |
| | Family rejection. |
| | Fear of losing custody of child/children. |
| | Limited services for prenatal care or parenting help. |
| | Limited number of centers that will take pregnant women. |

| | |
|---|---|
| Counter-objections | Become a better mother to the child/children.<br>Life of the baby.<br>Long-term health of the child/children.<br>Vitality and improved quality of life. |
| Other barriers to treatment | Cycle of abuse.<br>Cycle of neglect.<br>Lack of treatment staff training and knowledge about needs.<br>Poverty.<br>Scarcity of treatment; treatment programs and resources for pregnant women who abuse substances are scarce. A limited number of treatment centers will take a mother and young children. |
| Special considerations | Federal law requires that pregnant women receive priority admission into substance abuse treatment programs, allowing them to bypass waiting lists and gain immediate admission when a bed in a residential program is available.[7] The primary treatment provider must secure prenatal care if a pregnant woman is not already receiving such care.<br>Pregnancy creates an increased sense of urgency for both clients and counselors because of the temporary upswing in motivation to change and the need for problem resolution.[8] For some women, pregnancy creates a window of opportunity to enter treatment, become abstinent, quit smoking, eliminate risk-taking behaviors, and lead generally healthier lives.[9] These women can temporarily alter their pattern of use in response to pregnancy. For example, women might cut back on or establish abstinence of alcohol and illicit drugs while pregnant, even though they are as likely to resume use later on.<br>Brief interventions using motivational interviewing are sometimes effective in helping pregnant women stop using substances.[10] While in treatment, comprehensive case management that involves medical and social case management is an essential ingredient to treatment. Still, substance abuse habits often begin before and may continue after coming to term with pregnancy; education regarding disease of addiction, and its impact on physical, mental, and spiritual health, must be provided.[8]<br>For many women, having their children with them in treatment is essential to their recovery and removes a barrier to treatment entry.[8]<br>For a woman entering treatment, the tendency to focus on problems or stressors other than her substance use is quite normal. Women are socialized to assume more caregiver roles and to focus attention on others. Even if she has not appropriately cared for others (such as her children) during addiction, it does not mean that she will not see this as an important issue. Clinicians need to appreciate this gender difference; instead of assuming that worries and the tendency to be other-focused is a detriment, you can use these concerns as a means of motivation throughout treatment. |

*(continued)*

**TABLE 6.9** *(continued)*

|  |  |
|---|---|
|  | Some detox programs will not treat a pregnant woman because they lack the necessary obstetrical support and are concerned about liability. Indeed, there is concern here. Detoxification presents critical risks to a fetus, and withdrawal of a pregnant woman from addictive drugs or alcohol should always be accompanied by close medical supervision and monitoring. Detoxification should only be performed under medical supervision. |

1. Stone R (2015) Pregnant Women and Substance Use: Fear, Stigma, and Barriers to Care. *Health & Justice.* 3(2).
2. Forray A (2016) Substance Use during Pregnancy. *F1000Research.* 5 (F1000 Faculty Rev): 887.
3. Ross LE and Dennis CL (2009) The Prevalence of Postpartum Depression among Women with Substance Use, an Abuse History, or Chronic Illness: A Systematic Review. *Journal of Women's Health.* 18(4): 475–486.
4. Grella CE (1997) Services for Perinatal Women with Substance Abuse and Mental Health Disorders: The Unmet Need. *Journal of Psychoactive Drugs.* 29(1): 67–78.
5. Lewis RA, Haller DL, Branch D, and Ingersoll KS (1996) Retention Issues Involving Drug-Abusing Women in Treatment Research (pp. 110–122). *Treatment for Drug-Exposed Women and Their Children: Advances in Research Methodology, NIDA Research Monograph 166.* Rockville, MD: National Institute on Drug Abuse.
6. Office of Research on Women's Health (2013) *Trans-HHS Intimate Partner Violence Screening and Counseling: Research Symposium.* Rockville, MD: Women's Health Resources. Available at: http://whr.nlm.nih.gov/ipv-symposium.html#b00 (accessed March 4, 2018).
7. U.S. Congress (2011) *42 U.S.C. 300X-27: Treatment Services for Pregnant Women.* Washington, DC: U.S. Congress. Available at: www.gpo.gov/fdsys/granule/USCODE-2010-title42/USCODE-2010-title42-chap6A-subchapXVII-partB-subpartii-sec300x-27 (accessed March 4, 2018).
8. Center for Substance Abuse Treatment (2009) *Treatment Improvement Protocol (TIP) Series, No. 51. Substance Abuse Treatment: Addressing the Specific Needs of Women.* Rockville, MD: Substance Abuse and Mental Health Services Administration. Available at: www.ncbi.nlm.nih.gov/books/NBK83257/ (accessed March 4, 2018).
9. Hankin J, McCaul ME, and Heussner J (2000) Pregnant, Alcohol-Abusing Women. *Alcoholism: Clinical and Experimental Research.* 24(8): 1276–1286.
10. Miller WR (2000) Rediscovering Fire: Small Interventions, Large Effects. *Psychology of Addictive Behaviors.* 14(1): 6–18.

**TABLE 6.10** Women with children

| Characteristics | Women with substance use disorders frequently have to overcome feelings of guilt and shame, not only for how they treat children while using substances, but also for social reasons.[1] The societal stigma toward women tends to be greater than that toward men, and this stigma can prevent women from seeking or admitting they need help. In many states, parenting women can be reported to child protective services, lose custody of their children, or be prosecuted for using drugs.[2] |
|---|---|
|  | Women who are mothers and who face substance use problems must find a way to support themselves and their children, often with little experience or education and few job skills. Some |

rely on child support. Many have problems with money and financial stability.

A high proportion of women with substance use disorders have histories of trauma, often perpetrated by persons they both knew and trusted.[3] Sexual or physical abuse is common; many women witness such violence as children. Women with children may further be experiencing domestic violence such as battering by a partner or rape as an adult. Women self-medicate with addictive substances to mask pain associated with this underlying trauma, including past and ongoing domestic violence, as well as childhood abuse and neglect.

Breastfeeding women who experience substance abuse disorders can have adverse effects on infants, even while it may be beneficial;[4] risk of withdrawal in infants is high after drug dependence occurs. Finally, gender role expectations in many cultures result in further stigmatization of substance use; additional challenges face women who are of color, disabled, lesbians, older, and poor.

| | |
|---|---|
| Common signs of a problem | Caretaker. |
| | Low self-efficacy. |
| | Low self-esteem. |
| | Not liked by other women. |
| | Relationships are central to identity. |
| | Report emotional intimacy provided by shared drug use with a partner. |
| | Tendency to ignore own needs. |
| Common objections to treatment | Access to resources. |
| | Cost. |
| | Fear of no positive outcomes. |
| | Need for childcare. |
| | Single moms may work multiple jobs/take care of kids and can't make commitment. |
| Counter-objections | Consider the emotional/psychological impact on children. |
| | Her health determines the long-term health and vitality of children. |
| | Long-term recovery offers a life of satisfaction and contentedness. |
| | She is not alone; coordinated care can be arranged. |
| | The life and well-being of the mother is valuable. |
| Other barriers to treatment | Competing timetables and perspectives on the purposes of recovery from social services. |
| | Poverty. |
| | Scarcity of appropriate and available care; a limited number of treatment centers will accept women and their children. |
| Special considerations | Overall, women in residential treatment accompanied by their children showed better outcomes (abstinence, employment, child custody, and involvement with continuing care or support groups) than women not accompanied by their children at six months after discharge.[5] In fact, women who |

(continued)

**TABLE 6.10** *(continued)*

complete treatment that allows children in residence have less psychological distress and improved skills for independent living, parenting, employment, and relationships.[2]

Additionally, children of women in treatment have many of their own needs that cannot simply be addressed by the provision of childcare and residential living space. These needs are addressed when children are provided services directly, as well as when the needs of their parents are met.

Mothers in treatment continue to care for children, even if they do not have custody of them.[2] In some cases, the mother in treatment may not currently have custody and the daily responsibility for the care of her children. Those cases require special considerations by treatment providers to assist the woman in her efforts to regain custody if appropriate, and, when regaining custody is not an option, assist the mother as she transitions in the loss of her children.

1. Lal R, Deb KS, and Kedia S (2015) Substance Use in Women: Current Status and Future Directions. *Indian Journal of Psychiatry*. 57(2): S275–S285.
2. Center for Substance Abuse Treatment (2000) *Substance Abuse Treatment for Persons with Child Abuse and Neglect Issues: Treatment Improvement Protocol (TIP) Series, No. 36.* Rockville. MD: Substance Abuse and Mental Health Services Administration. Available at: www.ncbi.nlm.nih.gov/books/NBK64892/ (accessed March 4, 2018).
3. Center for Substance Abuse Treatment (2009) *Treatment Improvement Protocol (TIP) Series, No. 51. Substance Abuse Treatment: Addressing the Specific Needs of Women.* Rockville, MD: Substance Abuse and Mental Health Services Administration. Available at: www.ncbi.nlm.nih.gov/books/NBK83257/ (accessed March 4, 2018).
4. Reece-Stremtan S and Marinelli KA (2015) ABM Clinical Protocol #21: Guidelines for Breastfeeding and Substance Use or Substance Use Disorder. *Breastfeeding Medicine.* 10(3): 135–141.
5. Stevens SJ and Patton T (1998) Residential Treatment for Drug Addicted Women and Their Children: Effective Treatment Strategies (pp. 235–249). *Women and Substance Abuse: Gender Transparency.* New York: Haworth Press.

**TABLE 6.11** Women in prison

| | |
|---|---|
| Characteristics | The number of women in prison increased by more than 700% from 1980 to 2015.[1] In fact, since 2010, women have been the fastest-growing population in prison.[2] The average prison term for incarcerated women is 15 months. As a result, an increasing number of female prisoners are permanently banned from their children's lives, as state laws terminate parental rights when children are in foster care from 15 to 22 months.[3] |
| | Across the world, prison statistics show that a higher percentage of women than men are in prison for drug offenses.[4] Two of three women who go to prison have substance abuse problems.[5] Furthermore, according to the U.S. Department of Justice, an estimated 52% of females in comparison to 44% of males incarcerated in local jails were dependent on or abusing drugs.[3] |

Compared to their male counterparts, female inmates are more likely to have mental disorders, to be HIV-positive, to have been physically or sexually abused, and to have lived with their children in the month prior to their arrest.[3] In fact, the majority of these women suffered serious physical or sexual abuse as children. Furthermore, three-quarters have histories of severe physical abuse by an intimate partner in adulthood.[3] It is also estimated that one-quarter of women who enter prison are pregnant or have a child who is 1 year or younger.[3]

| | |
|---|---|
| Common signs of a problem | Do not feel safe. |
| | Feel guilty. |
| | Internalized sense of criminalization. |
| | Low self-awareness. |
| | Low self-esteem. |
| | Self-blame. |
| | Shame. |
| | Traumatized. |
| Common objections to treatment | Cost. |
| | Lack of addiction treatment programs through criminal justice system. |
| | Limited resources within prison. |
| | Who takes care of the children? |
| Counter-objections | We can work to develop therapeutic services offered at prisons to help with substance abuse/mental health. |
| | Legislation exists in some states to offer job training to incarcerated women. |
| Other barriers to treatment | Difficult to get a job/stable life when released from prison. |
| | Legislation or the current political will tends to place women – especially female minorities – into prisons over treatment programs. |
| | Limited resources make it very difficult for women in prison to get help. |
| | Limited rehabilitation programs within prisons. |
| Special considerations | Co-occurring disorders coupled with histories of sexual/physical abuse require ongoing treatment in this population. Diversion models such as TASC, DTAP, and SACPA have been shown to reduce drug use and recidivism.[6] Still, regardless of treatment duration, intermittent and ongoing access to supportive treatment personnel after formal programming is over are critical.[7] Counseling can address issues specific to women, such as dependency, physical and sexual abuse, job skills training, and parenting. |

For women, the more time spent in treatment, the more likely self-esteem will increase, especially in a residential/inpatient setting.[3] A residential treatment community helps women build awareness of their strengths and helps them "practice" having higher self-esteem. Unhealthy situations after treatment can occur (domestic abuse, a job with low pay and high stress),

(continued)

**TABLE 6.11** *(continued)*

and appropriate transition through social services advocacy or support groups is helpful.

The presence of children can be a mother's only link to a stable life. After losing child custody, some women increase substance abuse. Research suggests that it is in the best interest of both mothers and their children to have continued interactions while the woman is incarcerated.[3]

1. Carson EA (2015) Prisoners in 2014. Washington, DC: Bureau of Justice Statistics. Available at: www.bjs.gov/content/pub/pdf/p14.pdf (accessed March 4, 2018).
2. Glaze LE (2014) Correctional Populations in the United States: 2013. Washington, DC: Bureau of Justice Statistics. Available at: www.bjs.gov/content/pub/pdf/cpus13.pdf (accessed March 4, 2018).
3. Center for Substance Abuse Treatment (2005) *Treatment Improvement Protocol (TIP) Series 44: Substance Abuse Treatment for Adults in the Criminal Justice System.* Rockville, MD: Substance Abuse and Mental Health Services Administration. Available at: https://store.samhsa.gov/shin/content//SMA13-4056/SMA13-4056.pdf (accessed March 4, 2018).
4. Penal Reform International (2015) *Global Prison Trends 2015.* London: Penal Reform International. Available at: www.unodc.org/documents/ungass2016/Contributions/Civil/PenalReform/Drugs_and_imprisonment_PRI_submission_UNGASS.pdf (accessed March 4, 2018).
5. Grella C (2008) Quality Improvement for Drug Courts: Monograph Series 9. *Gender-Responsive Drug Treatment Services for Women: A Summary of Current Research and Recommendations for Drug Court Programs.* Washington, DC: National Drug Court Institute.
6. Belenko S, Hiller M, and Hamilton L (2013) Treating Substance Use Disorders in the Criminal Justice System. *Current Psychiatry Reports.* 15(11): 414.
7. Finfgeld-Connett D and Johnson ED (2011) Substance Abuse Treatment for Women Who Are Under Correctional Supervision in the Community: A Systematic Review of Qualitative Findings. *Issues in Mental Health Nursing.* 32(10): 640–648.

**TABLE 6.12** Chronic pain

| Characteristics | Some 133 million Americans experience or have had an episode of chronic pain.[1] Further, Americans spend $560–635 billion in medical costs treating and managing chronic pain annually.[2] In the United States, our culture has normalized consuming prescription drugs; prescriptions are easily obtainable, available, and relatively inexpensive. |
|---|---|
| | Doctors, who are simultaneously incentivized by big pharma and feel pressure to avoid lawsuits from patients, began prescribing opioid prescriptions in the 1990s. In fact, I am of the opinion that opioids are prescribed and overprescribed to manage pain. As a result, many people who are diagnosed pain patients become addicted to opioid prescriptions. Typically, analgesic and anxiolytic efficacy diminishes over the course of weeks, months, or years as tolerance develops. This often elicits dose escalation. With time, prescription pain pills have become a gateway to other drugs such as heroin and fentanyl (75% of heroin users started on prescription drugs).[3] |

It is important to note that chronic is different than acute pain; it persists and stresses the body. Continued pain can trigger emotional responses that create a feedback cycle and produce more pain. Physical pain increases when an emotional factor is present and is exacerbated by factors such as physical inactivity and overuse of sedating drugs. Additionally, chronic pain and addiction have many shared neurophysiological patterns, as well as similar physical, social, emotional, and economic effects on health and well-being. Insomnia, depression, anxiety, and impaired functioning are symptoms frequently reported when one or both conditions is present.

Further, research is showing us how chronic pain may stem from childhood and can fuel an addiction.[4] Therefore, physical pain (acute or chronic) brought on by a traumatic event (in addition to emotional pain) may also be a trigger for substance abuse disorders.

| | |
|---|---|
| Common signs of a problem | Anxious. |
| | Chronically irritable. |
| | Depressive. |
| | Disinterest in natural rewards. |
| | Dysphoric. |
| | Emotional pain. |
| | Lethargic. |
| | Preoccupation with substance that provides relief. |
| | Reactive, especially to stress. |
| | Seeking to escape pain, not necessarily euphoric effect. |
| | Suicidal ideation. |
| Common objections to treatment | Cannot function without opioids. This is, in fact, a medical issue of dependence and possible tolerance. |
| | Denial of the problem. |
| | Family expectations and shame. |
| | Fear of the condition of unbearable pain. |
| | Lack of alternative treatments; how else to treat chronic pain other than painkillers? |
| Counter-objections | Cravings pass when hedonic tone and conditioned responses resolve. |
| | Detoxification is usually quick and technically easy. |
| | Long-term health will improve. |
| | Long-term abuse of prescription pills can have lasting effects on brain chemistry and bodily function. |
| Other barriers to treatment | Disjointed, uncoordinated care. |
| | Inadequate clinical reimbursement for treatment and/or patient. |
| | Inadequate provider knowledge about treatment of pain or limited access to pain specialists. |
| | Lack of consensus on how to treat pain. |
| | Legal issues for controlled substances. |
| | Opioid-induced hyperalgesia; opioids heighten sensitivity to pain and make the person believe the pain is worse than it is. |
| | Stigma within healthcare system to treat pain. |

(continued)

**TABLE 6.12** *(continued)*

| | |
|---|---|
| Special considerations | Currently, huge public policy and health concerns exist for managing chronic pain with the opioid epidemic. The number one cause of death under age 50 is now prescription opioid drugs;[5] new technologies/studies/medical breakthroughs must be addressed to combat this public health crisis.<br><br>Patients must take on a significant amount of responsibility for optimal management of pain. Effective treatment goals are possible and should include improved functioning and pain reduction. But even the best treatment is unlikely to completely eliminate chronic pain; aiming for 100% total pain relief can be self-defeating.<br><br>To guide the process, treatment agreements document the treatment plan and the responsibilities of both the patient and the clinician. A team approach of psychologists, addiction counselors, pharmacists, and holistic care providers can help. A team approach that includes complementary and alternative therapies, including mindfulness, yoga, qigong, acupuncture, spinal manipulation, physical therapy, breath work, outdoor adventure, and life skill training, along with CBT, ACT, and DBT skills, is helpful with this population. |

1. Nahin RL (2015) Estimates of Pain Prevalence and Severity in Adults. *Journal of Pain.* 16(8): 769–780.
2. Institute of Medicine Committee on Advancing Pain Research, Care, and Education (2011) *Relieving Pain in America: A Blueprint for Transforming Prevention, Care, Education, and Research.* Washington, DC: National Academies Press. Available at: www.ncbi.nlm.nih.gov/books/NBK92521/ (accessed March 4, 2018).
3. Cicero TJ, Ellis MS, Surratt HL, and Kurtz SP (2014) The Changing Face of Heroin Use in the United States: A Retrospective Analysis of the Past 50 Years. *JAMA Psychiatry.* 71(7): 821–826.
4. Mirhashem R, Allena HC, Adams ZW, van Stolk Cooke K, Legrand A, and Price M (2017) The Intervening Role of Urgency on the Association between Childhood Maltreatment, PTSD, and Substance-Related Problems. *Addictive Behaviors.* 69(6): 98–103.
5. National Academies of Sciences, Engineering, and Medicine, editors Phillips JK, Ford MA, and Bonnie RJ (2017) *Pain Management and the Opioid Epidemic: Balancing Societal and Individual Benefits and Risks of Prescription Opioid Use.* Washington, DC: National Academies Press. Available at: www.ncbi.nlm.nih.gov/books/NBK458661/ (accessed March 4, 2018).

**TABLE 6.13** Professionals

| | |
|---|---|
| Characteristics | Extensive substance use can be a part of the work culture, in which high-pressure demands and competition are encouraged. Sometimes professionals misuse drugs for enhanced performance, while others self-medicate for stress relief. Or people may start out using these substances to treat pain or a mental illness and become addicted when they do not take them as prescribed. |

In my experience, some of the most commonly abused substances among workforce professionals and executives include alcohol, marijuana, prescription stimulants, cocaine, prescription sedatives, opiates, and prescription painkiller medications. In certain occupations, drugs or prescriptions for drugs are easy to obtain.

| | |
|---|---|
| Common signs of a problem | Aggression.<br>A sense of entitlement.<br>Frequent tardiness or work absence.<br>Frequent mood changes.<br>Increasing irresponsibility.<br>Irritability.<br>Lower performance at work.<br>Narcissism.<br>Paranoia or extreme anxiety.<br>Unsociable, or problems getting along with others. |
| Common objections to treatment | I have a company to run.<br>I'm in the middle of negotiating a big deal.<br>I have an important meeting.<br>No one else can know; I'll lose my license (nurses, doctors, lawyers, pilots).<br>I'm very important and can't take time away from my business.<br>I'm not an addict; those people are unkempt and unsuccessful.<br>I have control over my drug use.<br>My drug use helps me and doesn't get in the way of my responsibilities.<br>I don't want my social network to know about my addiction problem. |
| Counter-objections | Concierge treatment that allows the person to accommodate work demands and treat addiction at the same time.<br>Destigmatizing message: addiction is a medical condition.<br>HIPAA laws protect the privacy of a person seeking treatment.<br>Offer relatable examples of people in high positions who are in recovery.<br>"I understand that you have really important business priorities; we'll make special accommodations."<br>You are legally allowed to take a medical health leave. |
| Other barriers to treatment | License issues. |
| Special considerations | In this population, there is a difference between executives and licensed professionals whose license is dependent upon drug-free testing. Professions that face legal and professional licensure problems as a result of substance use disorders include:<br><br>• health professionals (medical doctors, dentists, nurses, pharmacists, etc.);<br>• lawyers; |

(continued)

TABLE 6.13 *(continued)*

- pilots;
- drivers; and
- heavy machinery operators.

These individuals face the loss of their profession and require special consideration during interventions. Confidentiality is of utmost importance, and professionals can be matched with treatment centers accordingly.

Many working professionals are used to being in charge and will need to be an active part in decision-making. Further, corporate or employee programs may offer subsidized funding for addiction treatment.

## TABLE 6.14 High wealth

| | |
|---|---|
| Characteristics | This demographic is wealthy, either self-made or having inherited money from a family legacy, including old and new business ventures as well as investments. There is immense pressure to succeed, accomplish, and add to family wealth. The IP is commonly surrounded by a group of enablers who perpetuate dysfunctional patterns. |
| | In terms of addictions, substance and alcohol use are typically present. In my experience, these may be accompanied by gambling, sex, shopping sprees, and other process addiction disorders. |
| Common signs of a problem | Arrogant. |
| | Belief in being indestructible. |
| | Belief in self-importance and being better than others. |
| | Entitled. |
| | Narcissistic. |
| | Unrealistic expectations. |
| Common objections to treatment | Collective denial (emperor's new clothes situation); the family, friends, or individual claim there is no problem. |
| | Enablers, including family and staff, cover up problems and abuse. |
| | Fear of legal consequences, loss of status or considerations. |
| | Fear of stepping away from business, duties, or responsibilities. |
| | Want to avoid media exposure or the family in the spotlight. |
| Counter-objections | This will end of the cycle of bailouts and abuse. |
| | Treatment will ensure the safety of employees and the longevity of the business enterprise. |
| | Validate victims and survivors of neglect and abuse. |

| | |
|---|---|
| Other barriers to treatment | Family expectations and secrets. |
| | Impact on business ventures or jobs for large groups of people. |
| | May not want to spend the money. |
| | Political/economic ramifications. |
| Special considerations | Clinicians are privy to the scope of wealth within the family. Therefore, confidentiality is necessary. It may also be helpful to consult with wealth managers, legal teams, accounting teams, and other members of their team |
| | Treatment providers or treatment centers must ensure the privacy of the individual, as well as show sensitivities to family and business privacy. |

**TABLE 6.15** Celebrities and other high-profile folks

| | |
|---|---|
| Characteristics | This demographic of people prioritizes their self-made brand identity and image in the spotlight. Their outer appearance takes precedence over inner turmoil. They are often under intense scrutiny. They often feel that they have unlimited power, influence, and money. Regardless of the substance of choice, their power and influence make them feel indestructible. |
| | This demographic can include athletes, creators of high-tech, or entertainment stars who characteristically have an unrealistic goal of being the best. They are in relentless pursuit to one-up themselves. |
| Common signs of a problem | Argumentative. |
| | Not being able to perform at the top level. |
| | Narcissistic and self-consumed. |
| | Helpers continually bailing out or covering up. |
| Common objections to treatment | "I am strong enough to overcome the problem on my own." |
| | Fear of hurting public image. |
| | Fear of ruining brand identity and losing endorsements, sponsorships, audience, or public opinion. |
| | Privacy concerns. |
| | Reliance on substance to perform, win, or be the best. |
| Counter-objections | Can use power and influence for good and create positive change. |
| | Exposure can shine spotlight on under-reported or invisible issue. |
| | For sports, long-term danger to health. |
| | The journey to recovery can boost brand image. |
| | The journey to recovery can be an inspiration to others. |
| Other barriers to treatment | Family or legacy issues. |
| | Fear of letting fans or audience down. |
| | Privacy. |

(continued)

**TABLE 6.15** *(continued)*

| | |
|---|---|
| Special considerations | Celebrities may require some special accommodations, recovery coaches to go on tour, and executive protection. Family work needs to be extended to include the business team as well as the nuclear family. Other powerful and media-exposed people with relationships will enable and hide destructive behavior. |

## Reference

1. Brown B (2015) *Rising Strong*. New York: Penguin Random House.

# 7

# DIFFICULT INTERVENTIONS

## Point-Counterpoint

## Why Are Some Interventions More Difficult than Others?

During an intervention, our task as clinicians is to always look for an opening within individuals and family systems. Openings keep the path to wellness clear. However, at times, an intervention can become difficult. Complications arise. The level of systemic dysregulation may be deeper that you initially observe.

*There will always be someone who's going to object to an intervention.*

Note that the objection does not always originate from the ILO. Within a family unit, homeostasis exists that unconsciously keeps someone in their current role as the "troubled" or "troublesome" family member. If the ILO gets help, members of the family also have to look at their behaviors and change. There is no longer a label of "troubled person" or "problem."

When addiction is present in a family, people start to identify an individual as the "troubled one," when in fact each member of the accountability team is actually playing a role in the illness. The people who are surrounding the IP may be just as problematic as the person using drugs or alcohol.

Many times, treatment represents the need to change; family members may resist. Sometimes the ILO will *want treatment*, but a parent or partner will find excuses to avoid or sabotage the intent of finding wellness. In these cases, a "reverse intervention" is required. A reverse intervention occurs when the IP asks for help but the payor and other concerned individuals require intervention. Other times, addiction may occur with co-occurring mental illness, or an intervention will lead to the discovery of multiple member mental illness. Still other times, trauma is at the heart of substance use.

This chapter aims to give you the tools that you need to identify more difficult situations so that you can apply different approaches to a complicated intervention.

Addiction nearly never occurs in a vacuum. Substance use disorder presents as a signal to larger, more complex family problems. This is why, as clinicians, it is imperative that we remain open and flexible. We must also be prepared.

Following are the most common types of difficult interventions that clinicians will encounter, with case studies for each.

## Dual Diagnosis

Many people who are diagnosed with substance use disorder also have mental health issues. This is called "dual diagnosis" or co-occurring disorder. The American Psychiatric Association's definition of a mental health disorder, as classified in the 5th edition of the *Diagnostic and Statistical Manual of Mental Health Disorders*, is rather broad.[1] In common parlance, the APA states:

*Mental illness is a condition that affects a person's thinking, feeling, or mood.*

A mental health condition isn't the result of one isolated life event. Research suggests that multiple, linking causes (comorbidity) affect the appearance of a mental health problem.[2] Scientists generally agree that a combination of genetics, environment, and lifestyle influence whether someone develops a mental health condition such as addiction, or not.[3]

Further, mental health problems are widespread. The National Alliance on Mental Illness reports that one in five American adults experiences a mental health condition every year.[4] Further, mental illness is frequently present with addiction. According to the 2016 National Survey on Drug Use and Health, an estimated 8.2 million people aged 18 or older in the United States (3.4% of the entire population) experience both a mental disorder and substance use disorder simultaneously; that's 43.3% of the 19 million adults with a past year substance use disorder.[5]

Symptoms for mental health disorders can vary greatly. Warning signs include extreme mood changes, confused thinking or problems concentrating, avoiding social activities, and thoughts of suicide. These symptoms can overlap with those experienced during addiction, but can be difficult to spot. The most common mental health illnesses diagnosed with addiction include:

- ADHD;
- anxiety disorders;
- bipolar disorder;
- borderline personality disorder;
- depression;
- dissociative disorders;
- early psychosis and psychosis;
- eating disorders;

- obsessive-compulsive disorder;
- post-traumatic stress disorder;
- schizo-affective disorder; and
- schizophrenia.

## Case Study 1: Dual Diagnosis, Where Mental Health Came First

Elena was a 22-year-old female who had dropped out of college. Soft-spoken and quiet, she spent hours alone in her room, contemplating what to do. When we spoke with her, she hardly spoke above a whisper and cried easily. Her mother reported a history of depression in the family, and Elena self-reported she was extremely sad and smoked marijuana daily to calm herself.

In looking for a treatment center, and in exploring her past, it became obvious that she spent long periods of time alone and was afraid to act. At age 17, she had been sent to wilderness treatment for her depression. In this instance, Elena was hurting, and she readily agreed to seek help as she was isolated, alone, and frightened. She hated the way she felt, and in truth a simple conversation was all it took to motivate her to treatment.

A center was chosen that excelled in mental health and offered an integrated life skill approach to recovery. Elena stayed in primary treatment for 120 days, then transferred to structured living, relapsed as she stopped taking her prescribed medication after seven months of healthy living, and re-entered the same primary treatment center for another 30 days to help her get back on track. She had experienced a severe setback: shaving her head, using pot and cocaine, and going off prescribed medications. However, reinitiating treatment stabilized Elena and led to a period of lasting recovery.

## Other Medical Conditions

There are a host of medical conditions that can occur when dealing with substance use. Indeed, people who suffer from addiction often have one or more accompanying medical issues, which may include stroke, cancer, and mental disorders, as covered in Chapter 6 as "dual diagnosis" cases. Some of the issues I've come across frequently include:

- asthma;
- cancer;
- cardiovascular/heart disease;
- chronic pain;
- diabetes;
- lung disease; and
- thyroid disease.

**TABLE 7.1** Dual diagnosis

| | |
|---|---|
| Characteristics | Either disorder can develop first. People experiencing mental illness may turn to substances as a form of self-medication. In the case of chronic pain, anxiety and depression may appear due to changes in mobility, work, or relationships. Research shows that alcohol and other drugs worsen the symptoms of mental illnesses. And while one disorder may be acting out, another one can go off in a different direction to avoid detection. |
| Common signs of a problem | Anxiety. Depression. Delusion. Isolation. Not medication-compliant. Psychosis. Repetitive behaviors. Stopped taking medication. Suicidal ideation. Lack of focus. |
| Common objections to treatment | "I can do this myself; I don't need treatment." "This place isn't qualified." "I've done this before." "How's it been working for you? Looks to me like . . ." [CONSEQUENCES] |
| Counter-objections | Self-reports from the accountability team. Teach about hyperalgesia. "What you're doing now is not working, so let's try something different." It can be helpful to include the ILO's primary physician in the intervention team. The physician has experienced them and knows that the use of mind-altering substances is not helping. They can be a professional witness to the abuse, as this individual puts much credence in medical experts. |

| | |
|---|---|
| Other barriers to treatment | Psychotic breaks may occur. However, you don't know what's going on with people because they may be experiencing substance-induced psychosis or a mental health triggered psychosis. It's hard to determine what is going on neurologically until the substance clears. In order to understand the nature of delusions, patients need to seek specialized dual diagnosis care. To find out which came first, it is essential to interview individuals separately, and to investigate: |

- legal history;
- physical medical history; and
- family history.

| | |
|---|---|
| Special considerations | This way, clinicians can create an accurate family map and develop a portrait of the ILO. Next, clients need to establish a period of abstinence (four to six weeks) so that clinicians can identify substance abuse as primary or secondary. The goal is to identify multiple issues and then prioritize appropriate intervention strategies or treatment. |

Family history and presenting issues are one way to signal possible mental health problems. Sometimes people may have been assigned a mental health diagnosis. During an initial assessment, one looks at these identifiers to help you understand the behaviors and understand how to deal with them. However, until people are detoxed, treatment facilities cannot complete neurological and psychological testing until three weeks into treatment. In the interim, use past medical records, self-reports about the individual, what they're doing, and your knowledge about who they are serve as indicators.

Picking the right treatment center is essential in cases of dual diagnosis. The best treatment for dual diagnosis is integrated, when a person receives care for both their diagnosed mental illness and substance abuse.

Any addiction treatment provider must be clear that they have the staff and modalities to treat underlying disorders. If it's a primary mental health disorder that presents, an addiction treatment center will not be able to adequately treat the problem. Interventions that involve dual diagnosis cases often do not end up in a group meeting. Indeed, they can take more than one gathering and can take time and a few repeated visits. These specialized interventions require an active facilitator. Further, they can be volatile and may involve courts, law enforcement, or medical facilities. Keep this in mind: teaching families and the ILO is imperative. Understanding the effect emotions have on chronic pain and how the brain affects chronic pain (hyperalgesia) as one prepares for an intervention is helpful.

From the outset, a medical history is paramount. One becomes aware of health issues while doing a biopsychosocial assessment for the ILO with the family of origin. Imaging scans, chest X-rays, and blood tests can show the damaging effects of long-term drug abuse throughout the body. In addition, some drugs of abuse, such as inhalants, are toxic to nerve cells and may damage or destroy them, either in the brain or the peripheral nervous system. Dental records are also important in identifying drug misuse and abuse, as well as disordered eating.

> *Identifying physical problems is one goal of completely a robust assessment; at times, there are limitations. If needed, refer an IP for more diagnostic testing or pass on case notes to the addiction treatment center for follow-up.*

Of note here is that illness can become the stabilizing force in maintaining family homeostasis. Interpersonal conflicts are overshadowed by dealing with a "sick" person or yielding a "sick role" within the family system. Further, pain can serve as an attention-getter. For example, a mother may feel abandoned by her grown children and illness can bring them back. Or a young adult child may get more attention than their siblings due to an illness.

However, a person experiencing illness may also manifest symptoms that are difficult for others to cope with. They may add stress to the family via emotional outbursts. They may shift increased responsibility for maintaining home and income to other members. Plus, they may seek an audience for their misery. They may receive excuses from chores or work, ultimately resulting in imbalance and resentment.

> *I've found that medical conditions combined with substance use are incredibly stressful. Not only does the IP despair; they may lose hope for the future. Paradoxically, family begin to doubt the veracity of the medical problem.*

**TABLE 7.2** Other medical conditions

| | |
|---|---|
| Common signs of a problem | Anger. |
| | Defensive. |
| | Dependence on medication. |
| | Doctor shopping. |
| | Fluctuating activity levels. |
| | Frustration. |
| | Repetitive surgeries. |
| | Isolation at home. |
| | Unpredictable mood swings. |
| | Loss of friends, job, and productivity. |
| | Loss of plans and hope for the future. |
| | Sleep problem. |
| | Weight gain. |

| Common objections to treatment | "I am sick; this is a medical problem and I'm not a drug addict."<br>"My doctor said so."<br>"I'm afraid I'll be in pain." |
|---|---|
| Counter-objections | Hope through explanation of brain changes and neuroplasticity.<br>You can respect pain and learn to live with it; alternative and complementary treatment modalities.<br>Leverage attachment to healthy living. |
| Special considerations | Treatment needs to take into consideration the medical needs of the ILO. For example, a treatment center must be selected that specializes in chronic pain if it is present. If needed, you can refer an ILO to more diagnostic testing or pass on case notes to the addiction treatment center for follow-up. |

In my experience, I've found that people don't hurt as much if they have something better to do. As an interventionist, I reshift focus to work and activities to set goals, not to pain tolerance. Empowerment through goal-setting is helpful to everyone. One can focus on change management of the three M's:

1. *Medical.* What signs, symptoms, or diagnosis of illness are present?
2. *Movement.* What type, how often, and how much exercise is the ILO getting?
3. *Mindful.* How does the person take care of the inner self?

## Multiple Addictions

Multiple addictions include cross-substance use and substances combined with process addictions. While there is much debate about the diagnosis of process addictions, it is important to recognize that these compulsive behaviors share significant clinical traits with substance use disorder, including:

- loss of control;
- loss of time;
- compulsive behavior;
- efforts to stop are futile;
- preoccupation with the behavior;
- inability to fulfill obligations;
- continuation despite negative consequences;
- escalation;
- losses; and
- withdrawal.

The most commonly diagnosed process addictions include:

- *Compulsive gambling.* The most well known of the process addictions, compulsive gambling is also known as pathological gambling or gambling disorder, and is diagnosed as an addictive disorder in the DSM-5. This is because gambling activates the brain's reward mechanisms in ways that are similar to psychoactive substances. Compulsive gamblers cannot control the impulse to gamble, even when it has negative consequences for them or their oved ones. Many people gamble to escape worry, gamble longer than planned, or gamble in spite of the desire to quit.
- *Compulsive spending.* Compulsive spending is a pattern of chronic, repetitive purchasing that becomes difficult to stop, and ultimately results in harmful consequences. Indeed, shopping causes distress or anxiety but is used to numb feelings. Compulsive spenders often purchase using credit cards or go on manic buying sprees. They often feel guilty, ashamed, or embarrassed after spending and can resort to lying about purchases. They are often juggling accounts to make them seem balanced.
- *Sex addiction.* An estimated 9 million Americans (3–6% of the population) are affected by sexual compulsivity or sex addiction.[6] While skeptics wonder is there such a thing, the effects of preoccupation with sex are devastating. Individuals relying on sex for comfort, nurturing, or relief from stress take sex to the next levels. Sex interferes with normal living and can create significant consequences. Sex addicts manifest obsessive behavior, unwanted consequences, are unable to perform daily tasks, and cannot stop their sexual behaviors. They spend a significant amount of time spent in sexual activity or recovering from sexual activity and experience severe mood changes around sexual activity. Included in this category is partner betrayals due to multiple affairs and/or pornography.
- *Technology addiction.* Technology addiction is also called Internet addiction, Internet use disorder (IUD), or Internet addiction disorder (IAD), and is a new phenomenon. It can be defined as frequent and obsessive technology-related behavior that occurs despite negative consequences. It's often described as a serious problem involving the inability to control use of various kinds of technology, the Internet, smartphones, tablets, and social networking sites.
- *Food and disordered eating.* There is a commonly held view that eating disorders are a lifestyle choice. Eating disorders are serious illnesses that cause severe disturbances to a person's eating behaviors. They can even cause death. Obsessions with food, body weight, and shape may also signal an eating disorder. Common eating disorders include anorexia nervosa, bulimia nervosa, and binge eating disorder.
- *Shopping.* Compulsive buying disorder, or oniomania, is characterized by an obsession with shopping and buying behavior that causes adverse

consequences. Compulsive buying is not limited to people who spend beyond their means; it also includes people who spend an inordinate amount of time shopping or who chronically think about buying things but never purchase them.

- *Gaming.* While technology addiction is not officially diagnosed through the DSM-5 at the moment, Internet use gaming disorder was added to the DSM-5 in 2013 as "recommended for further study." Gaming disorder is defined as a pattern of digital or video gaming behavior characterized by impaired control, increasing priority over other activities, and continuation or escalation of gaming despite the occurrence of negative consequences. For gaming disorder to be diagnosed, the behavior pattern must be of sufficient severity to result in significant impairment in personal, family, social, educational, occupational, or other important areas of functioning, and evident for at least 12 months.

- *Hoarding.* Hoarding disorder is a persistent difficulty discarding or parting with possessions because of a perceived need to save them. A person diagnosed with hoarding disorder experiences distress at the thought of losing items. Excessive accumulation of items, regardless of actual value, occurs.

## Case Study 2: A Cross-Addicted Woman in Her Fifties

I once worked with a woman in her fifties. She was compulsively shopping and spending and was facing an impending divorce. She had a diagnosis of mania and was drinking two bottles of wine per day. On top of that, she was gambling so much that she would lose time from work and would go back to win repeatedly. She sold, borrowed, or stole money to sustain the habit. Not surprisingly, this woman experienced sleepless nights, anxiety, and depression. In this case, the first issue addressed was substance misuse, the second issue was mania, and third shopping sprees and the efficacy of this obsessive-compulsive behavior. In doing so, past trauma was explored in treatment.

## Trauma-Informed

While doing an actual intervention, one is mindful of past experiences. However, the intervention meeting is not the time to address all the events of one's life; the goal is to move someone to change and to a safe place. Over time, clinical teams within a treatment setting use trauma-informed practices such as EDMR, somatic, or havening to adequately address these issues with the client. As the clinician-interventionist, your task is to provide the treatment center with a robust biopsychosocial history, which includes these events. You must be mindful. Your job is to understand that addiction and trauma are interwoven.

**TABLE 7.3** Multiple addictions

| | |
|---|---|
| Characteristics | Multiple addictions are defined as cross-substance addictions (addiction to two or more substances simultaneously) or a substance addiction that occurs at the same time as a process addiction. There is a strong component between chemical and process addictions, so it can be hard to recognize most acute issues or cross-addictions. Often one disorder may be acting out while another one is on hold, or off in a different direction. Process addictions (aka compulsive behaviors) include difficulties regulating behavior around food, sex, shopping, gambling, or technology. Compulsive behavior interferes with normal living and causes significant negative consequences; it causes similar physiological responses in the brain as psychoactive substances. However, behaviors often occur prior to first usage of a substance. The guiding theory for why this happens is that the shame or guilt associated with the process addictions often leads to the need to "medicate" with drugs or alcohol. Still, clinicians will determine, "What came first?" To do this, we first ask clients to establish a period of substance abstinence (four to six weeks). We complete a family history via triangulation of data, family mapping, and portraiture, and we obtain a longitudinal medical history of the IP. In this way, clinicians can establish primary/secondary/tertiary order of addiction. |
| Common signs of a problem | Anger. Depression. Excessive shopping, gambling, or sex partners. High levels of guilt and shame. Impaired thinking. Isolated. Manic. Obsessive–compulsive behaviors. Stop taking medications. Volatile. |
| Common objections to treatment | "I've already been to x amount of treatment centers; it's not going to work." "I'm not willing to give everything up." "I have no money; I'm incredibly in debt." |
| Counter-objections | "Let's look at what we call progressive abstinence. It is clear that if you continuing doing x, you will end up with more issues then you have now. Let's take a look at what's going on and figure out how you may become the person you want to be before more problems arise." Scholarship, family, or sliding scale fees. |
| Special considerations | When multiple addictions are present, clinicians can use an ecological approach to identify issues, prioritize intervention strategies, and identify therapeutic interventions for process addictions. One clinician question to keep in mind is, "Do we treat multiple addictions concurrently, or treat them one at a time?" In this case, we are talking about progressive abstinence dealing with one issue at a time. What are you going to treat first? This will be decided by treatment centers. The main principle is that the most volatile condition is treated first. The interventionist must do due diligence to connect families with appropriate centers, and if the treatment center cannot handle the situation, they need to refer out. |

**TABLE 7.4** Trauma-informed

| | |
|---|---|
| Characteristics | While experiencing trauma does not guarantee that a person will develop an addiction, research clearly suggests that trauma is a major underlying source of addiction. Indeed, the effects of trauma are cumulative:<br><br>• A child with four or more adverse childhood experiences is five times more likely to become an alcoholic and 60% more likely to become obese.[1]<br>• Survivors of illnesses, accidents, and natural disasters report between 10% and 33% experience alcohol abuse.[2]<br>• Sources estimate that 25–75% of persons who survive abuse experience addiction.[3]<br>• A diagnosis of PTSD increases the risk of developing substance use disorders.[4]<br>• Male[5] and female sexual abuse survivors experience a higher rate of alcohol and other drug abuse.[6]<br><br>Further, research shows that childhood or adulthood trauma can fuel an addiction.[7] Chronic physical pain brought on by a traumatic event (in addition to emotional pain) may also be a trigger for substance abuse disorders.[8] |
| Common signs of a problem | Anxiety.<br>Depression.<br>Excessively fearful.<br>Guilt.<br>Loss of ability to control certain behaviors.<br>Low self-esteem.<br>Motivated by fear.<br>Panic.<br>Reactive.<br>Shame and guilt.<br>Unworthy. |

*(continued)*

**TABLE 7.4** (continued)

| Special considerations | There are two components of trauma: first, the objective nature of an event ("My father killed himself," "My baby died of SIDS," "I witnessed a murder," "My boyfriend beat me," "My mother said I was no good," "I survived Hurricane Katrina," etc.); and second, the subjective experience of the event ("How do I perceive the occurrence?"). Per Michele Rosenthal, a behavioral health specialist and researcher, "Fear drives all post-trauma behaviors; healing focuses on resolving the fear." Therefore, treatment centers dealing with trauma must focus on healing rather than not tearing down. |
|---|---|
| | With trauma, clinicians need to educate families about PTSD, traumatic brain injury, and then provide specific matching to treatment facilities or professionals with trauma experience. |
| | Solid assessments must be completed for people who have a history of trauma. In fact, trauma can be uncovered with family mapping. The key is twofold. First, clinicians must remain open to what our clients say (start where the client is), rather than what we think of them or their situation. Second, clinicians must provide experiences that allow clients to communicate with their body, not necessarily communicating through talking. It's a process of observing how the body responds to different stimuli. |
| | When facilitating an intervention with trauma history, clinicians must be mindful. Understanding, attachment, attunement, and empathy are critical. If the perpetrator is a family member, assume others may be victims. You'll also need to have a perpetrator leave an intervention; instead, or not be present; this is why individual prescreening interviews is important. Do not let abuse become the focus of intervention; instead, focus on getting help. Pay special attention to manage anger. Track all members and ground when necessary. |
| | All therapeutic interventions must be trauma-informed, focusing on strength and resilience. Trauma treatment *will also* address loss and help people grieve; something of value is gone, and people need to experience a total response to an emotional experience. Some interventions in treatment centers may be more specific to somatic experiences of trauma, such as EDMR, challenge by choice, outdoor activities, psychodrama, art expression, mindfulness, massage, acupuncture, or seeking safety. Therapeutic interventions may offer a multitude of resources, including but not limited to an addiction and trauma recovery integration model, mental health, strategies, and recovery (TAMAR). |

1. Bellis M, Hughes K, Leckenby N, Jones L, Baban A, Kachaeva M, Povilaitis R, Pudule I, Qirjako G, Ulukol B, Raleva M, and Terzic N (2014) Adverse Childhood Experiences and Associations with Health-Harming Behaviours in Young Adults: Surveys in Eight Eastern European Countries. *Bulletin of the World Health Organization*. 92: 641–655.
2. Roth S, Newman E, Pelcovitz D, van der Kolk B, and Mandel FS (1997) Complex PTSD in Victims Exposed to Sexual and Physical Abuse: Results from the DSM-IV Field Trial for Posttraumatic Stress Disorder. *Journal of Traumatic Stress*. 10(4): 539–555.
3. Khoury L, Tang YL, Bradley B, Cubells JF, and Ressler KJ (2010) Substance Use, Childhood Traumatic Experience, and Posttraumatic Stress Disorder in an Urban Civilian Population. *Depression and Anxiety*. 27(12): 1077–1086.
4. Sareen J (2014) Posttraumatic Stress Disorder in Adults: Impact, Comorbidity, Risk Factors, and Treatment. *Canadian Journal of Psychiatry. Revue Canadienne de Psychiatrie*. 59(9): 460–467.
5. O'Leary P, Gould N, and Easton SD (2015) The Effect of Child Sexual Abuse on Men. *Journal of Interpersonal Violence*. 6: 2–23.
6. Fergusson DM and Lynskey MT (1997) Physical Punishment/Maltreatment during Childhood and Adjustment in Young Adulthood. *Child Abuse & Neglect*. 21(7): 617–630.
7. Alim TN, Lawson WB, Feder A, et al. (2012) Resilience to Meet the Challenge of Addiction: Psychobiology and Clinical Considerations. *The Journal of the National Institute on Alcohol Abuse and Alcoholism, Alcohol Research: Current Reviews*. 34(4): 506–515.
8. Substance Abuse and Mental Health Services Administration (2014) *SAMHSA's Concept of Trauma and Guidance for a Trauma-Informed Approach*. Rockville, MD: Substance Abuse and Mental Health Services Administration. Available at: https://store.samhsa.gov/shin/content/SMA14-4884/SMA14-4884.pdf (accessed March 4, 2018).

### Case Study 3: Paraplegic with Traumatic Brain Injury and Borderline Personality Disorder

Felix was a good looking 27-year-old gay Hispanic male who had been in a terrible car accident at age 21 that left him paraplegic and with a traumatic brain injury. We were called on to help by his trust attorney, as he was also abusing a variety of substances, including methamphetamines. He was not taking care of his dog and was missing multiple appointments due to his substance abuse.

Felix had two families, one consisting of wealth managers and custodial attorneys who helped him following the accident. The other was his family of origin, who did not speak English and from whom he had removed himself, as he wanted to be seen as independent. This intervention brought together two separate caretakers and a multiple host of providers, ranging from experts in brain injury to mental health professionals and translators. For this intervention, his "business family" was instrumental in getting him into treatment, and his family of origin played a part in helping him stay in treatment.

The selection of an appropriate placement was challenging, as it had to be skilled in mental health, substance abuse, and able to address his medical condition. The treatment center had to be willing to accept his service dog and required a bilingual staff member who could work with his family.

## Multiple Family Members with Mental Health Problems

The Collective Intervention Strategy can unearth mental health disorders within a family system. This can include addictions and/or mental illness listed in the dual diagnosis section above. In these cases, it is best to work with a team member or call in a professional colleague for assistance. You can read more about the benefits of working with additional clinicians in Chapter 5.

> *Family members come in with their own generational issues. The impact of trauma can be intergenerational.*

During interventions, it is critical that you exhibit patience when dealing with possible mental health disorders. Interventionists need to join with the client and align with them in a non-threatening way. In fact, when dealing with mental illness, you may over-empathize. Indulge obsessive-compulsive disorders, for example, or compliment narcissists. In this way, you avoid power struggles. Then you are free to instill hope.

### Case Study 4: An Entire Family in Need of Treatment

This family map was completed via phone. This was an unusual case, in the respect that the family map was not completed at the beginning. Rather, in keeping with starting where the client is, I met Jack and his family in a most

**TABLE 7.5** Multiple family members with mental health problems

| | |
|---|---|
| Characteristics | Multiple members of a family with any number of mental health problems (listed in the dual diagnosis section) who present symptoms or behaviors during interviews and meetings. |
| Common signs of a problem | Anxiety. Depressive. Manic. Obsessive. Reactive. Suicidal. Volatile. |
| Special considerations | Intervention strategies for this demographic should focus on low stimulation. In some cases, it is best to avoid a group setting. Also, take your time. A combination of patience, perseverance, and determination are required. Additionally, you'll need to practice flexibility in approaches. For example, adjust to a monotone voice. Use the legal system to help. Create a firm fence around the ILO. Do not be afraid to invite team members that are saboteurs to leave. Further, the situation can become volatile with little warning. Clients may enter a delusional system; you need to be skilled to decide whether or not to place them in involuntary commitment. During an intervention when a mental health issue is present, form a strategic partnership with colleagues, possibly a psychiatrist or forensic psychologist. Be in direct contact with the treatment center admissions team, a court liaison, or case managers. These clients can often face legal problems, so make sure to partner with a knowledgeable attorney; you can use legal problems as a motivator for long-term change. Still, be aware that you do not use treatment as an escape plan. You'll need to be consistent, understanding, direct, and firm during interventions where mental health illness is present. To support the family, you both educate about and then enforce strong boundaries. Then go flat when a client escalates. When stuck, use techniques of distraction. |

circuitous way. Jack was referred by a friend who called and asked if I could help get him transferred from one treatment center to another. I agreed.

The center where he was currently placed did not accept him, as they were not equipped to deal with his preliminary diagnosis. They wanted him to leave immediately, putting the family in a precarious position of needing to choose another treatment center immediately and doing another invitation to change. I agreed to do so, and the family had a treatment center picked out that was robust in its offering and had a good history. Thus, there was a mini intervention encouraging the transfer, and Jack entered treatment.

This was not his first treatment episode. He was a 54-year-old retired executive and had three other past treatment episodes. Jack was currently living with his 29-year-old son. He had three children, aged 19, 22, and 29, and his wife was in the process of obtaining a divorce.

After Jack was successfully in treatment, I asked permission to interview all family members and do a family map to get a better understanding of them all and to help find solutions. What was revealed had significant treatment implications. All members of the family had experienced trauma. The mother had been sexually abused by an uncle and the family had a history of mental health disorders. Both daughters had previous treatment experience in wilderness programs and one appeared to be oppositionally defiant, while the other experienced significant depression. The son had learning disabilities, was a daily pot smoker, had dropped out of a first-rate college due to daily usage, and had a symbiotic relationship with dad; they were codependent. Further, mom was highly enmeshed with family and had a difficult time giving up control and setting boundaries, and was always open to suggestions.

Upon completing these interviews, it was clear that daughter number 2, aged 22, was experiencing depression and was an occasional pot smoker. We discussed softly that it appeared she could use some inpatient treatment and options were given. She entered a program with a huge sigh of relief, engaging in treatment for over 180 days.

While she was in treatment, her younger sister, Polly, imploded. A freshman in college, she not only flunked her classes, but was arrested for hitting someone while under the influence. She was mad and angry. Again, starting where the client was, we determined a center that was known for young adults and could handle her acting out. Getting her there required the assistance of a trained escort well versed in addiction and safe transport who traveled with her mother, and I continually coached all through plane rides and stopovers. Polly proved to be a challenging client. With firm boundaries, she stayed in this center for 45 days, entered another center for 90 days, and then completed a stint in structured living with intensive outpatient treatment. She did well, though father continues to enable today, while mother sets boundaries and her success is yet to be determined.

With now three people experiencing treatment, the family's focus turned to their son, who was talented and yet had failed to launch. When offered treatment for his daily drug use (marijuana and cocaine) and his failure, so to speak, to launch, he refused, and his father agreed, as he was his caretaker. Tom did make some changes on his own, however it remains to be seen how he learns to thrive. He still lives in his father's home.

## Clinical Interventions

This is one of two types of interventions that take place inside of a treatment center. The most common type of clinical intervention occurs after detox and about a week of treatment within a facility. Clients often say, "I've had enough. I think I'm going to leave." Other times, clients may have been through treatment multiple times and their current treatment episode evolves new issues. In these cases, they may have achieved some period of abstinence, and underlying attachment issues or unresolved trauma compels them to old, unhealthy behaviors.

Best practices for clinical interventions include addressing the ILO in a group. Sometimes in the treatment center there may be a one-on-one conversation with a therapist. But when you go one-on-one with someone, one is not as successful at achieving treatment compliance.

In fact, we know that interventions work best in groups. We see again and again in early recovery that the power of the group helps bring about change. For this reason, clinical interventions must bring together community. In this way, these interventions can benefit from a team that consists of:

- accountability team members;
- treatment center addiction professionals; and
- professional interventionist.

The main idea here is that the accountability team continues to set and keep health boundaries with the ILO. You recognize progress but only support treatment continuation.

Clinical interventions may occur a number of times during residential treatment. It's a matter of collaboration, of openness, and the ability to take a look at treatment performance with a pause. We ask, "What's in the best interest of this client?" Then we adjust strategy and move forward.

In each of the following cases, there is preparation ahead of time. In truth, every day and in every way, teams are inviting residents to change. They are invited to look at behaviors that are not helpful. In the times when resistance is at such a breaking point, it is advisable to bring in family and other team members to help with a more formal invitation.

### Case Study 5: Clinical Intervention for a World Traveler

The IP is a 23-year-old woman with multiple treatment episodes. Prior to her last admit, she had purchased tickets to travel to Europe and is determined to go. Her current level of sobriety is less than 90 days. The clinical team is recommending that the client hold off on travel until she has developed and demonstrated life skills in structured sober living. Family are brought into this discussion; they provide both financial and emotional support. The family are present via Skype.

In this instance, the invitation that is presented by all is to delay this vacation and spend more time in an intensive program. Speaking from the heart, the family affirms the client's progress and makes a clear elucidation of what will and will not be supported.

## Case Study 6: Clinical Intervention during Detox for a Chronic Pain Patient

The ILO was a 37-year-old female who experienced chronic pain and substance abuse disorder. She was refusing to participate in treatment, and stood the risk of losing state licensure as an MD and of losing her child. As she was beginning medical detox, she was extremely argumentative and wanted to leave. Once she calmed down, the clinical team sat with her and attempted to join up and reinvite her to stay. Family members were also included. If letters are used in step 10 of the Collective Intervention Strategy, this may be a time when original letters can also be helpful.

## Case Study 7: A Lower Level of Care

A 25-year-old male wants to leave treatment against clinical recommendations. We call the family and discuss the consequences if he leaves. In this case, the clinical team has decided that the individual might benefit from experiencing a lower level of care, transitioning from residential to structured sober living. A verbal change agreement is proposed. The family is included in this discussion, and while the client is free to leave, it's clear that the only thing loved ones will support is going to structured sober living.

## Case Study 8: Involving Those Who Matter

A 63-year-old executive wants to leave treatment, as he wants to go back to work and his family. He has been resistant to looking at his entitlement, alcohol, and other drug use. He has a narcissistic personality. The clinical team believes it is advisable that the client stay 30 more days. The executive has given a consent form to his business advisor along with family members. In this instance, the clinical team include the business advisor in the treatment intervention, as he is the one person who can help move him to change.

## Reverse Interventions

Reverse interventions are the second type of intervention that occurs within the treatment center setting. These cases involve payor denial of an addiction problem in a dependent. They can also involve parents consciously prioritizing activities *other than treatment*. They require that clinicians work with the IP to intervene on the payor so that the patient may get the help they need.

These types of interventions often involve a young person who seeks treatment, while their parents' priorities may be tied to education, financial, or career goals. Another example that we often see in treatment centers is that the patient knows it is best for them to stay in extended care, where they are developing a robust support network, rather than return home.

## Case Study 9: College Junior Needs Help in Spite of His Parents' Plans for Medical School

Johnnie is a junior at a prestigious university. Over the last year, he stopped attending his classes and he has spent most of the semester partying. Last Saturday, he wrapped his car around the tree and did not remember he did so. When Johnnie met with the college's alcohol and other drug counselor, he self-revealed the challenges he was having with mind-altering substances.

In looking at his college career, it was clear that he was continually getting into trouble. Mom and dad were avid supporters of the school, and had big plans for Johnnie to go on to med school and to follow in his grandfather's footsteps. Johnnie was not sure that this would be possible, and he was currently flunking his courses.

Johnnie and I talked about taking a medical leave from school so his grades would not be jeopardized, and he was afraid his parents would not permit that. With Johnnie's permission, we invited his parents in and Johnnie shared what had been happening. At first, dad did not want to hear about this, as he had just given a large donation to the school and wanted to look good. After spending several hours explaining the options and assuring the parents that Johnnie could return once treatment was completed, his parents became open and willing to look at treatment centers and addiction treatment for Johnnie.

## References

1. American Psychiatric Association (2013) *Diagnostic and Statistical Manual of Mental Disorders* (5th edition). Arlington, TX: American Psychiatric Publishing. Available at: http://dx.doi.org/10.1176/appi.books.9780890425596 (accessed March 4, 2018).
2. National Institute on Drug Abuse (2008) *Research Report Series. Comorbidity: Addiction and Other Mental Illnesses*. Bethesda, MD: U.S. Department of Health and Human Services, National Institutes of Health. Available at: www.drugabuse.gov/sites/default/files/rrcomorbidity.pdf (accessed March 4, 2018).
3. National Institute on Drug Abuse (2016) *Genetics and Epigenetics of Addiction*. Bethesda, MD: National Institute on Drug Abuse. Available at: www.drugabuse.gov/publications/drugfacts/genetics-epigenetics-addiction (accessed March 4, 2018).

4. National Alliance on Mental Illness (2015) *A Long Road Ahead: Achieving True Parity in Mental Health and Substance Use Care.* Arlington, TX: NAMI. Available at: www.nami.org/Learn-More/Mental-Health-Conditions (accessed March 4, 2018).

5. Center for Behavioral Health Statistics and Quality (2017) *2016 National Survey on Drug Use and Health: Detailed Tables.* Rockville, MD: U.S. Department of Health and Human Services, Substance Abuse and Mental Health Services Administration. Available at: www.samhsa.gov/data/sites/default/files/NSDUH-FFR1-2016/NSDUH-FFR1-2016.pdf (accessed March 4, 2018).

6. Derbyshire K and Grant JE (2015) Compulsive Sexual Behavior: A Review of the Literature. *Journal of Behavioral Addictions.* 4(2): 1–7.

# 8

# FAMILY MAPPING AND PORTRAITURE

## Why We Need to Gather Data

Before we begin, I'd like to ask you to first put yourself in a client's shoes. Imagine how you'd feel if you were asked to open up the biggest can of worms – to reveal family secrets – to a total stranger! How would you react? Would you be courageous? Could you tell your life's story and be immune to self-criticism? Would the others around you listen without judgment?

Probably not.

Addiction, trauma, and shame are intertwined. In fact, shame affects our clients' ability to tell their own stories. Still, clients inherently come to us with feelings of trauma, shame, guilt, humiliation, embarrassment, grief, and loss. The way that they *feel* affects the stories they *tell* about themselves. Our goal is to encourage curiosity and personify possibility.

> As clinicians, we are there to motivate aspiration, to convey the message that a better life is possible.

Typically, we cannot rely on the first story that we hear from any one person. So, as clinicians, it is our job to allow the data to tell the story, to create an objective view of what's *really* going on. This is where the skills of family mapping and portraiture come in. These clinical tools can be used to visualize what you learn during the process of inquiry. In other words:

- *Family mapping* is what sociologists call a genogram – a snapshot of a person's past, including people, relationships, circumstances, and medical history. It is a way into the story of what is happening in the family unit.

- *Portraiture* is a qualitative, subjective research method developed by American sociologist Sara Lawrence-Lightfoot. The aim of portraiture is to blend art and science to create holistic, authentic narrative portraits that can capture the intricate dimensions and essence of human experience.

These two methods of qualitative inquiry work together to illuminate the stories behind the stories: the motivations, the causes, the driving forces of mental health disorders.

## What Is a Family Map?

Genograms were first used in clinical settings by Monica McGoldrick and Randy Gerson, and were outlined in their book *Genograms: Assessment and Intervention*[1] in 1985. Over time, the term "genogram" became loosely interchangeable with "family maps."

A family map is a snapshot of a person's life. However, it includes people, relationships, circumstances, and a full view of the family's medical history. The visual diagram helps clinicians define what is truly going on within the family system and to determine which issues to tackle first.

> *Basically, a family map is a pictorial representation of a family system that provides us with information about family-of-origin issues, which can then be used as a therapeutic point of reference. The purpose is to show simply and concisely whether a family is organized in a healthy way or not.*

Family maps use symbols to show how members relate to each other. While some symbols are standard, you can use family members' names, initials, cartoon figures, faces, or any other meaningful symbols in your illustrations. In fact, you can individualize maps to clients. You can use coloring and coding as you like. Get creative!

A family map shows the good *and* the bad; the trauma, resiliency, *and* the joy. Family mapping serves the group in educating about – then casting light on – repetitive behavioral patterns and generational tendencies. One maps out client's family history of substance abuse, mental health disorders, or any dramatic recent changes such as a death, trauma, finances, sexual addictions, shopping, spending habits, and even digital media usage. Indeed, family mapping is critical in helping clinicians and families picture "just the facts" as they work together to separate feelings, fears, or points of view during an intervention.

In sum, we are trying to achieve a robust picture of who the identified client is, what they are doing, and where they came from. Many times, the ILO feels like they are the only one with a problem. There is a long line of family members that have experienced complex problems. Helping to identify that also helps you when you are performing an intervention.

## How to Create a Family Map

Before clinicians begin a family mapping process, operational and administrative issues should be completed. You'll need to have in place:

1.  An engagement signed with the family.
2.  You have already learned a bit about them through phone calls and discussions.
3.  You have asked their permission to engage in the process.
4.  The client is informed you will spend 60–90 minutes together in doing this exercise.
5.  You set a time and date to talk.

Before we begin, it is best to stop, pause, and take a moment to recognize the difficulty in uncovering secrets. For this reason, I affirm clients for being courageous. I dance slowly with them and often talk circuitously for about 5–10 minutes before diving into particulars. Once their breathing settles a bit and they are ready, we begin.

As you begin to prepare for your first family mapping experience, you need about 90 minutes, paper, colored pens, and a genuine curiosity about the lives of others. The family map will illustrate each person, alive or deceased, born or unborn (including pets), that occupy historical space. Each has a story and a piece to contribute.

You begin by mapping out relationships closest to the ILO. So, map the IP and the nuclear family. Men are represented by squares. Women are represented by circles. The male symbol (upper left) relates to the female symbol (upper right) in the majority of family building maps. The ILO can be represented with the acronym "ILO" or as a square within a square (male) or a circle within a circle (female). An "X" within a circle of square means that the person is no longer living. Table 8.1 illustrates the common symbols used in family mapping.

*Note:* Family mapping is a directed activity, and conversations are nonlinear. So, as you paint this family map, you may go across generations. Still, always start by asking about the ILO and then branching out.

Add lines to represent family connections, much like a typical family tree. Keep members of the same generation on the same row. Then label each shape with the person's name. Then go back into the history of the family. Decide on how many generations to go back; three to four generations should suffice. You can start from the base of a family tree with current, living generations on the map.

From there, you'll focus on mapping issues, conflicts, or diagnoses. In addition to substance use disorders, you'll want to map out significant physical and mental illnesses. Addiction does not occur in a vacuum, nor does it present simply as chemical dependence. So, consider compulsive behaviors such as gambling, shopping, exercise, or food addictions. Also, map out behavioral problems, relationship problems, and personality traits. You can assign a letter to code each condition on the map (see Table 8.1 for common acronyms).

At this point, relationships will become more diverse on the family map. You'll map sibling rivalry, conflicts, divorce, or abuse. You'll show lines of alliance and hierarchy of influence. You may illustrate major trauma or family loss. As you begin to detail hereditary patterns, psychological factors, and history, the patterns from the past begin to illuminate the present. One discovers what problems are common, where/when they arose, and to whom they are connected.

Remember, life is messy.

The principle thing to understand about creating a family map is that your visual representation of a family evolves. The conversations you have with the accountability team will be nonlinear. Even in the course of one interview, the conversation will take you many places. This is purposeful. An accurate family map or portrait is the culmination of an open-ended yet guided conversation.

> The main idea is that you will record and plot data as they are collected. Toward the end of the process, the family map will accurately illustrate the past and the present, which in turn allows families and ILOs to step into the present on solid ground.

During steps 2, 4, 5, and 6, you will be speaking with many people. These conversations will take place over the course of several days or weeks. Therefore, the family map will be subject to lots of editing – exclusions, additions, minimizations, amplification. Still, we seek neither more nor less drama than the facts.

## Medical Definers

- Alzheimer's or dementia;
- anemia;
- autism;
- breast cancer;
- cancer;
- chronic pain;
- circulatory disease;
- diabetes;
- Down syndrome;
- heart disease;
- high blood pressure;
- HIV/AIDS;
- kidney disease;

**TABLE 8.1**  Common symbols used in family mapping

| | |
|---|---|
| "_____" | Family lines |
| "_ _ _ _ _" | Dashed lines signify communications are blocked; relations don't disclose honestly, hear well, or problem-solve effectively. |
| ◯ | Female |
| ☐ | Male |
| ✖ | Deceased |
| ⟋ | Separated |
| ⫽ | Divorced |

| | |
|---|---|
| ILO | Identified loved one |
| Color code | Addiction |
|   or pattern | Chemical: drug or alcohol |
|   of your | Death: sudden, suicide, or natural |
|   choosing | Behavioral: gambling, sex, shopping, disordered eating, exercise, digital |
| | Relationships: marriages, divorces, sudden deaths, extramarital affairs |
| | Family secrets |
| | Finance: financial debting, overspending, codependency or caretaking behaviors |
| | Legal issues |
| | Trauma: homeless, military, emotional abuse, multiple moves |
| | Mental health: suicide, suicide ideation, codependent, physical abuse, learning disabilities, ADHD, school problems, autism, religiosity, work, perfectionism |
| | Physical: chronic pain, physical, medical condition |
| | Anything else the person thinks is important or noteworthy |
| | *Note:* This a custom family map, so it does not have to be perfect. |

- liver disease;
- lung cancer;
- memory loss;
- respiratory disease;
- STDs;
- stroke;
- suicidal talk or attempt; and
- violence.

## Family Map Example

Figure 8.1 is a sample of a family map. As you can see, Jack is the ILO and has had a history of substance abuse, mental health issues, legal issues, trauma, and

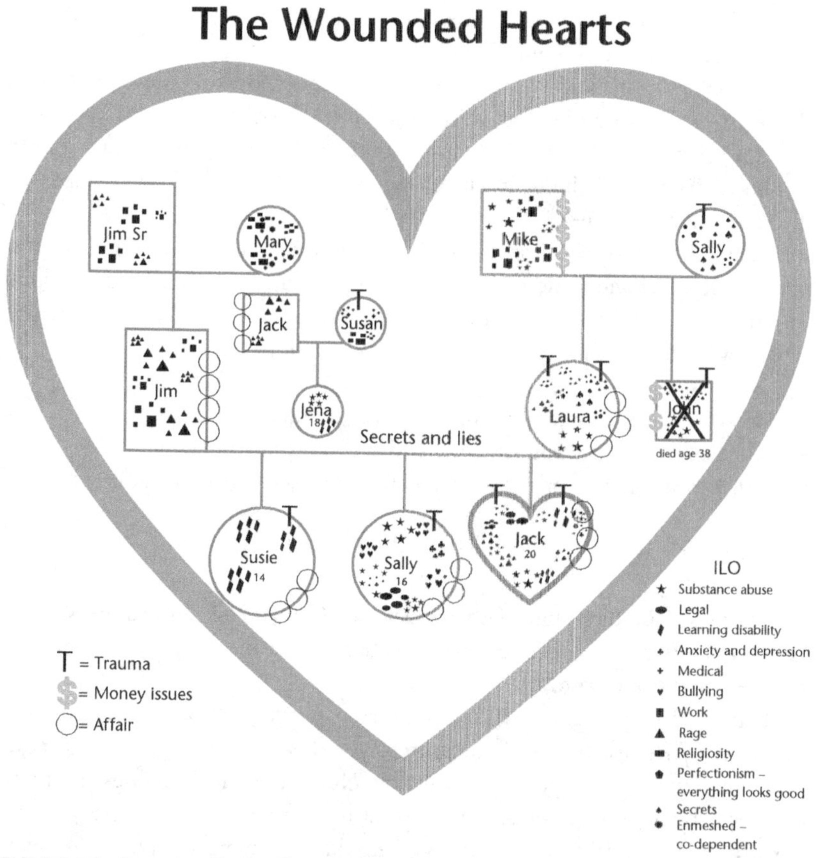

# The Wounded Hearts

**FIGURE 8.1** Sample of a family map

*Note:* For purposes of publication, this family map was produced in black and white; however, using different colored markers to highlight the many different issues facing the family makes mapping stand out. See the eResources for the color version of this image.

multiple partners. His parents, Jim and Laura, have been beset with complex issues, as has his sister, Sally. Little sister Susie has learning disabilities. In looking across generations, one can see that substance abuse, depression, anxiety (i.e. mental health issues), and partner betrayal span generations. Secrets and lies have dominated family conversations.

Now that Jack is in treatment, the family is taking the time to look at past hurts and to have the opportunity to become curious and rewrite their story.

## Guidelines for Family Mapping Conversations

If you want to get good at interventions, one must be an explorer who ho suspends judgment and fear. Your role is to affirm, summarize, and inquire.

You will be witness to the deepest emotions in people's lives. And how do you prepare for your role as a guide to recovery?

First, take on the role of an explorer. Ask open-ended questions. Start with the questions that are outlined in Worksheet 4.3 (How to Listen to Wounded Heart: Questions for Guided Conversations with Clients). You'll want to return to phrases such as, "Tell me about X" or, "Let's talk about X" or, "When was the last time X happened?"

Second, develop key listening skills. Listen with emotional attunement. It helps to be quiet and settle yourself to actively listen. Additionally, it is helpful to respond rather than react. Respond with a statement that accurately reflects what you've been told. Here are some key skills to use:

- *Reflection.* Repeating what someone has just said.
- *Rephrase.* Repeat what someone said and substitute a new word.
- *Paraphrase.* Reflect or rephrase a feeling, not necessarily the content.

> *It sounds like you are struggling and are frustrated.*

Exercise your listening skills with a colleague. Stop and ask for examples. How are you? How are you feeling today? Gather some basic data and then reflect, rephrase, and paraphrase.

Third, use metadiscourse to drive the conversation. Also, be aware of how clients use metadiscourse. Metadiscourse, or the way we talk about a conversation, can provide you with valuable clues about real feelings, motives, or perspectives. Note here that if we want to start practicing compassion, we have to start by setting boundaries and holding people accountable for their behavior.

Sometimes, for example, clients exaggerate. Clients may exaggerate as way to get a loved one's attention. Or you can use exaggeration to make a point. If you exaggerate, be careful not to be sarcastic:

> *So, if I hear you correctly, your son/daughter/husband/wife wants you to . . .*
> *So, if I hear you correctly, you want to . . .*

Sometimes you'll need to bring out new information through evoking responses that are relative. As clinicians, we ask clients to identify what's "good" or "not so good" about changing behavior. Other times we will explore ambivalence:

> *So, on the one hand, you want to stop smoking, and on the other hand you do not.*
> *So, on the one hand, you say you are angry with your loved one, and yet you have little emotion.*
> *On the one hand, you want to be able to leave the children with your wife, but you are afraid to.*

*On the one hand, you want to intervene with your wife and have her get help, and on the other you are afraid to.*

*On the one hand, you want Mark to get well and be a part of the family, and on the other you never want him to return to your home.*

It is always important to ask permission. At other times, it is helpful to invite. To do this, we develop an invitational vocabulary as we work with clients and loved ones to share their story. To reiterate the way in which we talk about family systems problems, the words that we use are very, very important!

With your permission, let's talk about . . .

I invite you to look at some of the boundaries you currently have in place. If I heard you correctly, they are . . . XYZ. How are those working for you? (In most cases, they are not.)

## Family Map Case Studies

These cases are a snapshot of my practice through the years. I hope they illustrate for you the power of family mapping, staying the course, and remaining flexible and open to the power of discovery.

### Case Study 1: Family Secrets Inspire Healing

A family map was completed in a treatment center with all family members present. Meet Sally, a 32-year-old music executive who is experiencing problems with opioids and disordered eating. She has a mother and father, and had a brother, Alex.

In doing their family map, Sally was clear that she had heard about this exercise from other clients and wanted to do it for the group. She was clear that she did not want to put an "X" through Alex's name, who had died a year before; rather, she wanted to design a halo. In doing this family map, unresolved grief became visually apparent.

According to family members, Alex was the perfect son. He had no issues, while Sally reported and confirmed she had experienced much trauma, had abused substances, and had an eating disorder. The family demonstrated visually how much they were not ready to deal with Alex's suspected cause of death; it was reported he fell to his death in a parking lot after a drug deal went poorly. There was no autopsy or further discussion. This was the family's secret.

Sally's mother's family kept secrets alive and presented to the world like the perfect family, while dad revealed the generational history of financial success, alcoholism, and mental health disorders. Doing the family map together, the family saw how secrets kept them under wraps. The family map then gave the clinician in the center much to work on with them.

## Case Study 2: Family Mapping Leads to Unexpected Resolution of Personal Identity Struggle

In this case, the family map was done in a treatment center with mom, dad, and Erik, 20 years old. His family looked like the perfect family: beautiful and all decked out. He is the only son of a high-wealth family and has three younger sisters, who, when doing the family map, all have their own learning and mental health issues. Mom self-revealed that she was in recovery and that her family had a history of substance abuse. Dad was very successful and hard-charging.

In doing the family map, many issues were revealed in front of the group. Erik has legal issues, substance abuse, anxiety, depression, and ADHD diagnoses. Erik's sisters experience bullying and depression. Mom has a family history of substance abuse, although she's in recovery. Dad also has a family history of substance abuse.

Then, mom said, "I have something to share about my brother, who died at the age of 38." The family – especially Erik – had been told he had a heart attack. And there in the confines of the room, mom shared, with tears softly streaming down her face, that he died at 38, he was gay, and he died of AIDS. The room fell silent. We hugged, and Erik hugged his mom, ever so grateful that the secret was out.

We took a break; during that break, Erik became animated and asked for a private meeting with his family and several lead staff. They agreed, and with the knowledge he gained from his family map he felt free to share his own sexual identity as bisexual. As an unintended consequence, the family map gave him permission to be the young man he was struggling to be, as well as freeing his mother from family secrets.

## Case Study 3: A Family Enters Treatment

Sometimes a family map will reveal the need for family members' own treatments. In this case, four placements for five family members took place over a six-month period: a mother, father, and two daughters. The son refused treatment.

Along the way, I connected this family to appropriate clinical resources and collaborated as best I could. This was one of the first families where almost everyone was open to treatment. Surely they all in their own way produced systemic change, and the changes were based on the mental health needs that were uncovered during family mapping. Overall, the family exhibited a readiness to change.

Mom throughout all this identified her role as rescuer, martyr, and hero. In truth, having multiple family members in treatment was a lot to handle over a six-month period, two children in treatment, and soon-to-be ex-husband in treatment, and a son who failed to launch. After several months more, mom was finally open to looking at her own behavior, citing that she had done her best for all the family and now she must look at herself, and agreed that once her teaching responsibilities were over, she would enter an intensive program that looks at how she relates to others and herself.

In two months, three out of five family members were ready to change. In seven months, three out of five family members had engaged in treatment that lasted more than 60 days. After that, one family member went for a two-week intensive and saw two private therapists. Only one of the five family members refused treatment. Today, dad is still abstinent, the youngest daughter is enrolled back in school and working, and the middle daughter stopped taking her medication and went back into treatment for stabilization. My work as an interventionist and solution-focused family recovery professional was complete.

## Case Study 4: Assessment Is a Tool, but Openness to Process Is Best

This case was referred to me by a family outlier who was concerned for Rock. Rock was respected in his Native American tribe for the work he was currently doing with film and media. Together, his producer and I sketched out a family map via the phone. I learned that Rock was a robust gentleman, a chronic relapser, who had endured years of sexual abuse and trauma in 37 foster homes. He was also feared as he was a gang leader and had multiple legal offenses. He was currently on parole. Rock was tremendously talented and liked to write poetry as well.

Married several times, he had children that lived on the reservation and that knew of his drug abuse. Given all that had transpired with him, we decided on a gender-specific treatment center – all-male – that worked well with chronic relapsers and was well versed in dealing with legal issues. But then the world I thought was the right world, based on what I have learned, was wrong.

As it turned out, Rock did not have permission to cross state lines. He had to travel back to his home state for violating parole. Confident we could work that out and get him back, I thought once again I did the right thing.

And then Rock called me and was gruff and rough, and I thought a bit entitled and ungrateful for all the work I had done. "I can't return to X treatment center," he bellowed. "It's not right for me." After getting over myself, I asked, "Why is it not right for you?" Then Rock said softly, "I am Racquelle, not Rock – I am a she, not a he." For a minute, I was speechless. I shook my head and wondered why I did not see this, nor ever wonder this. I was a seasoned clinician and had done due diligence. And I missed this completely. I asked with surprise, "Have you ever told anyone?"

He replied, "No."

I said, "You must tell your parole officer. I can't help you until you do." With some hesitation, he shared his news with his parole officer, as well as others.

Raquelle entered a treatment center that works with transgender clients. I sought out consultation from other experts, and after I got over being uncomfortable I could be of service to Raquelle. I share this case study with you, for as good as we think we might be with assessment, I have learned to always be open for the unexpected. I was grateful that Raquelle trusted me enough and was in pain enough to share her truth with me.

## What Is Portraiture?

Portraiture is a qualitative research methodology used to collect rich, meaningful data about the ILO and the family system they operate within. The seminal text *The Art and Science of Portraiture* by Sara Lawrence-Lightfoot and Jessica Davis outlines the method as a way for clients to feel seen, "fully attended to, recognized, appreciated, respected, scrutinized."[2] It is, in essence, the culmination of in-depth interviews and observation. It is the narrative of the family.

> *A good portrait creates a composite picture of the ILO and their family and friends; it captures the essence of the entire support system, using the group as its subject.*

We use portraits in a variety of ways:

1. We gather information as a portrait view of the individual so that we can gain insider standing of the person. This aids us in treatment referral.
2. In the pre-intervention meeting, we share a clinical portrait of the ILO within the family system. The accountability team listens and shares their own version of the narrative, always allowing for variation and nuance.
3. Accountability team members add to the portrait during the intervention meeting itself, as they share what's in their hearts, what they love about the person, and what is troublesome. In this way, their experiences and their portrait of the ILO is used to motivate and inspire change.

A portrait is a word rendering of who that person is: their strengths, foibles, and weaknesses. It may consider photographs of the family, as well as of the ILO. The clinician creates a portrait based on interviews so that one can understand the complexities of the case, as well as understand how one might intervene, what objections may arise, and how one enters a conversation with compassion, love, and facts.

As a clinical tool, portraiture has higher aims. Portraiture as narrative inquiry acknowledges that communities share knowledge through sharing stories. Therefore, portraiture works for families; it includes participants and embraces the complex reality of life. Ultimately, the process of portraiture guides the construction of a story and then relates the story to its wider contexts; a full portrait "seeks to illuminate the complex dimension of goodness."[2]

Indeed, an effective portrait offers a complicated view of an individual or a family system, with a deep appreciation for its failures and imperfections. It unearths the good and the bad, reflecting reality through the lens of change. In this way, family unity becomes a mixture of the parts that produce the whole.

## How to Create a Portrait of an Individual

### 1. Change Role from Clinician to Researcher

Using portraiture in an intervention requires first that clinicians take on the role of researchers; we become a discerning observer who is distanced from the action. This way, we can see the whole family system and identify patterns that actors in the system might not notice because of their involvement. To do this, we sit on the boundaries of the group and "witness" what is happening.

Note here that a clinician's perspectives as participant or observer ebb and flow many times in this process, from feeling like an insider to feeling like an outsider, and back again. This is the nature of the role we play. Complete objectivity is not possible because the developing of a portrait involves the active association of the researcher and the person being observed in constructing the portrait itself. This interaction considerably alters perspective but is a part of the process; a portrait is always the subjective reality reported by the researcher.

### 2. Define Data Sources and Collection Methods

Our main sources of data are both formal and informal conversations with accountability team members. Individual interviews are at the core of this context. Indeed, triangulation of data is foundational to the art of portraiture. It is essential to talk to every individual in a family when we perform an intervention; everyone holds a different portrait of the ILO and they see different things.

I have found that speaking with each person individually first – before we gather as a group – yields more truthful and richer data. This requires that every potential accountability team member be interviewed individually. This type of more extensive interview yields a much more comprehensive, far-reaching, and three-dimensional "portrait."

### 3. Hold Individual Interviews

We use the interviewing questions outlined in step 4, Worksheet 4.2 (Intake Questions for First Point of Contact), to begin the data collection process. These questions guide the clinician into understanding more. As a type of narrative inquiry, portraiture is event-driven. So, the identification of key events and the details are critical for understanding the lives of the ILO and their families. Here are the key elements to consider as you're preparing a portrait:

- *Context.* What is the context of where the ILO lives, works, or goes to school? What does the family look like? Are relationships enmeshed, tenuous, supportive, etc.?
- *Voice.* How does the person sound when you interview them? Are they sobbing so hard you cannot get a word in between gasping breaths? Are they so scared of their loved one that they are afraid to call you from their home and are locked in their car calling you? What does the voice communicate?
- *Relationship.* What is the relationship they have with the ILO? Are they a relative, friend, employer, assistant, etc.? How has that relationship altered over time? What fears do they have in speaking their truth? What will they stand to lose if the ILO gets help?
- *Emergent themes.* Emergent generational themes surface during the process of creating a family map. To build on these, look for a history of family secrets, multiple affairs, money problems, multiple moves, multiple marriages, sudden death or suicide, school problems, legal problems, trauma, abandonment, attachment issues, substance abuse, mental health (most common anxiety and/or depression, then bipolar and/or schizophrenia), enmeshment, or resilience.

Further, we can break down the process into the specific storytelling elements. We ask the following questions, which come directly from my work as a Certified Daring Way/Rising Strong Facilitator.

## The Reckoning

- Look at your fall down moments.
- What emotionally hooks you?
- Why do you need to give yourself permission to look at your past?
- How have you been offloading hurt?
- Are you willing to get curious?

## The Rumble

- What do you need to unleash your curiosity?
- How would you define uncertainty, risk, and your emotional response to them? What does it look like, feel like, show up as?
- How does shame show up in your story? Perfectionism, comparison?
- How do you see boundaries? Choosing courage over comfort, what is right over what is fun?
- How do you view generosity? Living big, anxiety, or criticism?
- How do you see forgiveness? Do you have the belief you'll come out the other side a better person not consumed by anger or hatred? No longer chained in victimhood and dependent on the perpetrator?

## The Revolution Story

This is our way home. We are the authors of our own lives. We write our own daring endings. We craft love from heartbreak, compassion from hurt. What is your vision for yourself? What is your vision for your loved one? What is your vision for your family?

## 4. Define Emerging Themes

Searching for patterns or emergent themes is the fourth component of portraiture. This systematic and rigorous process of empirical description, interpretation, and analysis is used to create a series of main points that comprise the final narrative portraits. Portraitists need to be well versed in flexibility and iterative research design. Iterative, in that as we collect data, we begin immediate analysis, which informs later observations and interviews. So, after talking with accountability team members about initial ideas to determine the narrative, it is important to conduct additional interviews and observations based on hypotheses.

## 5. Produce an Aesthetic Whole Narrative of the Life of the ILO

Finally, we craft a story from our findings; we give expression through storytelling. Indeed, we play an active role in this. We, as clinicians, can either type out the story into print format or share our subjective findings orally. Portraiture has been designed to use a verbal canvas. This opens narrative possibilities as complex, provocative, and inviting.

> *You are trying to be holistic, revealing the dynamic interaction of personality, events, and family system in a portrait.*

The main dimensions of an addiction intervention portrait include:

1. Initiation of use.
2. Outcomes.
3. A description of the person's strengths.
4. The fond memories we remember about the person.
5. What have we experienced in the last six months that (sometimes) more than frightened us, or made us worried?
6. What are some of the objections the identified client might have in going to treatment?

## The Final Product

Portraiture creates a dialogue between the clinician and the client(s). The process affirms that clinicians and family members are collaborators in a story. To put it another way, when we embark on an intervention, our job is not to provide a client with a definitive clinical diagnosis. Instead, the information we gather will help us differentiate between disorders so we can navigate an intervention course.

The narrative that clinicians create may be called "the portrait" because it is presented as a singular and totalizing picture. The story of the individual is put together with contextual detail. Taking on the role of clinician-portraitist, the story we tell is presented as an authentic view of reality. We speak with authority and try to capture the essence of clients' experience and perspective through the details of action and thought revealed in context.

The bottom line is that we create and mold a story instead of merely searching for one. Understand that interventions are a science *and* an art; portraiture is a constructivist activity involving intervention instead of a passive observation of life in context. Clinicians join up alongside families in search of goodness, strength, and resilience. These points of entry are also exit points; it is easier to intervene with honey and veracity then with anger and confrontation.

## An Example of Portraiture

### Case Study: Sally

Sally was a 37-year-old woman, beautiful, a showstopper in any room. She dabbled in the design business, always trying to create but never finishing up. As a young girl, she was always sought after by the boys in the class; she was pretty. But early on, she had trouble reading and focusing, and may have had an ADHD diagnosis. Her charm and photographic memory helped her remember absolutely everything. She reminded me of a newscaster.

Her looks took her far and she was the apple of her father's eye. She always seemed to get out of trouble with him. In junior high, she had trouble with math and focusing on things. She lived in an area that had so many people around her. Going off with her friends to parties, she was introduced to cocaine by a friend at a time when cocaine was just being introduced in the area. It took her to places she never thought she could be: she was stronger, faster, better, prettier, and became highly sexually active and best friends with Nancy. Nancy was a year older and she just loved hanging out with her.

Suddenly, her appearance changed. What once was a clean-cut, preppy-looking young gal turned into someone whose mascara was running down her face and whose hair was disheveled. Mom and dad were popular in the community, well-respected professionals. They never thought that this could be their child.

She got argumentative, she yelled and screamed. Her parents went away and left her with a schoolteacher. Then they discovered that their princess took their car at 15 years old for a joyride. During their absence, she also had friend over who stole their electronic equipment. They had their blinders on; they thought she was going through a phase.

She was invited to leave private school and was now in a public school. Here, there was a counselor who she often saw and who she related to. They laughed. They talked. And one day, she was in the bathroom and was caught with a little tiny wrapped up piece of aluminum foil. In her purse were pills.

The counselor spoke with her and they talked about getting help. She was sort of miserable, was failing classes, and wasn't attending, rapidly spiraling into undiagnosed mania. So, the counselor, in her presence, called her family, who only lived in Denial Land. He had researched, just like any good interventionist, a place where she could go.

They met; the mom, having seen but not knowing what to do, was devastated. She felt it was all her fault. The father thought that this was ridiculous, there was nothing wrong. He disagreed. But mom knew that something was wrong. Dad was angry, and even though he had money would not support treatment. Mom borrowed money, and this was the first treatment episode for this girl. She was bright, pretty, attractive, smart, but had an undiagnosed mental health disorder and parents who didn't want to see.

Without the outside intervention of a counselor trained in substance abuse, who knows what else would have happened. Who knows how long people could have stayed with the cashmere blanket of denial wrapped around them. It was the clarity of someone to stand up and advocate to help the client to go to treatment that changed Sally's trajectory of misery.

## References

1. McGoldrick M, Gerson R, and Petry S (2008) *Genograms: Assessment and Intervention* (3rd edition). New York: W.W. Norton & Company.
2. Lawrence-Lightfoot S and Davis JH (1997) *The Art and Science of Portraiture*. San Francisco, CA: Jossey-Bass.

# PART 3
# Troubleshooting

# 9

# WHAT'S GOING WRONG?

## Planning and Risk Management

Like life, interventions can be messy. Just when you think you've made all preparations you can possibly make, an unforeseen contingency occurs that requires response. How can you plan for the unknown? Flexibility is key. Just as you're inviting the accountability team to think outside the box, you must too.

*In sum, be prepared for the unexpected. Then adjust your style on the spot.*

While I am a big advocate for the invitational approach to an intervention, I would be remiss if I did not share that sometimes a surprise may be the only way to do a meeting. For example, you may discover last minute that the invitation has not been delivered while waiting for the intervention meeting to begin! Hence, the meeting may be a surprise for you and the ILO.

Here are some other cases I have experienced:

- While you and the family have selected a safe, neutral place to hold the intervention, you wind up in a parking lot where the loved one is locked inside a car – not exactly the boardroom that was planned for.
- Not only is the ILO unaware of an invitation; she is currently in the process of shooting up heroin in a locked bathroom.
- The ILO flees the scene and goes underground. He cannot be located via telephone and is untraceable.
- The entire family is skeptical that the ILO will not show up to the family cottage up in the mountain, a safe place that was chosen for its neutrality. What do you do?

It is paramount that one takes time to plan for any contingency that you can think of. Still, know and accept that things can happen outside of your well-orchestrated control. Here's a simple formula to keep with you throughout the challenges that you will face:

1. Hit pause.
2. Regroup.
3. Allow for breathing space. The problem is not going away.
4. Then think outside the box and join up.

See Worksheet 4.10 (Intervention Planning Checklist) to help mitigate and plan for problems in advance.

## Location, Location, Location

A long time ago in 1963, the anthropologist Jules Henry wrote a seminal piece, *Culture Against Man*,[1] on how American institutions help and hinder health services. While the book is over 50 years old, Henry made an argument that entering a person's home invited could share more information on how the family lives than any clinical visit. When you see how a person within a family operates at home, clinical insights outweigh any family session. His truth rings clear today as we continue to meet clients where they are in their native habitats.

Interventions take place out in the field, in boardrooms, hotel suites, and people's homes; they do not (for the most part) take place in a clinician's office. So, it is wise that you locate meeting places outside of your private office. For example, a meeting room or conference space, or any rentable, safe location that is neutral for the family, can work.

## What Could Go Wrong?

### 1. The Invitation Was Never Given

#### Problem

While you have coached the family on how to give an invitation, when you arrive at the designated venue, you discover the person has no idea that you are coming.

#### Solution

Hit pause. Regroup. Allow for breathing space. The problem is not going away. Then think outside the box and join up.

## Case Example

This scenario happened recently; we arrived to discover the ILO was locked in the bathroom, shooting up. She eventually wandered out of the bathroom, called her supplier – the drug dealer – and then packed up her belongings with a package of popsicles and proceeded to walk down a large hill. There was no intervention that day, except that she met us, the interventionists.

Her drug dealer came and carted her back to her apartment. The family was devastated for a moment. We had to process the event and what happened. Things got worse for this 37-year-old female; a week later, we traveled by invitation to her apartment. Again, she was with similar using friends and would not open the door, though now she knew our names and we were talking. She liked my male teammate better than me, which was fine.

A few days later, while I was present, he was invited in, no family, no other people. She was run-down, sleepless, slight, and tired. She agreed to go with him for help and entered treatment.

## 2. The ILO Doesn't Show Up

### Problem

In this case, the ILO does not arrive at the event location on time. In these cases, assess the amount of time and energy it would take to locate the person and invite them to the meeting. In some cases, the ILO goes underground.

### Solution

Ideally, you will have someone close to them find out where they are. You might be able to track people by their phones or by calling some of their acquaintances. Send two people. If you are hopeful that the IP is nearby, you might go with these representatives and hold a meeting elsewhere. In other cases, you may have to hire a private investigator to find them.

## 3. The ILO Flees the Scene

### Problem

People run away during the intervention.

### Solution

To prevent this from happening, assign two people to stay with the ILO at all times. They can alternate on this responsibility. Make sure if possible that you collect the IP's phone, driver's license, passport, and keys before the intervention begins.

Sometimes *not running after someone* is the best solution. Folks often need to experience the consequences of their behavior. Ultimately, one is not a cowboy on a bucking bronco or speeding across country trying to rope in a wild horse. Sooner or later, the person will need help. For today, an invitation was extended, and they know folks are committed to trying to get them the help they need.

## 4. The ILO Locks Themselves or Passes Out in a Closet, a Bathroom, on the Terrace, or in a Room

### Problem

In this case, you haven't planned ahead of time and gathered all the keys to the house. Or the IP panics and isolates, and takes advantage of an opportune moment to show their resistance.

### Solution

This can be dealt with mainly through de-escalation talk. See if you can talk them out of the closet. If they won't come out, you may have to call 911. Additionally, one can mitigate the risk of a freak-out by having someone assigned to them, perhaps their best friend or a close confidant.

### Case Example

Early on, when I started teaming with professional colleagues, we were inviting a tall, gauntly, 47-year-old gentleman to enter treatment. Unsteady on his feet and wobbly, he was softly unhappy that my teammate and I were present. He had a history of trauma and addiction in his family, and he had unwittingly inherited a bar where he went most every day. While married, his partner preference was unclear.

He bumbled around his home and regrettably decided his only way out was to lock himself in a big walk-in closet. We heard a huge clump and heard him fall. Our first concern was that he was safe and had not injured himself. We learned last minute that he kept a gun by their bed. While it was still there, we wanted everyone to be safe. He was crying and saying he wanted to end his life.

I did an assessment for self-harm and found him to warrant mental health intervention. My partner and I switched off in talking to him, and he did open the door slightly, and my teammate sat with him as he was sobbing. I placed a call to the police and we discussed the situation with their mental health team. They became a partner in this meeting, as he needed to be hospitalized first before he could be transferred to a dual diagnosis center.

## 5. Logistical Issues with a Pet

### Problem

Pets may be significantly attached to the ILO and may cause logistical problems during and after the intervention meeting. Sometimes many pets are present.

### Solution

Assess and see if there are pets involved, including dogs, cats, horses, birds, snakes, etc., during the process of portraiture and individual interviews. Clinicians must identify any motivating factors, as multiple pets can especially be an objection to going to treatment and a deterrent to the process. You must assess to what extent these are a part of the IP's lifeline, and how you may or may not separate them. Obviously, taking care of them while they are gone is a must.

### Case Example

Sarah was a 23-year-old female who had repetitive hospitalizations and treatment episodes for alcoholism. She recently purchased a puppy to be her friend. In her disease, the puppy was uncared for and untrained, as reported by her mother who visited her apartment, took photos, and was prepared to share them if necessary at the intervention. Sarah had just gotten out of the hospital and was pulled over by the police for another DUI.

Reluctantly, with dog in hand, Sarah showed up at the hotel suite to meet with family members. She held her puppy in her arms and steadfastly stated she would not go once again to treatment without her dog. At the meeting, Sarah was childlike and bullish, insulting her grandmother, who resembled a Rockwell painting and who was dying of cancer.

Before she huffed off, her parents shared they would take care of the puppy should she choose to enter treatment. She was also told that she could expect no more financial support from her folks, who knew full well she still had money from a trust fund. She left the meeting with a huff and a puff, wanting to make sure that any choice was on her terms.

Later that day, she spoke to the treatment facility, and around dinner time called and said she was willing to go and see what it was like. The next day, she was accompanied by a female escort to the center. Our task as interventionists is to get her to the best possible treatment center. After that, it is the center's responsibility to work with her resistance. She is still in treatment, though has had several lapses. The puppy has a new home with her parents and she is talking about getting another dog.

## 6. Animals Are in Danger in a Home

### Problem

In performing an intervention where the primary presenting problem is hoarding, it may happen that multiple animals are also living with minimal or no care with the ILO.

### Solution

Making sure that the pets are contained and cared for is important. Think safety first and do not do an intervention on a property with multiple pets unless there is no other choice. Call animal control when necessary. Be sure to think outside of the box.

### Case Example

While preparing for an intervention, we found that in addition to hoarding numerous figurines, boxes of clothing, and other objects, the property had over a dozen cats and some stray dogs. From the photos provided by the accountability team, the home was unkempt and we saw evidence of these great numbers of animals. In this case, I employed a specialist who works with hoarders to help during the intervention, along with animal control. It was later learned that many neighbors had already complained of the stench.

In this case, we aligned ourselves with animal rescue. However, we had no other choice but to do the intervention on site. And in addition to team members and family, we had with us a representative of animal rescue and a professional who was an expert with people who are hoarding.

## 7. The Situation Escalates beyond Your Scope

### Problem

In this case, the ILO indicates they will harm themselves or attempts to harm you or others. Additionally, the ILO may exhibit violence, such as slamming a wall.

### Solution

You call the police (duty to warn). If you have a professional license in which you are bound by confidentiality, duty to warn, duty to protect, or privileged communication, you must share that up front with the payor and with the person that you are intervening on. Taking a full biopsychosocial history at the beginning and assessing previous self-injury attempts and violence during your data-gathering phase can help you know what problems might arise.

## Case Example

Zack was an overly entitled 32-year-old male who had exhibited oppositional behavior since he was a teen. In a fit, he threw a large rock and broke the family's sliding glass and smashed holes in the wall.

In reviewing his history, his parents reported he had been arrested twice on domestic violence charges, his apartment had holes in the wall, and he was extremely loud and boisterous. The family was beset with an undercurrent of anger, caused mainly by partner betrayal and lies. Father carried on affairs while mother drank. He bullied her, kept separate bank accounts, and had other nefarious activities while he put a plastic face forward to the community. She, in turn, controlled the family finances and would lash out in rage and hit her husband.

Given the overt nature of violence, it was decided early on to include executive protection (someone highly trained in safety and security who is licensed and accredited) in the process. Executive protection helped identify a safe location for the intervention that could be secured, and were prepared if things got out of hand, so no one would be in danger prior to having to call law enforcement.

## 8. Gun Safety Issues

### Problem

Guns. You arrive and find that the drug dealer is present or that the location is a drug den. This happens more often in a surprise intervention then an invitational one, though it can happen.

### Solution

If guns show up at any point during an intervention, exit – you are not Wonder Woman or Superman. I recommend regrouping and taking a different tact. You are not hired to be directly in harm's way. So, stop, pause, regroup, and de-escalate if necessary.

To prevent the presence of firearms, do a safety assessment before the intervention meeting begins and make sure that all arms are locked in a gun vault. Also, be flexible and hire executive protection or call the police when you need to. If you have executive protection with you, they are often former police, Israeli Secret Service, or Navy Seals; they may want to assess before the intervention also. If needed, find an alternative time or location for the meeting. And do not be afraid to turn down an intervention if it is clear that there are guns in the home and the payor is insistent that is where the intervention must take place.

## 9. Invasion of Privacy

### Problem

The ILO calls the police to report intruders. While the intervention meeting can be held in a variety of places, this case most frequently occurs when the intervention is held in the IP's home.

### Solution

Get permission and consent forms to enter the home in the pre-intervention meeting, or hold an intervention in a neutral space. Otherwise, one must be respectful and not intrude on someone's property.

### Case Example

A husband hired us to intervene on his wife, who had been abusing pills by the handful. Since he was a doctor, she was getting them from his colleagues. In addition, while extremely religious, she had decided that her marriage was not enough, and she was engaging in extramarital affairs. She had six children – the youngest was in kindergarten, and the school principal was gravely concerned. Her home was full of religious artifacts, pills, and objects used for sexual intimacy.

The wife ILO was angry that we had been invited to her home and was uncontrollable with rage. She called the police and said we were trespassing. The police came and spoke with the husband and us. Given her prolixity for upset, we did leave. However, the information gleaned and the condition of the home, plus reports from others, prompted a report to the Department of Child and Family Services.

## 10. Drug-Induced Psychosis or Mental Health Psychosis

### Problem

Co-occurring disorders can create situations that trigger paranoia, delusions, or extreme anxiety.

### Solution

With respect to a substance abuse/mental health intervention, if the person presents in a psychotic state when they enter for stabilization, the protocols for treatment are similar. A robust biopsychosocial history may well give you clues as to what the primary treatment might be. Hit pause. Regroup. Allow for breathing space. The problem is not going away. Then think outside the box and join up.

## Case Example

A young man who graduated college and had failed at several jobs had been living in a local run-down motel for the past three weeks. His grandfather's death caused him much distress, as did his cousin's suicide, coupled with a family history of mental health disorders (including schizophrenia). He was at times disoriented.

He comforted himself by ordering pizza and beer, and on occasion took pills. He was somewhat oriented to time and place, and certainly knew his whereabouts. His car had been a secondary home, and looking in the window one could see how unkempt the car was. His family wanted to speak with him as they were very worried, as his rantings and ravings were troublesome.

We arrived at the motel hoping that his brother could check on him. He knew we were coming to visit through texts. His room was on the second story overlooking the parking lot. His father and brother went up to see him. He knew we were all here and that we had reserved a boardroom across the street to meet.

That day, no meeting took place. Instead, the ILO walked out onto the open air and started to scream at the top of his lungs, causing a major disturbance among guests who were just starting to rise. The owner of the motel came by and informed the parents that he had a daughter in recovery, and while he was empathetic to their plight, he would not interfere with his motel guest who had paid for a month to stay here. Local law enforcement also made their way to the motel, and again the family politely explained their concerns.

We all hit pause and regrouped, as it was obvious nothing would happen today. Yes, the young man did eventually go to treatment (mental health primary), but on that day we hit pause to allow for a clearer opening in his mental state.

## 11. Family Members Backpedal or Say That the ILO is "Not That Bad" or Doesn't Need Help

### Problem

The intervention can be undermined during the process by a member or members of the accountability team. When denial pops up, be prepared for it. An ILO may leave an intervention with their chief enabler.

### Solution

You can quietly challenge any statements that are against the movement to family health. Speak with accountability team members directly about what they have said, or the process may fall apart.

### Case Example

When I first started doing interventions, I had a wide range of financial options and allowed people to pay after the intervention. I no longer do that (see

Chapter 10 on the business of interventions). In this case, a therapist had asked that I see his client in his office, and I agreed.

She was a lovely young woman who was deeply concerned about her boyfriend, who was a race car driver. He was abusing uppers and downers and using cocaine. His father was one of his sponsors and a regular marijuana and polydrug user. His mother and siblings also dabbled in drug use and abuse. They were, however, greatly alarmed by the change in their loved one's behavior and demeanor, and feared that he could harm himself or someone else at 180 miles per hour.

We held a pre-intervention meeting in the therapist's office. Father was the payor. We set a date and time for the intervention, which precluded him from any more races, and then the father said, "No, he must drive the race first." In my softest voice possible, I explained that it was unsafe for his son to race.

The father stood up, glared at me, and turned to the group and said a few expletives. Then he made it clear that in no way, shape, or form would he help with treatment or an intervention unless his son suited up and drove at 180 miles per hour. The car and his career were at stake.

I felt the sweat pour out of me, and I invited the father to leave and the others to stay. I had no idea what would happen. I explained the options and asked the group to decide. I left them alone for 20 minutes while they talked over their options. Money was a large issue. When I came back in, the room was slightly divided; two people left, and agreed not to interfere with the process.

We figured out how the intervention could be done without the primary payor. The finance was key to her loved one's well-being. Dad, with all his bark, did not interfere any more than withholding money, and we could successfully intervene the next day. The young man never drove in that race, and there were many more sober races after that.

## 12. Transport Problems

### Problem

The ILO misses connections for transport or attempts to jump out of the car during transport.

### Solution

Refundable tickets or flex tickets. Always be flexible with transport. Make sure tickets purchased are changeable and refundable.

If you are transporting, it is best to have the IP in the back seat with someone else, or even two people with them in the back of the vehicle. Be sure that the car has child locks and use them.

## Case Example

There are times when you can coach a person to treatment. Such was the case with Rock. This was not his first rodeo, and he knew the drill and was out of options. He had little money with him except a plane ticket, so we had to arrange for someone to help him get food.

Did you know airport information can be extremely helpful if you explain what is happening? He had been up many nights in a row, and while he was stationed near his plane's gate he feel asleep and missed his plane. Airport officials were most helpful, and a day later he was on his way after much coordination.

## Reference

1. Henry J (1963) *Culture Against Man*. New York: McGraw-Hill.

# 10

# THE BUSINESS OF INTERVENTIONS

## So, You Want to Be an Interventionist?

People call a professional interventionist when they are desperate, fearful, angry, sad, mad, and confused. Consciously or subconsciously, however, folks are attached to the problem, both cognitively and emotionally. Dysregulated attempts to change have failed. Now the family truly doesn't know what to do. Are you ready to direct the chaos?

If the process of CIS attracts you, there are a few more qualifiers that can make it your dream job. These include:

1. The opportunity to be true to yourself.
2. The job fits into your life.
3. Mental health, substance abuse, process addictions, or chronic pain interventions incorporate your ethics and values.
4. Being an interventionist allows you to tap into your own gifts.
5. The work gives you energy.
6. Interventions allow you to align with your passion and do what you love.
7. Interventions help you to make a difference in something you believe.
8. The job is enjoyable and doesn't seem like work.
9. You are able to earn a living.
10. It fulfills you.
11. It matches your professional credentials, values, and ethics.
12. You are entrepreneurial.

One must be honest about one's skills. Not only do you need the skill set to do the clinical work; you also need to operate – most times – as an entrepreneur.

*So, what do you know about self-employment?*

Interventions are ultimately a form of private practice. However, this work is very different than most clinical work, as you need to build flexibility into your schedule. One must understand the nature of booking, traveling, and lack of face time with day-to-day clients.

## Getting Down to Business

My main advice to you when considering self-employment as an interventionist is:

*Say what you do and do what you say.*

Self-employment offers many rewards. As a freelance professional intervention-ist, you are your own boss. There is more control over your time, as you set your own hours. Plus, your earning capacity increases, and you can participate and contribute within your community.

However, consultancy work has its downsides as well. Not only are you going to need to work long hours; employment can be seasonal. In fact, you may not know where the next intervention is coming from. The bottom line is that intervention work offers great flexibility, and at times is an irregular source of income. It may be helpful for you to take the time to explore the career change first with an expert executive coach. This way, you can work through the choice before making the commitment.

The work of running and operating your own business also comes with many associated or hidden costs. You must grow your business and engage in strategic planning. "Failing to plan is a plan to fail." You must pay attention to business name and branding, plus file state and federal incorporation or business licenses. Banking or business accounts that offer access to debit accounts, debit cards, and credit cards require setup. Dedicated telephone lines, office space, and computer hardware are also considerations.

Plus, you'll need to set some standards on how connected you are going to be. Will you be available 24/7? Will an answering service or a personal assistant help field calls and make bookings? What devices will you use for your work (laptops, iPads, phones, earpieces)? How much texting will you do per day? Online marketing can be tricky, and the digital world requires a presence, espe-cially on social media sites such as Facebook, Twitter, and LinkedIn.

You should have written materials in the form of:

- business cards;
- brochures;
- banners;

- direct mailings;
- letterhead;
- website;
- engagements;
- confidentiality forms; and
- information sheets.

Further, you must identify and define data requirements. What data will you track? Some examples of data tracking include the number of calls, closes, referral sources, site visits, types of visits, or types of engagements. Meanwhile, you have to identify, connect with, and nurture business contacts. Then there's the accounting, billing (when and how?), not to mention legal consideration of your contracts or external consulting work.

In general, business expenses of intervention can include (and are not limited to):

- advertising or promotion via mailings, constant contact, or MailChimp;
- consultants and colleagues such as lawyers, accountants, business coaches, publicists, mentors, web developers, and editors;
- office or rental expenses;
- phones, answering services, Skype, Webex, and email;
- relationship-building, including gifts or dinners;
- staff, associates, payroll, and independent contractors;
- travel and transport; and
- website development.

What else should you keep in mind?

First, training is most important in this arena and will be an ongoing cost of investment. No matter who you are or where you are from, whether you are a PhD, a PsyD, an MFT, LCSW, MD, CAADE, or have only a "hard knocks" degree, do not be fooled – training is a necessary ingredient in becoming an interventionist and maintaining up-to-date skills. Taking a weekend course does not make one an interventionist, and taking part in a supervision group does not make one an interventionist either. Ongoing consultation is recommended. Further still, being in recovery does not mean you know everything, nor does it mean you know how to conduct an intervention.

> *Interventions require training, ongoing supervision, and confidence! Do not be arrogant; it will do you and your clients in.*

Malpractice insurance and professional licenses and certifications must be kept up to date. I find it imperative to join national organizations. You can consider membership to organizations such as the Association of Intervention Specialists

(AIS) and the Network of Independent Interventionists (NII), and other related professional organizations that you are eligible for. These professional guilds provide training, plus they are an excellent source for mentorship or supervision.

Indeed, mentoring is important in the training process. Practice makes perfect. As you learn to always expect the unexpected, one must be nimble, flexible, and humble. You are dealing with wounded folks in crisis and the issues are sensitive. Shadow along and get good at interventions before venturing on your own.

Not every type of intervention will be your forte. For example, disordered eating or chronic pain interventions are a skill in and of themselves, as are aging and adolescents. One will not be all things to all people. You must identify in this vast arena what types of clients you work with best. The rule of thumb is to get additional training in the areas that interest you.

If, for example, you are interested in sexual addiction and partner betrayal, get additional training as a CSACT. If you are interested in somatic experiences, try EDMR, havening, etc. Culturally, if you work with the military, know what it's like to have been on four tours of duty, understand that way of life. Ethnicity, religion, and cultural expectations all play a part. Learning and exploring will never end, so I invite you to be a seeker.

Other considerations that will play into your decision to start working as an interventionist can include:

- the time you have available for this work;
- working with an outside provider;
- multicultural considerations and your expertise; and
- your personal and professional ethics and values.

## Ethical Considerations

Ethics are highly important to behavioral healthcare. Ethics are the beliefs an individual or group maintains about what constitutes correct or proper behavior. In our industry, these are the standards of conduct an individual uses to make decisions.

A word of precaution here: do not confuse ethics and morality! The word morality comes from Latin word "*mores,*" which translates into customs or values. Morality involves the judgment or evaluation of an ethical system, decision, or action based on social, cultural, or religious norms. In reality, ethical problems occur because people are human; we make mistakes. Clients misreport symptoms. Our own inexperience and ignorance can leave us in a lurch. Or lack of planning for unpredictable or unforeseen situations catches us by surprise.

The truth is that anyone who is working within this niche must be internally clear about where they stand on certain issues. The industry accommodates many professions: psychologists, nurses, doctors, lawyers, technicians, business investors, each with related associations who have come together as a guild. These professional associations ask that members behave within certain guidelines. The most popular of the associations include:

- Association of Intervention Specialists (AIS);
- Network of Independent Interventionists (NII);
- American Association of Advertising Agencies;
- Direct Marketing Association;
- Public Relations Society of America;
- American Marketing Association;
- Foundation for Public Affairs;
- American Hospital Association;
- National Association of Addiction Treatment Providers (NAATP);
- National Association of Alcoholism and Drug Abuse Counselors (NAADAC);
- American Psychological Association (APA);
- National Association of Social Workers (NASW);
- Marriage and Family Therapists (MFT);
- Commission on Accreditation of Rehabilitation Facilities (CARF); and
- California Association of Alcohol and Other Drug Counselors (CADAC).

## Ethical Principles in the Addiction Treatment Industry

As a healthcare institution or provider, it is imperative that you set yourself apart from those who are breaking (or even bending) the bounds of our ethical pledge to help patients and clients to recovery.

Indeed, the clinician should be held to higher standards of ethics in both clinical practice and personal life.

There are a few ethical principles common to the professional organizations within the treatment industry. The importance of human relationships is central to our work. This implies a deep respect for others. But how do we govern our overall clinical behaviors? The most recognized ethical principles in the addiction treatment industry include:

- *Autonomy.* Autonomous individuals act intentionally, with understanding and without controlling influences. Autonomous clinical practice infers that clinicians have an obligation to create the conditions necessary for autonomous choice in others. This includes respecting an individual's right to self-determination, as well as creating the conditions necessary for autonomous choice.
- *Beneficence.* To do good. Beneficence is action that is done for the benefit of others. Beneficent actions can be taken to help prevent or remove harms, or to simply improve the situation of others.

- *Fidelity.* To keep one's promise or word. This includes the duty to report and the traits of honesty and trustworthiness.
- *Integrity.* This principle upholds that the honesty, truthfulness, or accuracy of one's actions are highly important. In other words, do what you say, and tell the truth.
- *Justice.* This principle covers the duty to treat all individuals fairly and to distribute services equally.
- *Non-maleficence.* The duty to cause no harm.
- *Reparation.* The duty to make up for a wrong.
- *Universality.* Individuals are similar and human rights are supreme.
- *Utility.* The duty to provide the greatest good or least harm to the greatest number of people.

## Applying Ethics to Your Work

For the purposes of this textbook, I have tried to contain my discussion of interventionists and styles and referenced those that have actually written and published books on the subject (with the exception of the action model).

Plato, perhaps the most famous of ancient philosophers, laid the groundwork for our modern social mores. Plato believed that ethics were the pillars of good human behavior. Believing in thoughtful consideration and wise deliberation in all matters, he wrote that "human well-being is the highest aim of ethical thought and action."[1]

As such, ethical standards have made a home in our daily lives. In essence, the world's ancient philosophers posited that if life is a series of choices, ethics are the oil that greases our gears and keeps us moving forward with integrity, dignity, and concern. So, what position do you take in the following scenarios? The most common ethical issues and their governing laws at the moment include:

- *Billing.* Insurance, billing, and reimbursement are major sore spots in the industry. The Affordable Care Act (ACA) requires insurers to pay for all substance abuse treatment, including drug testing.[2] This benefit has been highly leveraged by unethical treatment facilities. In some cases, treatment centers or clinicians claim to take a patient's insurance when reimbursement is low. In other cases, the law is abused, especially when it comes to drug testing. In one case, a treatment center used nutrient supplements that were proprietary and billed the patient directly for the expenses. The False Claims Act makes it unlawful for anyone to knowingly or willingly submit or cause a fraudulent claim to the government for payment.[3]
- *Boundaries.* We must establish clinical boundaries between ourselves and our clients. These boundaries address the length of a counseling relationship, self-disclosure by a counselor, giving of gifts, and the limits of touch or personal communication between counselor and client. Boundaries also

set limits for intimate relationships, especially among peers, colleagues, or supervisors. A boundary will also define or limit personal benefit in the domain of monetary goods or services that you receive as a clinician. The emotional or dependency needs of a counselor should also be in check. Note that altruistic gestures can be misinterpreted, and unexpected situations occur within clinical practice. Set your boundaries and maintain them, or your reputation could be on the line.

- *Call centers.* These hotlines have been known to share patient prospect information between treatment providers or run their operations through 501C-3 nonprofit agencies to appear more objective. Internet marketing scams redirect visitors from multiple off-brand websites to one call center. Still further, the use of pay-per-click advertising allows treatment centers to bid for keywords on Google AdWords and receive inbound calls that convert directly to "sales." The reality is that most call centers operate to fill the beds – and pockets – of business investors in specific treatment centers.
- *Competence.* How do you achieve and maintain professional competence? To what extent do you exhibit cultural competence when working with specific groups? Is it OK to practice outside of one's competence?
- *Confidentiality.* Keeping private information private is the hallmark of a therapeutic relationship. HIPPA forms attempt to clarify the confidential nature of our work. However, strict confidentiality should be kept in the work of addiction interventions from the first phone call. The principle of confidentiality will govern your record-keeping, accounting, informal and formal conversations about clients, or client treatment decisions, as well as your progress notes. Any wireless devices, software, or hardware must be 100% protected from intruders. You'll need to be sure that you are familiar with state laws about confidentiality and have necessary consent forms signed and on file. Mandated reporting, "duty to warn" laws, and exceptions to confidentiality law (drug court, federally assisted treatment programs, confidentiality and minors, age of consent) will vary by state. I find it helpful to also make a statement describing the extent to which confidentiality of records identifying a client will be maintained, and include an explanation on limits of confidentiality, plus who to contact in emergency, in my official documentation.
- *Dual relationships.* These principles govern friendships between client and counselor, supervisor and supervisee. They cover sexual relationships, professional relationships (where a client and a counselor are professional colleagues), business relationships (where a counselor and client are business partners or have an employee/employer relationship), and communal relationships (where both belong to the same community such as AA, NA, Al-Anon, SA).
- *Fiduciary relationships with providers.* Treatment centers have been known to pay bounties for referrals. This leads to a practice called "patient brokering."

In return for referring a patient to a drug treatment facility, the broker receives a generous compensation of $500 to $5,000. Brokers will offer to share this money with patients, or entice them with drugs to leave an existing facility and qualify for another because they have relapsed, leading to a revolving-door syndrome.

- *Gifts and kickbacks.* Federal laws such as the Anti-Kick Back Statute make it a criminal offense for anyone to give a kickback with the intent of influencing referral of patients.[4] Some examples include trips, hotels, or gifts. Further, the Stark Law tries to prevent physicians' self-referral, or when a physician refers a patient to a facility they own or their family has financial interest.
- *Informed consent.* It is necessary to complete informed consent paperwork with families. They need to officially grant clinicians permission to carry out an intervention, in full knowledge of the possible consequences, risks, and benefits. An informed consent should include a description of any reasonable foreseeable risks or discomforts (consequences of early withdrawal), a description of any benefits to the subject or others, and disclosure of any alternative treatments, including medications.
- *Truth in advertising.* Advertising should contain clear, objective, and truthful statements. Be wary of treatment that promises to be "number one," "totally unique," or "a cure for addiction." Marketers or website owners can lie online. Websites can be misleading and include photos of amenities that do not exist. Some websites have fake addresses. In one case, a clinic claimed to be using brain scans with other unproven treatments and billing the patient. This is why I recommend site visits: to vet treatment center clinical settings and to verify their professional standards.

## Eight-Step Model for Ethical Decision-Making

There are myriad of ethical decision models. Among those most often cited are the Congress five-step model and eight-step model.[5] These weave nicely with ethical guidelines produced by the various professional entities. The one I tend to use the most has been created by Elaine Congress, and uses the acronym "ETHIC" to guide decision-making. See Worksheet 10.1 (The Congress Model of Ethics) for a quick reference to this model:

- E. Evaluate relevant personal, societal, agency, client, and professional values.
- T. Think about what ethical standard of the NASW code of ethics applies, as well as relevant laws and case decisions.
- H. Hypothesize about possible consequences of different decisions.
- I. Identify who will benefit and who will be harmed in view of social work's commitment to the most vulnerable.
- C. Consult with supervisors and colleagues about the most ethical choice.

Ethical decision-making can follow a specific process. In some cases, a decision may be in conflict with the law. Does that make the decision unethical? In other cases, laws may not explicitly guide behaviors. But will your decision or action do harm? These are the questions that we ask.

> *The reality is that inadequate policies currently govern the landscape. Further, the guidelines that we, as professional, have set out may not be not adequate for every situation.*

So, how do you proceed? First, I think it best to consider any clinical decision you make within the context of your ethical responsibility:

- as professionals;
- to colleagues;
- to clients;
- to practice settings;
- to professional affiliations; and
- to broader society.

Then I think that you can follow a simple model when making a decision. When I teach about ethics, I also teach a model for making decisions about any ethical dilemma. These steps can help you resolve issues so that you can feel an internal alignment in any decision that you make. The main steps are:

1. Identify the problem or issue. Is the issue clinical, legal, systemic (polices), cultural, ethical, or personal? Does the issue affect your own "issues"?
2. Apply a code of ethics.
3. Determine the nature and dimensions of the dilemma.
4. List the pros and cons.
5. Choose a course of action.
6. Implement a course of action.
7. Evaluate the outcome.
8. Evaluate the implications.

## Ethical Concerns and Sample Ethical Problems

In my work, I have asked for feedback on ethical concerns from individual behavioral healthcare thought leaders. Here is just a sample of the top four concerns that peers and colleagues have voiced:

- competence, dishonesty about services, and lack of compassion;
- misrepresenting your capabilities and preying on vulnerable people;
- overselling and over-administering urine analysis;

- kickbacks;
- accreditation and standardization of care;
- "cures" promised as opposed to solutions; and
- lack of training and supervision.

Further, dilemmas will always exist between yourself, clients, agencies, and the outside world. Take some of these case studies and consider how you might act ethically:

1. A 25-year-old mother is referred to you after her third DUI. She tells you that her father is a recovered alcoholic and drinks socially. She does not think she has a problem and does not believe she needs treatment or to be abstinent. What do you do?
2. In an employer relationship, a handsome admissions person is your subordinate. He is also in a 12-step program. You invite him for coffee after the meeting.
3. A former counselor calls to ask if they can hire a former client from a different treatment center that has less than a year's recovery.
4. An admissions officer offers you money for referrals. Or a former client gives you a $100 Starbucks card. Or a client gives you courtside Lakers tickets.
5. A mother wants to know what her daughter is saying about their relationship. Her 19-year-old daughter has not signed a consent form for her mother.
6. You are a substance abuse/mental business professional and are attending the same 12-step meeting as your client. Do you need to share? What do you do?
7. Someone has had an extramarital affair witnessed by their son. You are the husband's counselor. What do you do?
8. You are offered a kickback for bringing people into a particular center.
9. You use social media and want to let the world know you are off doing an intervention. What do professional guidelines say?
10. You are called by a TV show and asked if you might join the production company and preform on-air or filmed interventions. What do professional guidelines say about that?
11. Your client has been asked to star in a reality TV show and she wants to be able to have them come into your office. She has signed a consent form with the TV show to film her. What's your ethical responsibility?
12. You are called by CNN to talk about "the opioid crisis."
13. You are a licensed clinician performing an intervention across state lines. What do you need to find out?

## My Philosophy on Collaboration

Before I start this discussion, it is fair to let you know that my philosophy is that collaborating with an experienced interventionist or other behavioral healthcare expert is 100% in the client's best interest. When we are aligned, clinicians and interventionists can work together so that clients get the most consistent, accessible, effective, and supportive treatment they can get. This ushers in healing.

> *It is always my aim to make sure the family, clients, therapists, and clinicians of record know how valuable they are and that they are an integral part of treatment.*

Somehow that does not always translate into a clinician's mind.

With substance abuse, process addictions, mental health disorders, and chronic pain, moving someone into appropriate treatment *takes a village of concerned persons.* So, why don't more clinicians call in professional interventionists to handle substance use disorders? It might just be fear.

## Confronting the Fear

As you may know, I am a licensed clinician. I have been a trainer of trainers, as well as a trainer of up-and-coming clinicians as a faculty member at the SDSU School of Social Work and as an outside supervisor. As someone who is senior in this field, I have unfortunately recently experienced clinicians who:

- are not knowledgeable;
- have misconceived notions of what and who interventionists are;
- think they can do it all themselves;
- are afraid they will lose their long-standing client if the client goes to treatment; and
- are downright argumentative.

Some clinicians are unwilling to let go of their client and their client's family so that the loved one in question can use the services of a skilled, licensed and/ or certified, and trained interventionist. I have witnessed clinicians who, upon learning a family member has contacted an interventionist, do the following:

1. Are unwilling to explore or even talk to the potential collaborator-interventionist, and shut down communications.
2. Proclaim, "I know best" and, "You do not need any other professional."
3. Say using outside help will be detrimental as we need to keep "everything confidential."
4. Disregard building a vast knowledge of current treatment centers because that is not their area of expertise. They can then make faulty recommendations.
5. Directly sabotage intervention efforts. As a result, the family stays stuck. The therapist can create entanglement in their issues and inadvertently keep the status quo.

Clinicians who operate out of fear do not serve clients' best interests. It is wise to imagine an interventionist as a skilled orchestra leader conducting, for the moment in time, a symphony. You need the conductor's expertise for that concerto. It does not replace your individual talent. Rather, working collaboratively creates a synergy of health and wellness.

On the flipside of that token, I have had grand experiences with clinicians who understand the complexity of substance abuse and co-occurring disorders. They join hands with a skilled interventionist and collaborate to get the family and their loved one much-needed help.

And to all of you, I applaud your efforts.

## Interventions Are Adjunct Therapies

To all the licensed professionals out there:

> *Interventions are an adjunctive treatment to family therapy, psychotherapy, trauma work, and behavioral healthcare interventions. These primary therapies help people and their loved ones unlock unhealthy secrets and behaviors that keep the system unhealthy and ill – and the loved one in question still using mind-altering substances, being cognitively impaired, and engaging in harmful behaviors.*

However, using the skills of a talented interventionist in conjunction with the work that you do allows clients to be present to their:

* relationship patterns;
* underlying challenges;
* boundary-setting; and
* subconscious patterns of shame and trauma.

The experience of collaboration will give you a platform to work on a cornucopia of issues while working directly to move the ILO into treatment. Also, an intervention and the hiring of a skilled and talented interventionist, as well as having a loved one enter an accredited Joint Commission (JACHO) treatment center, *does not take the place of the work you do.*

> *Instead, your work is enhanced. When you outsource a professional intervention, it ultimately makes the work you do with your clients richer, deeper, and more effective.*

After working with a skilled interventionist, your clients have a more tangible ability to work through new issues that arise and new ways of relating to themselves as others so that there can truly be systemic change.

## When Can Your Client Benefit from an Interventionist's Help?

I believe interventions are a process in which one must be agile, ever present in the moment, and always starting where the client is, not where the model lies. A person must be well versed in different modalities, strategies that work with a team that challenges and complements their skills, and always be open to learning, growing, sharing, and transforming.

No two families are alike in the same sense that no two interventions are alike. Lastly, an interventionist needs to be humble and truthful enough to give work to another colleague, not because they are too busy to take on the task, but because they are not the right fit for that family and/or friends. Your client (and client's family, friends, etc.) might be a good fit for the skills of an interventionist if they:

- are still supporting (consciously or unconsciously) a loved one who is using mind-altering substances;
- have difficulty setting healthy boundaries or even knowing what boundaries are;
- have a history of complex trauma, substance abuse, and co-occurring disorders in their family of origin;
- have diminished capacity for functioning due to their fear of doing something different to change their loved one;
- have gotten to a point of disconnecting from the world around them as looking at the situation is too painful;
- are experiencing somatic symptoms, lack of sleep, rage, endless tears, repeated illness, stomach aches, migraines, etc.; and/or
- have been unsuccessful in addressing a loved one's substance abuse, mental health disorder, chronic pain, co-occurring disorder, legal trouble, or school and professional failures.

### How to Find an Interventionist

If you think you may have a client or a family who might get unstuck by working with a skilled interventionist who is highly trained in this arena, reach out. Call and interview a trained interventionist. Some interventionists are licensed clinicians, and some have other trained experiences through an integrated collaborative approach. I personally refer families that are not the right fit for me to my colleagues or someone else who is better suited for the case, based on their areas of expertise.

Remember, the professional realm of the behavioral healthcare interventionist is still something like the Wild West, by degrees. Clinical skills are helpful and desired, though not a prerequisite. I also like working with trained attorneys, psychiatrists, psychologists, and others who themselves are in recovery. Regardless of a colleague's background, one needs to figure out:

- what they know;
- who they've been trained by;
- what mentoring they've had; and
- what skills they bring to the table.

When choosing to refer out to a professional interventionist, it is important to find someone with experience, the appropriate licenses/certifications for your needs, and a strong code of ethics. This subject is one I talk about frequently at lectures across the country, and it's something about which I am very passionate.

To look for an interventionist, check out these two industry website listings:

1. The website of the Network of Independent Interventionists (NII).
2. The website of the Association of Intervention Specialists (AIS).

These professional guilds list members' credentials, licenses, and certifications. Note here that fees are not necessarily less if you pick an interventionist in your state vs. across the country. So, where finances are concerned, be sure that you clarify fees and services up front. Then I recommend picking up the phone and interviewing three. Finally, check with colleagues through other professional organizations to confirm references. See Worksheet 10.2 (What to Look for in an Interventionist) for a checklist, with a section for your own notes.

In sum, selecting and working with an interventionist is based on the decision of who is best for your particular client. Your choice will be informed by their needs, situation, and specific case.

## References

1. Cooper JM and Hutchinson DS, editors (1997) *Plato Complete Works*. Cambridge: Hackett Publishing Co.
2. U.S. Congress (2010) *Affordable Care Act, Public Law 111–148*. Available at: www.gpo.gov/fdsys/pkg/PLAW-111publ148/pdf/PLAW-111publ148.pdf (accessed March 4, 2018).
3. U.S. Congress (2012) *False Claims Act, Title 31 – Money and Finance, Subtitle III – Financial Mismanagement, Chapter 37 – Claims, Subchapter III – Claims against the United States Government, Section 3729 – False Claims*. Available at: www.gpo.gov/fdsys/granule/USCODE-2011-title31/USCODE-2011-title31-subtitleIII-chap37-subchapIII-sec3729 (accessed March 4, 2018).

4. U.S. Congress (2010) *Title 42 – The Public Health and Welfare, Chapter 7 – Social Security, Subchapter XI – General Provisions, Peer Review, and Administrative Simplification, Part A – General Provisions, Section 1320a–7b – Criminal Penalties for Acts Involving Federal Health Care Programs.* Available at: www.gpo.gov/fdsys/granule/USCODE-2010-title42/USCODE-2010-title42-chap7-subchapXI-partA-sec1320a-7b (accessed March 4, 2018).

5. Congress, EP (2000) What Social Workers Should Know About Ethics: Understanding and Resolving Practice Dilemmas. *Advances in Social Work Practice.* 1(1): 1–25.

# GLOSSARY

**Abuse or misuse**  Clinically, people abuse drugs for euphoric effect. Misuse means taking a medication in a manner or dose other than prescribed, taking someone else's prescription, even if for a legitimate medical complaint such as pain, or taking a medication to feel euphoria. So, there is some overlap in these definitions.

**Accountability team**  The family group or those closest to the ILO, the members of which we call the "accountability team." This can include members of the family of origin, family of choice, or both.

**Addiction**  According to the American Society of Addiction Medicine, addiction is defined as "a primary, chronic disease of brain reward, motivation, memory, and related circuitry." People experience a substance use disorder, addiction, or substance misuse. In this book, we use the word "addiction" interchangeably with "substance use disorders."

**Behavioral change agreement (BCA)**  A written document in which accountability team members clearly articulate what they are willing to do to support a loved one in recovery. The key notion is that healthy boundaries are critical for personal health and happiness. Once a loved one experiencing addiction seeks treatment, all family members, friends, and colleagues and business associates must take a hard look at their own behaviors and redraw these boundary lines to find change.

**Drug-free**  Saying "I am drug-free" or "I am free from illicit and non-prescribed medications" can be more affirming as opposed to "I am clean and sober."

**Drug of choice**  It is important to highlight a person's drug of use and start where the client is by focusing on the drug(s) the client feels is creating problems for them, rather than "a drug is a drug" approach.

**Drug poisoning**   This term is preferred to "drug overdose"; in other words, people poison themselves with drugs to the point of overdose.

**Identified loved one (ILO)**   The use of the term "identified loved one" (ILO) we can attribute to Brad Lamm. It has now become fairly standard in the treatment industry when describing the client or the identified patient. I find calling the identified client or identified patient the "identified loved one" to be an honorable way of speaking about the person you are about to ask get help. Still, this term can be interchangeable with "identified patient" (IP) or "identified client" (IC), especially in contractual agreements or when working with addiction treatment providers.

**Intervention letters**   These are letters written to the ILO that describe an individual's heart, hurt, and hope. Consequences are sometimes included, and sometimes not. These are often boundaries. It's useful to outline the following: What's special about the person? Why are you worried? What exact events have occurred? What are your hopes for the person?

**Mutual aid groups**   Refer to peer groups as "mutual aid groups" as opposed to "self-help groups."

**Not yet in recovery**   A person who experiences a substance abuse disorder may be seen as an individual who is not yet in recovery. Avoid the use of the words "untreated alcoholic" or "addict."

**Recovery**   Recovery management is a lifetime process of strength-building. This may be a better way to look at recovery than relapse prevention strategies.

**Relapse**   A return to drug use. "Recurrence or return to use" may occur as part of the disease, as opposed to using the term "relapse is a part of recovery." This can lead to developing recovery management plans as opposed to relapse prevention plans.

**Treatment completion**   It is helpful to describe that "one has left treatment" as opposed to saying, "I graduated from treatment," as if there is a diploma waiting. This can be followed by a statement that "I am commencing or beginning lifelong recovery."

# BIBLIOGRAPHY

Allen JG (1995) *Coping with Trauma: A Guide to Self-Understanding.* Washington, DC: American Psychiatric Press.

American Psychological Association (2016) *Ethical Principles of Psychologists and Code of Conduct.* Adopted August 2016, effective January 1, 2017.

Amodeo M and López LM (2013) *Alcohol and Drug Problems: Practice Interventions. Encyclopedia of Social Work.* Boston, MA: National Association of Social Workers Press and Oxford University Press. Available at: http://socialwork.oxfordre.com/view/10.1093/acrefore/9780199975839.001.0001/acrefore-9780199975839-e-516 (accessed March 4, 2018).

Bonow JT and Follette WC (2009) Beyond Values Clarification: Addressing Client Values in Clinical Behavior Analysis. *The Behavior Analyst.* 32(1): 69–84.

Bradshaw J (2014) *Post-Romantic Stress Disorder: What to Do When the Honeymoon Is Over.* Deerfield Beach, FL: Health Communications.

Brown B (2007) *I Thought It Was Just Me.* New York: Gotham Books.

Brown B (2010) *The Gifts of Imperfection.* Center City, PA: Hazelden.

Brown B (2015a) *Daring Greatly: How the Courage to Be Vulnerable Transforms the Way We Live, Love, Parent, and Lead.* New York: Penguin Random House.

Brown B (2015b) *Rising Strong.* New York: Penguin Random House.

Brown B (2017) *Braving the Wilderness.* New York: Random House.

Burton P (2017) *Confidentiality, Privileged Communication, Rules of Evidence and Social Work: Jaffee vs Redmond-Us Supreme Court-Oct. 1995.* Association of VA Social Workers. Available at: www.vasocialworkers.org/Documents/Jaffee%20v%20Redmond_byPaulBurton_July2017.pdf (accessed March 4, 2018).

Butler JF (2008) The Family Diagram and Genogram: Comparisons and Contrasts. *The American Journal of Family Therapy.* 36(3): 169–180.

Center for Behavioral Health Statistics and Quality (2016) *The TEDS Report: Gender Differences in Primary Substance of Abuse across Age Groups.* Rockville, MD: Substance Abuse and Mental Health Services Administration. Available at: www.samhsa.gov/data/sites/default/files/sr077-gender-differences-2014.pdf (accessed March 4, 2018).

Center for Behavioral Health Statistics and Quality (2017) *2016 National Survey on Drug Use and Health: Detailed Tables.* Rockville, MD: U.S. Department of Health and Human Services, Substance Abuse and Mental Health Services Administration. Available at: www.samhsa.gov/data/sites/default/files/NSDUH-FFR1-2016/NSDUH-FFR1-2016.pdf (accessed March 4, 2018).

Center for Substance Abuse Treatment (1998a) *Substance Abuse among Older Adults: Treatment Improvement Protocol (TIP) Series, No. 26.* Rockville, MD: Substance Abuse and Mental Health Services Administration. Available at: www.ncbi.nlm.nih.gov/books/NBK64419/ (accessed March 4, 2018).

Center for Substance Abuse Treatment (1998b) *Treatment Improvement Protocol (TIP) Series, No. 26: Substance Abuse among Older Adults.* Rockville, MD: Substance Abuse and Mental Health Services Administration. Available at: www.ncbi.nlm.nih.gov/books/NBK64269/ (accessed March 4, 2018).

Center for Substance Abuse Treatment (1999) *Treatment Improvement Protocol (TIP) Series, No. 34: Brief Interventions and Brief Therapies for Substance Abuse.* Rockville, MD: Substance Abuse and Mental Health Services Administration. Available at: www.ncbi.nlm.nih.gov/books/NBK64936/ (accessed March 4, 2018).

Center for Substance Abuse Treatment (2004) *Treatment Improvement Protocol (TIP) Series, No. 39: Substance Abuse Treatment and Family Therapy.* Rockville, MD: Substance Abuse and Mental Health Services Administration. Available at: www.ncbi.nlm.nih.gov/books/NBK64269/ (accessed March 4, 2018).

Center for Substance Abuse Treatment (2005a) *Treatment Improvement Protocol (TIP) Series 44: Substance Abuse Treatment for Adults in the Criminal Justice System.* Rockville, MD: Substance Abuse and Mental Health Services Administration. Available at: https://store.samhsa.gov/shin/content//SMA13-4056/SMA13-4056.pdf (accessed March 4, 2018).

Center for Substance Abuse Treatment (2005b) *Treatment Improvement Protocol (TIP) Series, No. 41: Group Therapy.* Rockville, MD: Substance Abuse and Mental Health Services Administration. Available at: www.ncbi.nlm.nih.gov/books/NBK64214/ (accessed March 4, 2018).

Center for Substance Abuse Treatment (2006a) *Substance Abuse: Clinical Issues in Intensive Outpatient Treatment, Treatment Improvement Protocol (TIP) Series, No. 47.* Rockville, MD: Substance Abuse and Mental Health Services Administration. Available at: www.ncbi.nlm.nih.gov/books/NBK64093/ (accessed March 4, 2018).

Center for Substance Abuse Treatment (2006b) *Client's Handbook: Matrix Intensive Outpatient Treatment for People with Stimulant Use Disorders.* Rockville, MD: Substance Abuse and Mental Health Services Administration. Available at: https://store.samhsa.gov/shin/content//SMA15-4154/SMA15-4154.pdf (accessed March 4, 2018).

Center for Substance Abuse Treatment (2009) *Treatment Improvement Protocol (TIP) Series, No. 51. Substance Abuse Treatment: Addressing the Specific Needs of Women.* Rockville, MD: Substance Abuse and Mental Health Services Administration. Available at: www.ncbi.nlm.nih.gov/books/NBK83257/ (accessed March 4, 2018).

Center for Substance Abuse Treatment (2010) *The Next Step: Towards a Better Life.* Rockville, MD: Substance Abuse and Mental Health Services Administration. Available at: https://store.samhsa.gov/shin/content/SMA12-4474/SMA12-4474.pdf (accessed March 4, 2018).

Center for Substance Abuse Treatment (2012a) *Treatment Improvement Protocol (TIP) Series, No. 54: Managing Chronic Pain in Adults with or in Recovery from Substance Use Disorders.* Rockville, MD: Substance Abuse and Mental Health Services Administration.

Available at: https://store.samhsa.gov/shin/content//SMA13-4671/SMA13-4671. pdf (accessed March 4, 2018).

Center for Substance Abuse Treatment (2012b) *A Provider's Introduction to Substance Abuse Treatment for Lesbian, Gay, Bisexual, and Transgender Individuals.* Rockville, MD: Substance Abuse and Mental Health Services Administration. Available at: https://store.samhsa.gov/shin/content/SMA12-4104/SMA12-4104.pdf (accessed March 4, 2018).

Center for Substance Abuse Treatment (2013) *Treatment Improvement Protocol (TIP) Series, No. 56: Addressing the Specific Behavioral Health Needs of Men.* Rockville, MD: Substance Abuse and Mental Health Services Administration. Available at: www. ncbi.nlm.nih.gov/books/NBK144286 (accessed March 4, 2018).

Collerran C and Jay D (2002) *Aging and Addiction.* Center City, PA: Hazelden.

Connors GJ, DiClemente GC, Velasquez MM, and Donovan DM (2013) *Substance Abuse Treatment and the Stages of Change: Selecting and Planning* (2nd edition). New York: Guildford Press.

Dayton T (2012) *The ACOA Trauma Syndrome.* Deerfield Beach, FL: Health Communications.

Dayton T (2017) *Codependency: What's It All About?* Available at: https://journal.thrive global.com/codependency-whats-it-all-about-9f7448327350 (accessed March 4, 2018).

Erikson E (1993) *Childhood and Society* (2nd edition). New York: Norton.

Forray A (2016) Substance Use during Pregnancy. *F1000Research,* 5 (F1000 Faculty Rev): 887.

Galindo I, Boomer E, and Reagan D (2016) *A Family Genogram Workbook* (1st edition). Educational Consultants.

Goldstein R, Craig AD, Bechara A, Garavan H, Childress AR, Paulus MP, and Volkow ND (2009) The Neurocircuitry of Impaired Insight in Drug Addiction. *Trends in Cognitive Sciences.* 13(9): 372–380.

Gorski T (1991) *Getting Love Right: Learning the Choices of Healthy Intimacy.* New York: Fireside.

Green C (2006) *Gender and Use of Substance Abuse Treatment Services.* Rockville, MD: National Institute on Alcohol Abuse and Alcoholism. Available at: https://pubs. niaaa.nih.gov/publications/arh291/55-62.htm (accessed March 4, 2018).

Greenfield SF and Grella CE (2009) What Is "Women-Focused" Treatment for Substance Use Disorders? *Psychiatric Services.* 60(7): 880–882.

Halabuza D (2014) Guidelines for Social Workers' Use of Social Networking Websites. *Journal of Social Work Values and Ethics.* 11(1): 23–32.

Hartman A and Laird J (1983) *Family-Centered Social Work Practice.* New York: Free Press.

Hurley PM (1982) Family Assessment: Systems Theory and the Genogram. *Children's Health Care.* 10(3): 76–82.

Jay D (2014) *It Takes a Family: A Cooperative Approach to Lasting Sobriety.* Center City, PA: Hazelden.

Johnson V (1972) *I'll Quit Tomorrow.* New York: Harper & Row.

Jones T (1991) Ethical Decision Making by Individuals in Organizations: An Issue-Contingent Model. *The Academy of Management Review.* 16(2): 366–395.

Kopp, S (1972) *If You Meet the Buddha on the Road, Kill Him: The Pilgrimage of Psychotherapy Patients.* Toronto: Bantam Publishing.

Lamm, B (2010) *How to Help the One You Love: A New Way to Intervene and Stop Someone from Self-Destructing.* New York: St. Martin's Griffin.

Landau J and Garret J (2008) Invitational Intervention: The ARISE Model for Engaging Reluctant Alcohol and Other Drug Abusers in Treatment. *Alcoholism Treatment Quarterly*. 26(1–2): 147–168.

Landau J, Garrett J, Shea R, and Brinkman-Sull D (1998) The ARISE Intervention: Using Family and Network Links to Engage Addicted Persons in Treatment. *Journal of Substance Abuse Treatment*. 15(4): 333–343.

Landau J, Mittal M, and Wieling E (2008) Linking Human Systems: Strengthening Individuals, Families, and Communities in the Wake of Mass Trauma. *Journal of Marital Family Therapy*. 34(2): 193–209.

Latkin C and Knowlton AR (2015) Social Network Assessments and Interventions for Health Behavior Change: A Critical Review. *Behavioral Medicine*. 41(3): 90–97.

Lawrence-Lightfoot S (2000) *Respect: An Exploration*. Cambridge: Perseus Books.

Lawrence-Lightfoot S (2016) *Growing Each Other Up: When Our Children Become Our Teachers*. Chicago, IL: University of Chicago Press.

Lerner R (1988) *Boundaries for Codependents*. Center City, PA: Hazelden.

Lerner R (2008) *The Object of My Affection Is in My Reflection: Coping with Narcissists*. Deerfield Beach, FL: Health Communications.

Martin WM and Hemphill P (2013) *Taming Disruptive Behavior*. Tampa, FL: American College of Physician Executives.

Mason, PT and Kreger R (2010) *Stop Walking on Eggshells: Taking Your Life Back When Someone You Care About Has Borderline Personality Disorder*. Oakland, CA: New Harbinger.

Meyers RJ and Wolfe BL (2004) *Get Your Loved One Sober: Alternatives to Nagging, Pleading, and Threatening*. Center City, PA: Hazelden.

NAADAC (2016) *NAADAC/NCC AP Code of Ethics*. Alexandria, VA: NAADAC. Available at: www.naadac.org/assets/2416/naadac-code-of-ethics.pdf (accessed March 4, 2018).

NASW Delegate Assembly (2017) *National Association of Social Workers Code of Ethics*. Washington, DC: NASW. Available at: www.socialworkers.org/About/Ethics/Code-of-Ethics/Code-of-Ethics-English (accessed March 4, 2018).

NASW, ASWB, CSWE, and CSWA (2017) *Standards for Technology in Social Work Practice*. Washington, DC: NASW.

National Institute on Drug Abuse (2014) *Principles of Adolescent Substance Use Disorder Treatment: A Research-Based Guide*. Bethesda, MD: National Institutes of Health. Available at: www.drugabuse.gov/publications/principles-adolescent-substance-use-disorder-treatment-research-based-guide (accessed March 4, 2018).

National Institute on Drug Abuse (2016) *Substance Use in Women*. Bethesda, MD: National Institutes of Health. Available at: www.drugabuse.gov/publications/research-reports/substance-use-in-women (accessed March 4, 2018).

National Institute on Drug Abuse (2017) *Substance Use and SUDs in LGBT Populations*. Bethesda, MD: National Institutes of Health. Available at: www.drugabuse.gov/related-topics/substance-use-suds-in-lgbt-populations (accessed March 4, 2018).

National Institute on Drug Abuse (2018) *Principles of Drug Addiction Treatment: A Research-Based Guide* (3rd edition). Bethesda, MD: National Institutes of Health. Available at: www.drugabuse.gov/publications/principles-drug-addiction-treatment-research-based-guide-third-edition (accessed March 4, 2018).

Newman J (2010) *Raising Lions: The Art of Compassionate Discipline*. CreateSpace.

Patterson K et al. (2012) *Crucial Conversations: Tools for Talking When Stakes Are High* (2nd edition). New York: McGraw-Hill.

Pozatek K (2011) *The Parallel Process: Growing alongside Your Adolescent or Young Adult Child in Treatment.* Brooklyn, NY: Lantern Books.

Prater CD, Zylstra RG, and Miller KE (2002) Successful Pain Management for the Recovering Addicted Patient. *Primary Care Companion to the Journal of Clinical Psychiatry.* 4(4): 125–131.

Raheb G, Khaleghi E, Moghanibashi-Mansourieh A, Farhoudian A, and Teymouri R (2016) Effectiveness of Social Work Intervention with a Systematic Approach to Improve General Health in Opioid Addicts in Addiction Treatment Centers. *Psychology Research and Behavioral Management.* 9: 309–315. Available at: www.ncbi.nlm.nih.gov/pmc/articles/PMC5118021/#b14-prbm-9-309 (accessed March 4, 2018).

Raitner W (2008) *The Forgiveness Myth: How to Heal Your Hurts and Move on and Be Happy Again.* Richfield, MN: Original Pathways Press.

Reedy BM (2015) *The Journey of the Heroic Parent: Your Child's Struggle and the Road Home.* New York: Regan Arts.

Rosenthal M (2015) *Trauma and Addiction: 7 Reasons Your Habit Makes Perfect Sense.* San Diego, CA: Behavioral Health, Living in Recovery, Living with Addiction. Available at: www.recovery.org/pro/articles/trauma-and-addiction-7-reasons-your-habit-makes-perfect-sense/ (accessed March 4, 2018).

Sack D (2012) *Emotional Trauma: An Often-Overlooked Root of Addiction.* Newburyport, MA: Psych Central. Available at: https://blogs.psychcentral.com/addiction-recovery/2012/03/emotional-trauma-addiction/ (accessed March 4, 2018).

Stanger L (2015) *Triple Threat: Beyond Dual Diagnosis.* New York: Huffington Post. Available at: www.huffingtonpost.com/louise-stanger-edd-lcsw-bri-ii-cip/triple-threat-beyond-dual_b_6586904.html (accessed March 4, 2018).

Stanger L (2016) *Falling Up: A Memoir of Renewal.* Los Angeles, CA: WZY Press.

Stevens S (2012) Meeting the Substance Abuse Treatment Needs of Lesbian, Bisexual and Transgender Women: Implications from Research to Practice. *Substance Abuse and Rehabilitation.* 3(1): 27–36.

Substance Abuse and Mental Health Services Administration (2014) *Projections of National Expenditures for Treatment of Mental and Substance Use Disorders, 2010–2020.* Rockville, MD: Substance Abuse and Mental Health Services Administration. Available at: https://store.samhsa.gov/shin/content/SMA14-4883/SMA14-4883.pdf (accessed March 4, 2018).

Walker S (2012) *Effective Social Work with Children, Young People and Families: Putting Systems Theory into Practice.* London: Sage.

Weiss R (1994) *Learning from Strangers: The Art and Method of Qualitative Interview Studies* (1st edition). New York: Free Press.

Wells EA, Kristman-Valente AN, Peavy KM, and Jackson TR (2013) Social Workers and Delivery of Evidence-Based Psychosocial Treatments for Substance Use Disorders. *Social Work in Public Health.* 28(3–4): 279–301.

Whitfield C (1994) *Boundaries and Relationships: Knowing, Protecting and Enjoying the Self.* Deerfield Beach, FL: Health Communications.

# INDEX